# Heavy Vehicle Technology

# Heavy Vehicle Technology

**D. J. Leeming** TEng, HNC(Mech.Eng), LCG, FIMI, MIRTE, MBIM
*Senior Lecturer in Automobile Engineering, Tameside College of Technology*
**and R. Hartley** TEng, MIME, MIRTE
*Senior Lecturer in Automobile Engineering, Accrington College of Technology*

**HUTCHINSON**
*London Melbourne Sydney Auckland Johannesburg*

Hutchinson & Co. (Publishers) Ltd
An imprint of the Hutchinson Publishing Group
17–21 Conway Street, London W1P 5HL

Hutchinson Group (Australia) Pty Ltd
30–32 Cremorne Street, Richmond South, Victoria 3121
PO Box 151, Broadway, New South Wales 2007

Hutchinson Group (NZ) Ltd
32–34 View Road, PO Box 40–086, Glenfield, Auckland 10

Hutchinson Group (SA) (Pty) Ltd
PO Box 337, Bergvlei 2012, South Africa

First published 1976
Second edition 1981

© D. J. Leeming and R. Hartley 1976, 1981

Set in Times

Printed in Great Britain by The Anchor Press Ltd
and bound by Wm Brendon & Son Ltd,
both of Tiptree, Essex

**British Library Cataloguing in Publication Data**
Leeming, David John
  Heavy vehicle technology. – 2nd ed.
  1. Commercial vehicles
  I. Title  II. Hartley, Reg
  629.22    TL230

ISBN 0 09 144690 2 cased
        144691 0 paper

# Contents

# Preface and Acknowledgements

This second edition has given the authors and publisher an opportunity to correct the minor errors and omissions that inevitably appear in a first edition of any textbook. It has also made it possible to make some additions and bring the book into line with the new City and Guilds of London Institute syllabuses for Heavy Vehicle Technology and the TEC standard units in Engine Technology and Vehicle Technology at Levels 1 and 2. Most of the matter contained in the TEC Level 3 units 'Diesel Engine Technology' and 'Steering, Brakes and Suspension' is amply covered in this new edition.

We would like to thank those firms and companies listed below that have so willingly and generously co-operated with us in furnishing information on their products thus making it possible to bring the book up-to-date on topics where technical developments are moving forward at a rapid pace. As the design, development and complexities of trucks and buses are likely to continue to change in the future we recommend this book to students at all levels as it has been written to keep the more mature student abreast of developments in vehicle technology as well as being of use to students who are currently pursuing courses in colleges for technical qualifications.

*D. J. Leeming and R. Hartley*

## Acknowledgements

Automotive Products Ltd
Bendix Westinghouse Ltd
Borg and Beck Co. Ltd
British Leyland
Chrysler (UK) Ltd
Clayton Dewandre Co. Ltd
Crane Fruehauf Ltd
Cummins Engine Co. Ltd
E. R. F. Ltd
Filtration Ltd
Ford Motor Co. Ltd
Gardner Engines Ltd
General Motors Ltd
Girling Ltd
GKN Farr Filtration Ltd
The Goodyear Tyre and Rubber Co. Ltd
IMI Marston Ltd
Jacobs Manufacturing Co. Ltd

Joseph Lucas Ltd
Lucas/C.A.V. Ltd
Merlin International Ltd
Neate Brake Controls Ltd
Perkins Engines Ltd
Rolls Royce
Sandbach Engineering Ltd
Scammell Lorries Ltd
Scania Vehicles (UK) Ltd
Schrader Automotive Products Division
Self-Changing Gears
Smiths Industries Ltd
Start Pilot Ltd
Telma Retarder Ltd
Turner Manufacturing Co. Ltd
Volvo (GB) Ltd
York Trailer Co. Ltd

# 1 Vehicle types and layouts

## Vans

Vans and light commercial vehicles (Figures 1 and 2) account for a large proportion of the goods vehicles operating in the United Kingdom. A common range of vans falls within the limits of 350 kg (7 cwt) to 500 kg (10 cwt) capacity based on a standard motor car chassis. Door-to-door deliveries by traders are made with these vans which are up to date in style and made from the simplest mechanical units requiring low-cost maintenance. The bodies are usually welded steel pressings with large doors to facilitate entry and exit, and access for loading and unloading is provided by one or two rear or side doors.

The power unit is usually a four-cylinder in-line petrol engine which is reliable and economical to operate, and it often has a low compression ratio, allowing low octane fuel to be used. Most large vans are powered by petrol engines, although compression ignition engines are fitted as alternatives by some manufacturers.

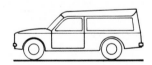

Figure 1  *Light van*

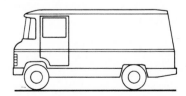

Figure 2  *Medium van fitted with petrol or compression ignition engine*

## Light commercial vehicles

The light, four-wheeled rigid commercial vehicle (Figure 3) with an unladen weight of less than 3.05 tonnes (3 tons) may be driven legally by a person holding a normal driving licence, making these vehicles popular with many operators in the distributive trades. The cab, which on many models may be tilted, is ergonomically designed to contribute to driver–salesman performance and must be easy to enter and leave, as many of these vehicles are used for door-to-door deliveries. The driving controls are very accessible as they are constantly in use, and good visibility from the cab is necessary for safe operation in busy urban areas.

The frame is usually made from pressed steel channel section and the body may be a flat or a van. The van body may have rear doors or side doors, or in some models both, for loading and unloading. A pull-down step is sometimes used to enter and leave the van, the step being of the internal type on vehicles where high standards of hygiene are required. Roller shutters or up-and-over doors are used for full-width rear access to the van interior.

The power unit is usually a petrol or compression ignition engine coupled to a four- or five-

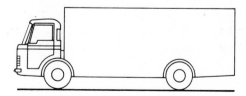

Figure 3  *Light four-wheeled rigid vehicle with box van body*

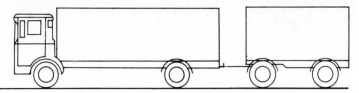

Figure 4 *Rigid vehicle with draw-bar trailer*

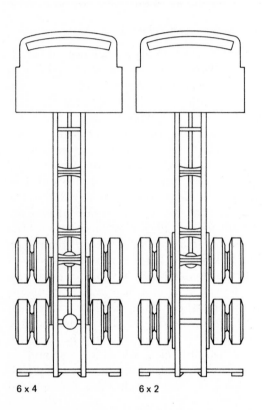

6 x 4          6 x 2

Figure 5 *Configuration of models*
*Different versions of the total number of wheels and the number of driving wheels are identified with the use of a number system, e.g. 6 × 4 indicates that a vehicle has a total of six wheels, of which four are driving wheels. Two separate road wheels secured to one hub are regarded as one wheel for this purpose*

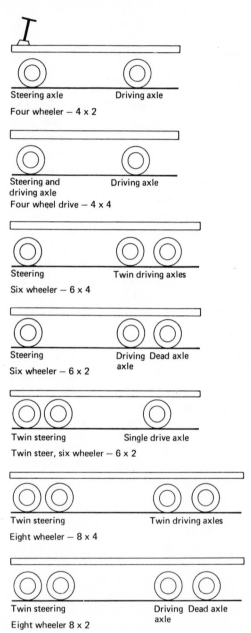

Steering axle          Driving axle
Four wheeler — 4 x 2

Steering and          Driving axle
driving axle
Four wheel drive — 4 x 4

Steering          Twin driving axles
Six wheeler — 6 x 4

Steering          Driving Dead axle
Six wheeler — 6 x 2          axle

Twin steering          Single drive axle
Twin steer, six wheeler — 6 x 2

Twin steering          Twin driving axles
Eight wheeler — 8 x 4

Twin steering          Driving Dead axle
Eight wheeler 8 x 2          axle

Figure 6 *Alternative versions of rigid vehicles*

speed gearbox and driving through a one- or two-piece propeller shaft to the final drive.

## Heavy goods vehicles

These vehicles are more heavily constructed than motor cars and vans and are specifically designed to transport goods. A compression ignition engine which has a comparatively low engine speed and high torque is usually fitted and it is normally located at the front of the chassis. The body may be in the form of a flat platform, a tank, a container van, or be specially built to suit a particular type of operation. A rigid vehicle (Figures 4, 5 and 6) may have two, three or four axles and can be adapted to haul a draw-bar

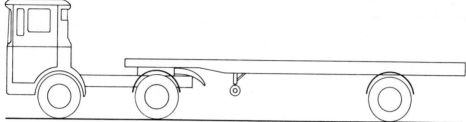

Figure 7    *Articulated vehicle: tractive unit and semi-trailer*

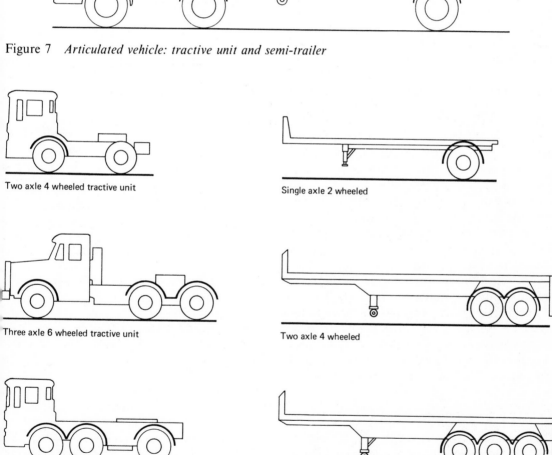

Two axle 4 wheeled tractive unit

Single axle 2 wheeled

Three axle 6 wheeled tractive unit

Two axle 4 wheeled

Three axle 6 wheeled twin steer

Three axle 6 wheeled

Figure 8

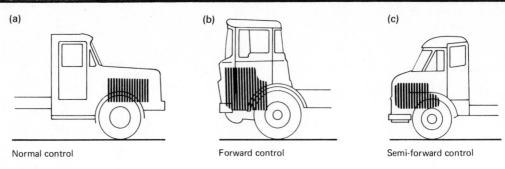

(a)                          (b)                          (c)

Normal control          Forward control          Semi-forward control

Figure 9

trailer. An alternative to the rigid vehicle is the articulated outfit (Figure 7) consisting of a tractive unit and semi-trailer.

Most goods vehicles have their cab and flat mounted on a chassis frame and they are designed with normal or forward control. A normal control vehicle (Figure 8) is designed with the engine located forward of the cab. A forward control vehicle (Figure 9a) is designed with the engine located forward of the cab. A forward control vehicle (Figure 9b) has its cab built over the engine include engine noise in the cab and heat which must be tolerated by the crew. Engine maintenance can be more difficult with forward control unless specialized equipment is available to overcome the inaccessibility of the engine.

The function of the main components of heavy vehicles is similar to that of light vehicles, but the components are designed to withstand much heavier loads. The chassis frame sections are heavily constructed and assembled with bolts or rivets, and flitch plates are often used to add stiffness to the members. The gearbox, which may be conventional, semi or fully automatic, is coupled through a two-piece propeller shaft to the final drive, and a centre bearing is normally used.

## Rigid vehicles (Figures 10 and 11)

There are applications in which a rigid vehicle is preferable to an articulated vehicle. Rigid tippers, bulkers and tankers often give operating advantages over articulated vehicles for a given similar capacity. Where hopper, grab or pressure loading

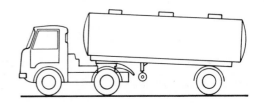

Figure 10    *Articulated vehicle-tanker*

Hydraulic tipping ram          Detachable taildoor swung from top & held at bottom

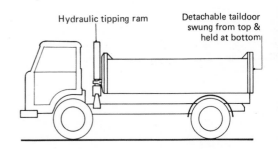

Figure 11    *Rigid vehicle-tipper with steel body*

is employed and discharge is equally rapid, the advantage of using one articulated tractive unit with several trailers does not always compare favourably.

An operator can benefit from the greater frame rigidity and strength of the rigid vehicle, this being particularly important where off-the-road and site work is involved. Tippers on rigid chassis are less subject to strain fracture in frame and body than some types of articulated outfits. For off-the-road work, multi-axle rigid vehicles have the advantage that four-wheeled drive can be made available at

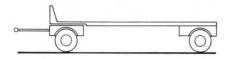

Figure 12    *Two-axle, four-wheeled type*

Figure 13    *Three-axle, six-wheeled type*

Figure 14    *Draw-bar showing steering linkage*

the rear bogey which greatly improves traction on soft ground.

The initial cost of a rigid vehicle can be less because the body is mounted on the chassis without the need for a separate trailer frame, brake system and fifth-wheel coupling. For many operations the rigid vehicle has greater stability and better road-holding qualities, giving improved safety margins; some drivers prefer rigid vehicles to articulated outfits because of the dangers of jack-knifing, trailer swing and overturning.

## Draw-bar trailers

A draw-bar trailer (Figures 12, 13 and 14) is similar in basic construction to a four-wheeled rigid vehicle with the exception that it does not have its own power unit and transmission system. It is connected to the drawing vehicle by a draw bar which tows and steers the trailer front wheels so that it follows the path of the drawing vehicle.

The most common draw-bar outfit is the four-wheeled rigid vehicle and trailer, although six- and eight-wheeled vehicles are sometimes operated with a trailer.

There is a wide range of trailers in use. Some are constructed with a flat platform or sided body, others are built as vans or skeletals for other kinds of operation. The size and capacity vary up to approximately 30.5 tonnes (30 tons) and bigger models are purpose-built with a greater number of axles. Trailer suspension is either by conventional semi-elliptic springs, rubber or air. By using a converter dolly, some semi-trailers are converted into draw-bar trailers for particular operations.

Most drivers find that draw-bar trailers are easier to handle than semi-trailers for normal driving purposes even though the combined length of the vehicle and trailer is often longer. There is less cut-in and no swing-out of the headboard when cornering with draw-bar trailers and they can be skilfully nosed into position by the vehicle if circumstances do not allow them to be drawn.

## Towing jaws, hooks and eyes

Towing equipment used with goods vehicles and draw-bar trailers is designed with a high safety factor to withstand the stresses and shock loads to which it is subjected in use. The equipment is also designed to minimize wear on the transmission of the towing vehicle and to give the payload as smooth a ride as possible.

Figure 15 shows a double spring jaw designed to be bolted on the rear member of the towing vehicle. This type of jaw is fitted by removing the split-pin, lock buts and exterior spring, and re-assembling after passing the shaft through the

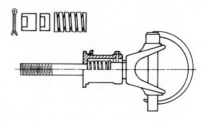

Figure 15    *Towing jaw*

clearance hole in the rear member. Similar in construction to the double spring jaw is the hook (Figure 16) and the eye which are sometimes preferred by vehicle operators. Self-aligning corner stays (Figures 17 and 18) are sometimes fitted to strengthen the rear member, which is subjected to many of the stresses caused by towing.

## Articulated vehicles

These are vehicles designed to carry their payload on a semi-trailer. The tractive unit and semi-trailer are coupled together in such a manner that the semi-trailer pivots on the tractive unit, allowing the combination to 'articulate'. The tractive unit has a comparatively short chassis which carries a coupling attachment for the semi-trailer. Tractive units normally consist of four or six wheels, and the six-wheeled unit may have twin drive axles or twin steer axles. Semi-trailers normally have one, two or three axles with either single or double wheels and have retractable wheels on which the front end can be supported when it is detached from the tractive unit. Articulated vehicles are more manoeuvrable than rigid vehicles for operating purposes, particularly with having a small turning circle. They are often more economical to operate than rigid vehicles, one advantage being that a number of semi-trailers can be operated with one tractive unit.

## Fifth-wheel coupling

This is normally used on tractive units whose unladen weight exceeds 2.032 tonnes (2 tons). It is more robust in construction than the automatic coupling which makes it suitable for maximum permitted loads on the biggest vehicles. The type shown (Figure 19) has two principle moving parts, these being known as the hook and the wedge lock, both manufactured with high tensile manganese steel.

*Operation*   Before coupling, the unit is 'cocked' by pulling out the release handle (Figure 20). As the tractive unit backs up, the semi-trailer kingpin enters the coupling throat and engages the hook

Figure 16    *Towing hook*

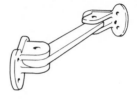

Figure 17    *Self-aligning corner stay*

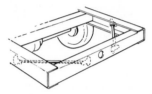

Figure 18    *Rear member with self-aligning stays fitted to chassis frame*

which pivots through 90° so that both shoulder and shank of the pin are totally enclosed by the hook and the coupler's jaw. As the hook turns (Figure 21), the wedge lock is released and the double coil spring pulls the wedge lock to its 'lock' position across the jaw. The kingpin pulls against the wedge which forms a 'bridge' across the coupler's throat when the vehicle is mobile. To release the kingpin, the release handle is pulled out and secured on the notch (Figure 22). The hook is now free to pivot, releasing the pin and leaving the coupling 'cocked' ready to re-couple, with the release handle free of the notch ready to re-lock automatically.

## Automatic coupling

This coupling gear consists of two ramps or runways (Figure 23) to take the flanged wheels fitted to the semi-trailer undercarriage, at

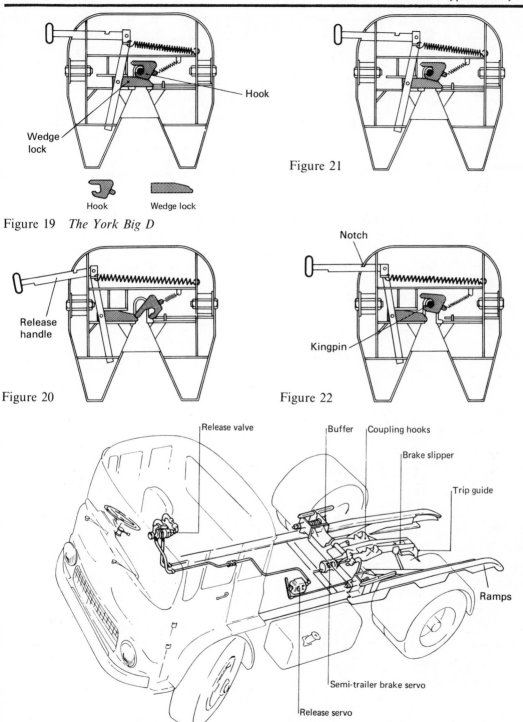

Figure 21

Hook

Wedge lock

Hook   Wedge lock

Figure 19   *The York Big D*

Release handle

Figure 20

Notch

Kingpin

Figure 22

Release valve   Buffer   Coupling hooks

Brake slipper

Trip guide

Ramps

Semi-trailer brake servo

Release servo

Figure 23   *Scammell coupling gear*

whatever angle the tractive unit may be coupled to the semi-trailer. At the front end of the ramps are two adjustable combination rubber spring buffers which absorb the shock of coupling up, and load the two coupling hooks in order to keep the trailer securely locked to the unit. The hand-operated control valve in the cab is provided with a safety catch and guard to ensure that the lever is not operated accidentally.

*Operation*   To uncouple the trailer, the control valve is depressed thereby creating air pressure in the release servo which operates the release rod and coupling hook level for lowering the coupling hooks and releasing the semi-trailer. The double locking hooks are provided so that, should initial coupling be incorrectly carried out, the rear hook will prevent the semi-trailer from breaking away.

The turntable operates on a rubbing plate attached to the front cross-member of the trailer frame and is secured by two horseshoe locking plates. A wearing ring is fitted to avoid undue wear on the rubbing plate and turntable (Figure 24).

A retractable undercarriage attached to the turntable carries two wheels to support the semi-trailer when detached. A transverse beam on the turntable carries two flanged wheels at its extremities; these wheels run on to the ramps at the rear of the tractive unit. The undercarriage shown has the advantage of a safety mechanism which prevents complete collapse of the undercarriage in the event of the locking gear failing to operate correctly owing to lack of maintenance, or uneven ground, or any other reason.

## Special types

*Pole wagons*   Pole semi-trailers and draw-bar trailers are used to carry logs, telegraph poles and

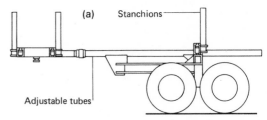

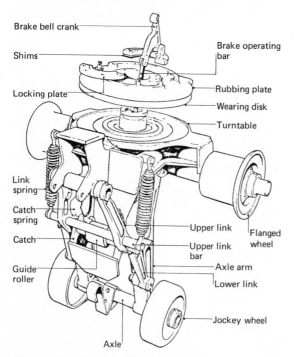

Figure 24   *Semi-trailer undercarriage*

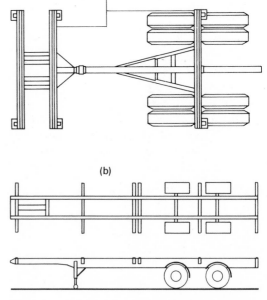

Figure 25   *(a) Pole wagon; (b) skeletal semi-trailer*

other similar loads. The central tubular pole and outer tube (Figure 25) can usually be adjusted for length. The load is supported on bolsters which are constructed with a number of removable upright stanchions between which the load is carried.

*Skeletals* Some trailers are constructed in the form of a skeletal, this being a frame consisting of two longitudinal members and a number of cross-members projecting outwards. A container is carried on the skeletal and secured with twist locks.

*Other types* It is not possible to illustrate every type of special application owing to the wide variety in use. A few are shown in Figure 26.

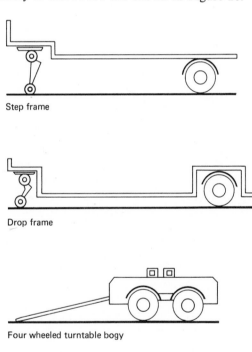

Step frame

Drop frame

Four wheeled turntable bogy

Four in-line removable axles

Figure 26 *Various types of trailer*

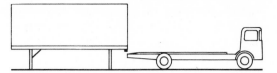

Figure 27 *Demountable body*

## Demountable body systems

Demountable bodies (Figure 27), swop bodies and stillages are all various names for types of body-work that can be transferred on and off commercial vehicles. The principal advantage of these systems is the facility of allowing one vehicle to operate with a number of bodies which can be left at a number of points for either loading or unloading whilst the vehicle is used to ferry other bodies for distribution. This operation reduces waiting time, both for the vehicle and the driver, when compared with fixed-body systems operating under similar circumstances. Demountable systems are also suitable for operators who handle products that take consider-able time and labour to load on their vehicles.

Since the introduction of containerization and Freightliner services, an increasing number of demountable systems have been used. The most popular systems are fully hydraulic, although some are pneumatic where air bellows are used to raise the demountable body. A common system in use has bellows incorporated on the underside of the container which raise it in one operation and the body support legs are lowered simultaneously. Air in the bellows is released by a gradual-flow valve and the weight transferred to the support legs. A normal platform vehicle requires no modification for this system, but bare chassis are fitted with a skeletal sub-frame to support and secure the body.

The hydraulically operated system has the lifting equipment mounted on the chassis with the body built on to an integral sub-frame to which the body support legs are attached. The lifting equip-ment incorporates four hydraulic rams, a control valve unit, fluid tank, relief valve and supply pipes. Hydraulic pressure is provided by a pump driven by a power take-off from the vehicle's gearbox.

Cones mounted on the chassis locate with centralizing rings in the body frame which is securely locked to the chassis by twist locks specifically designed to avoid accidental release. The body frame is lifted clear of the chassis by the extension of the hydraulic rams, and the body support legs are secured in their extended positions by mechanical locks. The hydraulic circuit is designed to enable a level lift to be made under any conditions, and the rams provide sufficient lift to cater for spring deflection, chassis clearance and uneven ground. The rams are retracted when the body support legs are lowered to allow the chassis to be driven clear.

### Goods vehicle cabs

The study of a driver in his working environment is known as ergonomics and has led to improvements in cab design to give the occupants the maximum comfort and visibility. Two doors are usually provided for easy access, and two seats are normally fitted for the driver and co-driver or mate. A third seat is fitted in some cabs to accommodate a third person, and legislation in some countries permits sleeper cabs for long-distance journeys so that cab crews can rest on a fitted bunk in the rear of the cab.

The driver's seat is usually designed to accommodate any size of occupant and is normally adjustable for height and distance from the steering wheel to promote relaxed driving. Most steering wheel positions are virtually horizontal and easily controlled by the driver. Instrument panels are normally arranged so that the instruments can be observed at a glance and they can be illuminated for reading during the hours of darkness.

Most cabs are built around a rigid frame of sturdy box-section members and panelled with sheet steel. An alternative material in use is glass-fibre-reinforced plastics which is lighter than steel but will not withstand impacts and vibrations to the same extent as steel. Windscreens are often made with wrapped-round double plate glass designed to give clear and unobstructed vision, and rear windows are fitted to improve visibility

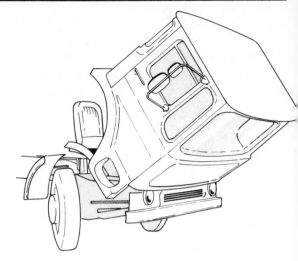

Figure 28   *Tilt cab*

and lighting. Cabs are mounted on the vehicle frame by rubber mountings which minimize chassis flexible vibrations on the cab and reduce cab vibration. Roof panels often consist of layers of glass fibre covered with PVC cloth to improve heat and sound insulation, and the engine is boxed-in by sound-absorbing panels to minimize engine noise. Heating and ventilation systems are used with demister vents for the windscreen and side windows to improve comfort and safety when driving.

*Tilt cabs (Figure 28)*   Some cabs can be tilted to allow access to the engine and its auxiliary units. Tilt cabs simplify engine maintenance and they are designed to tilt in a forward direction by a simple and easily operated balance mechanism when a safety lock catch is released.

### Passenger vehicles

*Buses*

Most buses and coaches are basically four-wheeled rigid vehicles, although a greater number of wheels and axles are occasionally employed, and articulated buses are operated in some countries.

The conventional layout of single-deck and

double-deck buses consists of a front-mounted engine slightly off-set towards the nearside, providing more room for the driver's compartment, and the final drive is slightly off-set to allow greater clearance for the centre gangway in the lower deck. The exhaust pipe usually discharges its gases to the offside where they will do least harm to the public. The fuel tank is situated on the offside which helps to counterbalance the boarding platform on the nearside. Safety rails are attached below the body sides to reduce the risk of accidents caused by people or animals becoming trapped under the sides, and an emergency door is fitted on the side of the saloon opposite the main entrance to comply with legal requirements. Some double-deck buses are built with low-bridge bodies for operating in districts where tunnels and bridge heights are low. These bodies can usually be recognized by their side gangway and bench seats each seating four passengers in the upper deck.

Older buses (Figure 29) have an open rear platform for passengers to board and alight, a disadvantage of this layout being that the driver does not have a good view of the platform from his compartment, even with the assistance of interior mirrors, and one-man operated buses further increase the risk of accidents to passengers during loading and unloading.

Most modern single-deck and double-deck buses (Figure 30) are built for one-man operation and have their doorways at the centre or the front, and in some layouts both at the centre and the front. Door action is power-operated and normally under the control of the driver who can see passengers boarding and alighting. Some larger single-deck buses operating in overseas countries are built with four doorways, one at the front, two at the centre and one at the rear.

Many modern single-deck layouts have their engine located beneath the floor in the centre (amidships) (Figure 31), or at the rear. This layout gives more room at the front of the saloon for a front entrance and a driver's compartment. Modern double-deck buses have a rear-mounted transverse engine which affords a front entry for passengers, has a low noise level and leaves the engine accessible for maintenance.

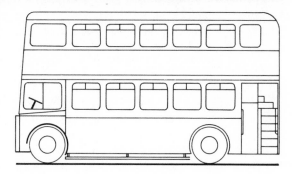

Figure 29    *Conventional double-deck bus*

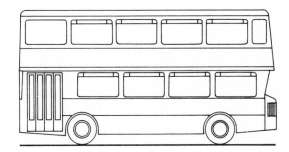

Figure 30    *Double-deck bus*

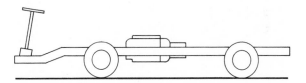

Figure 31    *Frame and layout with amidships, vertically mounted engine*

The passenger capacity of buses varies with the design and the type of operation. Many single-deck models have a seating capacity of fifty-two, although they can be designed to seat fewer and accommodate a large proportion of standing passengers. A typical 11.3 metre version has two doors, twenty-eight seats and space for forty-six standing, this vehicle having a total passenger capacity of seventy-four. Double-decked buses are also designed for different operation and have a passenger capacity of approximately sixty-five to seventy-five, although higher capacities are occasionally used for service.

## Midi buses

The demise of the bus as a mode of public transport in many towns and urban areas in the United Kingdom over the past years has brought personal hardship to the elderly, youngsters, the poor and the handicapped, in addition to others unable or unwilling to drive. In an attempt to prevent further reductions in the use of buses, some passenger transport operators have introduced the midi bus. There are a number of these vehicles now in use propelled by both conventional compression ignition engines and battery electrics. Many midi buses have a total passenger capacity of about twenty-six with comparatively large passenger standing area and few seats. These buses are popular for suitable short-route town operations as they are easily manoeuvred in congested areas and are economical to operate.

## Coaches

These vehicles are similar in construction to single-deck buses but they are more luxurious and tend to have heavier bodywork. Coaches are normally designed to seat between twenty-eight and fifty-three passengers and they usually operate on long-distance journeys, often overnight. They are designed with ample luggage lockers and a boot, comfortable seating, window curtains, air conditioning and heating, soft lighting, radio and tape music and a public address system. Some are also equipped with toilet facilities and a cocktail bar.

Many coach bodies are designed with a length of 11 metres and some coach engines are vertically mounted (amidships), located low in the frame to provide for a flat floor and low centre of gravity. The absence of the engine with its obstructive hump at the front of the saloon facilitates entry and gives extra floor space and a low noise level. The entrance is usually situated at the front or behind the front wheels, and an emergency exit is always provided at the rear of the coach.

## Electrically propelled buses

Electric vehicles have been operated for many years for the delivery of milk and bread, where the vehicle's workload is fairly constant and the daily mileage is comparatively low. Recent study of environmental pollution has prompted some vehicle manufacturers to investigate the possibility of using battery electrics to propel heavier vehicles, and a number of buses are now in operation – many for evaluation purposes.

Traction power is provided by batteries which are recharged overnight and during off-the-road periods. These supply current to an electric motor which drives the vehicle through a conventional transmission system and rear wheels. The batteries are usually the lead–acid type, although nickel–iron and nickel–cadmium can be used as alternatives with an anticipated longer life but a higher initial cost.

Interior heating is supplied by night storage heaters, often with fan assistance, these being recharged at the same time as the traction batteries. The front windscreen demisting system consists of a cold air supply which is electrically heated.

Vehicle mileage on fully charged lead–acid batteries is claimed to be between 50 and 80 km (30 and 50 miles) depending upon operating conditions and traffic density, with a maximum road speed of about 48 km/h (30 mile/h) for a passenger capacity of about twenty-five. Full size battery electric buses are being developed for future operations.

## Gas-propelled buses

Gas-propelled vehicles are by no means a new technical innovation. During the Second World War, developments took place with the use of producer gas as a fuel for fleets of vehicles. Many buses were equipped with trailers on which was assembled the gas producer unit which supplies the engine with fuel.

Recently, there have been a number of experimental steps in the search for a low-pollution, low-noise-level city bus. One type of experimental bus uses natural (North Sea) gas as its fuel and is being developed for operation on the Continent.

Natural gas has over 95% methane and has a high hydrogen and low carbon content which produces an exhaust gas mainly in the form of water vapour with very little carbon content, thus dramatically reducing carbon monoxide exhaust emissions – a common pollutant emitted from petrol-engined vehicles. Some manufacturers claim that, if a high volume plant were used to produce gas, fuel costs per mile would be comparable with the compression-ignition-engined vehicle. Engine power developed is also comparable with the compression ignition engine and there are the added advantages of smooth running and quietness.

One disadvantage of gas-propelled vehicles is the bulk and weight of gas storage bottles and their potential danger for causing fire and explosions. Research is being carried out with liquid gas which can be stored in a liquid state at –160°C. From the tank, the fuel passes to a heat exchanger where the cooling action in vaporization helps to cool the engine coolant, and then passes to a fuel mixer where gas and air are blended and fed to the engine cylinders.

## Frames

*Conventional layout*
The normal frame construction (Figure 32) for goods vehicles and many passenger vehicles consists of two longitudinal (side) members in the form of steel channel sections, and they are virtually straight both in plan and side elevation. These members are braced by a number of cross-

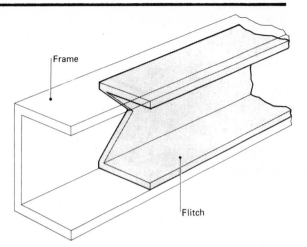

Figure 33   *The chassis frame may be reinforced by adding flitches*

members which are of channel or tubular section and may be riveted, bolted or welded in position. The front axle is normally the conventional beam type and the rear axle contains the final drive gear which is a double reduction unit on many vehicles.

*Frame reinforcement*
The frame must be able to withstand stresses placed upon it by numerous loads and forces. Section changes within a frame are prone to high stressing and indiscriminate drilling weakens the frame. Frames are strengthened (Figure 33) by the addition of flitches. These are plates designed to fit within the channel section to increase its strength and rigidity. The risk of fracture caused by vibration, overloading, overstressing and fatigue is reduced by adding flitches.

Flitches are designed so that the loading on the frame is spread uniformly over a considerable length and not concentrated at one point. The flitches are normally staggered in length and angled at their ends to provide even spreading of the stresses. Flitches should be snugly nested within the channel if they are to provide maximum reinforcement and reduce stressing to a minimum. If improperly fitted in the parent frame, flitches can cause excessive stress-raising at the fastening points which defeats the purpose of their use and unnecessarily increases the weight of the frame.

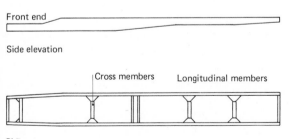

Figure 32   *Conventional layout – frame for rigid goods vehicle*

*Integral construction (Leyland National)*

Some later models of buses and coaches are built with the body and underframe structure as a complete integral unit (see Figure 34). The underframe of the vehicle shown is constructed from

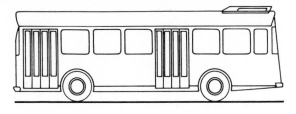

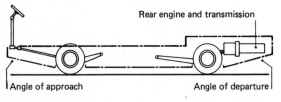

Figure 34  *Single-deck bus – integral construction*

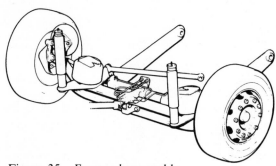

Figure 35  *Front axle assembly*

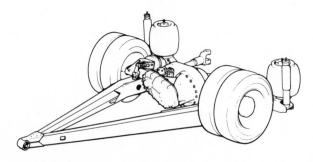

Figure 36  *Rear suspension assembly – 'A' frame type*

varying-size steel channel members together with pressed steel cross-members and pressed steel wheel-arch risers. The angles of approach and departure are important and are designed to allow ample ground clearance at the front and rear which is necessary on a long-wheelbase vehicle that operates in hilly districts. The main assembly is riveted and steel panels are used above waist height with high-strength aluminium alloy panels below the waist. The roofstick is the main structural member and is an assembly of substantial depth which forms a high-strength transverse member at the top of the pillar. The stick consists of a two-piece pressing screwed back-to-back along the line of abutment of the flanges and around the circumference of the opening in the member. The longitudinal members are of roll-formed section and form the sides of the heating and ventilation system duct.

The front axle (Figure 35) is a forged I-section beam constructed with the steering gear mounted directly on it. The rear suspension (Figure 36) is in the form of an A frame with three moving connections, one at the apex and one at each end of the Panhard rod.

## Air deflectors

The total resistance to the motion of a vehicle is the combination of rolling, gradient and air resistance. The latter is influenced by wind conditions and can be of a considerable magnitude at high road speeds, particularly on box vans.

By fitting deflectors, alternatively known as foils or fins, to the cab top, a streamlining is given to the air flow as it passes over and around the box; this reduces resistance or drag on the vehicle. Some further streamlining is also achieved by fitting air dams to the lower part of the cab front and nose panels to the front of the trailer box.

By improving the aerodynamics of goods vehicles an improvement in fuel consumption is gained, together with a saving in engine power. Further benefits include a slightly longer engine life, transmission life, less maintenance and less vehicle 'downtime'. Vehicle top speeds and performance are also slightly increased by using

Labels in Figure 34:
Rear engine and transmission
Angle of approach
Angle of departure

Turbulent air flow along
the top and sides of the box

Figure 37   *Air flow without deflector*

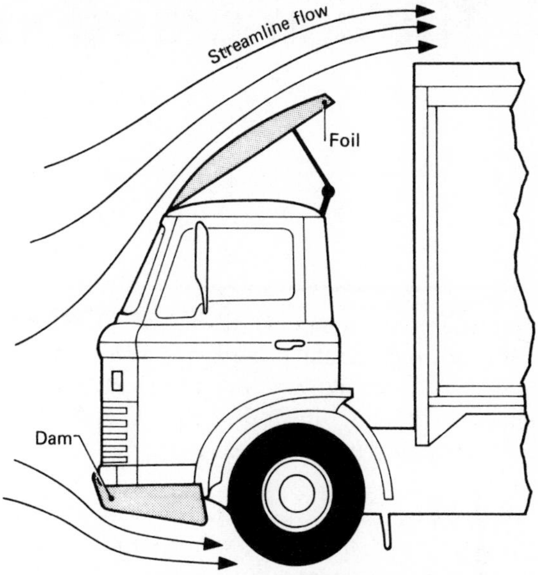

Streamline flow

Foil

Dam

Figure 38   *Air flow with deflectors fitted*

deflectors, leading to a reduction in journey time. Other benefits to drivers are improvements in vehicle stability, particularly with cross-winds, where less yaw and sway occurs thus reducing steering corrections and driver fatigue.

Deflectors are usually made from glass-reinforced plastics and can easily be fitted and removed from the vehicle. It is important that roof deflectors are fitted at the correct angle and height to obtain maximum advantage from them.

# 2 The compression ignition engine

Compression ignition (CI) engines are used in most goods vehicles and passenger vehicles. These engines are alternatively described as 'diesel engines' in honour of Dr Rudolph Diesel who pioneered and developed heavy engines of this type.

Most CI engines operate with the four-stroke cycle in the order: induction, compression, power, exhaust. The important difference between the CI engine and the spark ignition engine is that ignition of the fuel in the engine cylinders occurs at the high temperature of the induced air at the end of its compression stroke without need of an electrical spark. The compression ratio of this type of engine ranges from about 12:1 to about 22:1 depending upon engine design, many British engines having a ratio of about 16:1. The temperature at the end of the compression stroke depends to a large extent upon the temperature at the beginning of the stroke and upon the amount of heat lost during compression, but it is usually about 450°C. This temperature is higher than the self-ignition temperature of diesel fuel oil, so that when an atomized spray of fuel oil is forced into the combustion chamber, containing compressed and turbulent air, the burning process commences.

## Four-stroke cycle

*Induction*   The inlet valve opens just before top dead centre (t.d.c.) and air is induced into the cylinder by the descending piston which creates a depression in the cylinder. The inlet valve closes after the piston has just passed bottom dead centre (b.d.c.) and air is sealed in the cylinder.

*Compression*   The piston ascends and compresses the charge of air to about 1/16 of its original volume with the cylinder pressure rising to a value between 3100 and 5100 $kN/m^2$ and the temperature rising to approximately 450°C. The atomized fuel is injected into the cylinder just before the piston reaches the top of its stroke.

*Power*   The combustion process occurs when the piston is passing through t.d.c., causing the temperature of the gases to rise well above 1500°C with a corresponding pressure of about 5000 $kN/m^2$. The expansion of the burning gases forces the piston downwards on its power stroke producing a torque on the crankshaft. The exhaust valve opens just before the piston reaches b.d.c.

*Exhaust*   The spent gases are forced out of the cylinder as the piston ascends for its exhaust stroke. The cylinder is scavenged and the inlet valve opens before the piston reaches the top of its stroke. The next cycle commences as the piston descends on induction stroke and the exhaust valve closes just after the piston has passed t.d.c.

## Two-stroke cycle

In the two-stroke engine (Figure 39), inlet and exhaust of the gases take place during part of the compression and power strokes, respectively, in contrast to a four-stroke engine which requires four piston strokes to complete its operating cycle with two of the piston strokes functioning as an air pump.

A blower or supercharger is normally used to force air into the cylinders for expelling the exhaust gases and to supply the cylinders with

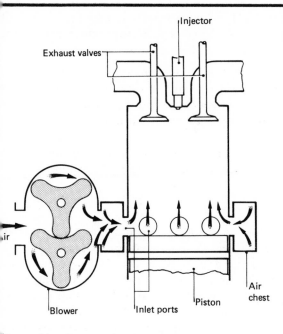

Figure 39   *Two-stroke CI engine*

engine. The port admits air from the blower into the cylinder as the piston uncovers the ports as shown in part *(a)*. The unidirectional flow of air towards the exhaust valves produces a scavenging effect, leaving the cylinders charged with air when the piston again covers the inlet ports. As the piston continues on the upward stroke, the exhaust valves close and the air charge is subjected to compression as shown in part *(b)*. Shortly before the piston reaches t.d.c., fuel is injected into the cylinder and combustion occurs as shown in part *(c)*. The resulting increase in cylinder pressure forces the piston downwards on its power stroke. The exhaust valves are again opened when the piston is about halfway down the cylinder allowing burned gases to escape into the exhaust manifold as shown in part *(d)*. Further downward movement of the piston uncovers the inlet ports and the cylinder is again scavenged and charged with air from the blower.

Another development of the two-stroke engine is the horizontal opposed-piston type in which two pistons are arranged in one long and open-ended cylinder (Figure 41). The inlet ports are controlled by one of the pistons and the exhaust ports are controlled by the opposing piston, when they are at their outer positions. The combustion chamber is formed by the two pistons coming together at the centre of the cylinder.

Two-stroke engines have the advantage of a higher power-to-weight ratio but their disadvantages usually include higher fuel consumption

fresh air, under a pressure slightly greater than atmospheric pressure. A common type of two-stroke engine has twin, poppet-type, rocker-operated exhaust valves, and inlet ports are arranged in the cylinder walls. These ports communicate with an air chest, which is charged with air under pressure, and piston movement controls the flow of air from the chest into the cylinder. Figure 40 shows a vee-type of two-stroke

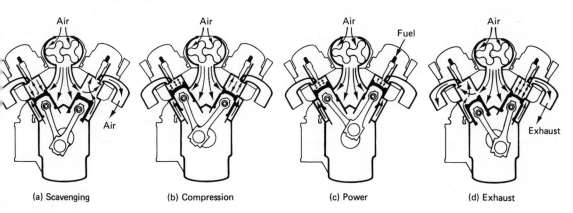

(a) Scavenging        (b) Compression        (c) Power        (d) Exhaust

Figure 40   *Two-stroke engine – vee type*

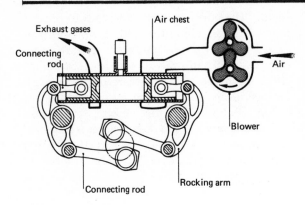

Figure 41   *The two-stroke engine – opposed-piston type*

than four-stroke engines due to their lower volumetric efficiency, less complete combustion and incomplete scavenging of exhaust gases in the cylinders.

## Valve timing

Valve timing of a four-stroke CI engine is set to give the best desirable engine performance. A typical valve-timing diagram is shown in Figure 42.

### Lead, lag and overlap

*Lead*   During the induction stroke the inlet valve is open and the descending piston creates a depression in the cylinder causing atmospheric pressure to force air through the air cleaner and inlet manifold to charge the cylinder. The inlet valve 'leads' by opening just before t.d.c. and 'lags' by remaining open after b.d.c. This arrangement allows maximum time to charge the cylinder allowing for the momentum of the induced air.

*Lag*   Both valves are closed during compression as the piston ascends and compresses the air charge to about 1/16 of its original volume. The valves remain closed during combustion and the piston descends on its power stroke. The exhaust valve 'leads' by opening before b.d.c., remaining open during the exhaust stroke and 'lagging' after

t.d.c. This allows maximum time for the exhaust gases to leave the cylinder and scavenge the combustion chamber.

*Overlap*   Both inlet and exhaust valves are open at the same instant, this is known as 'overlap' and occurs when the piston is passing through t.d.c. between its exhaust and induction strokes. The purpose of overlap is to take advantage of the momentum of the high-velocity outgoing exhaust gases to assist in scavenging the cylinder.

## Port timing

Most two-stroke CI engines have valves through which the burned gases are released from the cylinder and ports are machined in the cylinder walls through which the fresh charge enters the cylinder. Figure 43 shows the periods of crankshaft rotation during which the exhaust valves are open and the inlet ports are uncovered by movement of the piston. Pressure charging largely compensates for the shorter period the inlet ports are uncovered when compared with the longer period the inlet valves are open in a four-stroke engine.

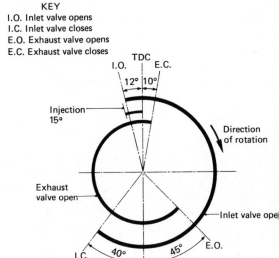

Figure 42   *A typical four-stroke CI engine valve timing diagram*

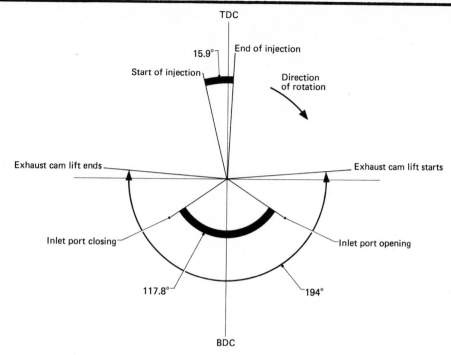

Figure 43   *A typical two-stroke CI engine port-timing diagram*

## Three phases of combustion

The combustion process in the cylinder of a CI engine (Figure 44) is usually described in three phases. The graph shows the variations in cylinder pressure plotted on a continuous crank angle base.

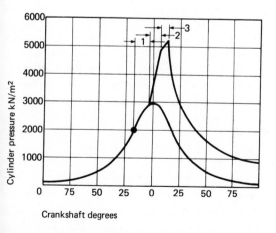

Figure 44   *Phases of combustion*

### First phase or delay period

Injection commences about 15° before t.d.c. as indicated by the dot on the compression line. Fuel oil is sprayed into the cylinder and combined with the air under a very high pressure. During this period ignition is being initiated but combustion does not occur immediately. The droplets of fuel are heated and mixed with the air, but their surfaces only are vaporized and only a small amount of heat energy is released. There is no noticeable rise in cylinder pressure and the pressure curve follows the normal compression curve which would be recorded if there were no combustion. The delay period occupies about 10° of crank rotation.

### Second phase

During this phase, there is a sharp rise in cylinder pressure to about 5000 kN/m². Turbulence of the air has assisted in combining the atomized fuel with the air, and sufficient heat has been absorbed to vaporize the fuel completely. The steepness of this pressure rise is a determining factor in causing 'diesel knock', the steeper the rise the louder the knock. This phase of combustion usually extends over a period of about 10° and is completed about 5° after t.d.c. In general, the longer the delay period the steeper will be the pressure rise during phase two and the louder will be the knock. The design of combustion chamber, nature of the fuel, pressure and temperature of the air during compression and the rate of fuel injection are all factors in deciding the length of the delay period and the steepness of the pressure rise in phase two.

### Third phase

During this phase, combustion continues as fuel is injected into the cylinder. There is sufficient heat available to vaporize and ignite the fuel as it issues from the injector. The rate of combustion during this phase is directly controlled by the quantity of fuel injected into the cylinder. Combustion and expansion of the gases takes place as the piston descends on its power stroke producing a sustained torque on the crankshaft during burning of the gases.

## Diesel knock and fuel

A disadvantage of the CI engine when compared with a spark ignition engine is its noise. One of the noises of the CI engine is known as 'diesel knock'. This is caused by the sudden increase in cylinder pressure during the second phase of combustion. During this phase the first particles of the injected fuel are heated to self ignition temperature and the whole of the injected fuel rapidly burns resulting in a sudden rise in cylinder pressure causing this characteristic knock.

One of the most important properties of a CI engine fuel is its ability to self-ignite, and this is known as its 'ignition quality'. The higher the ignition quality, expressed as a Cetane rating, the shorter the ignition delay, and the less pronounced is the diesel knock. Fuels with a higher Cetane rating are regarded as the better fuels as, in addition to being less prone to knock, they give smoother engine running and make cold starting easier.

## Combustion chambers

The CI engine relies on the heat produced in the cylinder during compression for ignition of the mixture of atomized fuel and air, and differs on this principle from the spark ignition engine which employs a spark plug for igniting the mixture. The CI engine is therefore designed with a relatively high compression ratio to produce sufficient heat during compression, and it must have a low surface-to-volume ratio in its combustion chambers to keep heat losses from the cylinders to a minimum.

### Types of combustion chamber

If the air and atomized fuel are to mix and burn efficiently in the combustion chamber, the air must be made to move at a high velocity in order to combine with the fuel droplets and form a combustible mixture. There are two basic designs of combustion chamber in use, both designed to give a smooth and controlled process of combustion together with a high degree of combustion efficiency and a minimum amount of 'diesel knock'. One of the designs is known as 'direct injection' and can be recognized by the combustion chamber which is in the form of a cavity in the piston crown. The alternative design is known as 'indirect injection' and the combustion chamber is wholly or partly in the cylinder head.

*Turbulence*  Turbulent movement of the air and injected fuel in a cylinder is often described by the words *squish* and *swirl*. Squish is the word normally used to describe the path of turbulent air and fuel in the cylinder. This movement is caused by the ascending piston, which is specially designed, compressing the air charge whose motion is directed in a circular path as shown. Swirl is the path of the air and fuel in the cylinder observed in the horizontal plane. This is caused by the angle and shape of the inlet ports and, in some engines, aided by a masked inlet valve.

### Direct injection

In this design of combustion chamber the fuel is directly injected (Figure 45) at a pre-determined time in the cycle of operations and combines with

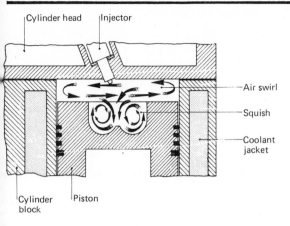

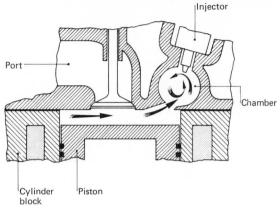

Figure 45   *Direct injection*         Figure 46   *Indirect injection*

the turbulent air. Briefly, combustion takes place as a result of the atomized fuel combining with the heated air in the cylinder. The atomized fuel in the form of minute droplets vaporizes as the outer surface of each particle absorbs heat from the air. As the temperature of combustion is reached, the vapour spontaneously ignites causing a further rise in temperature of the burning charge and produces a rapid increase in cylinder pressure.

Multi-hole injectors with four or five holes in their nozzles are normally used with direct injection and they operate at a comparatively high injector opening pressure, usually in the region of 170 atm. The injectors operated by a high-pressure fuel injection pump produce a penetrating type of fuel spray with enough 'reach' in the cylinder to seek and combine with the necessary oxygen for combustion.

Maximum cylinder pressures are high with direct-injection engines and tend to cause diesel knock, rough running and higher levels of exhaust smoke emissions than the indirect-injection designs. However, their easy starting, without the assistance of starting aids, together with their high thermal efficiency and fairly constant torque output make them popular for use in heavy vehicles.

*Indirect injection*
This design of combustion chamber (Figure 46) is more popular in small CI engines used in light commercial vehicles, vans and taxis. Air is forced through the narrow throat into the combustion chamber by the ascending piston which has the effect of promoting air turbulence. The injectors used in this design usually have fewer holes than those used with direct injection, and the single-hole pintle type with its soft conical spray and short reach is used in some of these engines.

The designs of most indirect-injection combustion chamber layouts have a larger surface-to-volume ratio than direct-injection layouts, and this causes greater heat loss from the cylinders. These losses of heat together with that lost by the passage of air from the cylinder into the combustion chamber all contribute to difficulties encountered when starting the engine from cold.

This disadvantage is overcome by using a higher compression ratio than in the direct-injection engine and, in addition, using a starting device such as a heater plug in each cylinder. A comparatively low injection pressure is required with indirect injection as it operates with an increased amount of air turbulence when compared with direct injection and the injector pressure is usually in the order of 100 atm.

The better turbulence achieved with indirect injection when compared with direct injection promotes smoother running over the entire speed range of the engine, there is more control of cylinder pressure increase and there is a shorter delay period causing less diesel knock. Indirect-injection engines also emit less nitric oxide with the exhaust gases which is likely to make them more popular in the future if more stringent legislation for exhaust smoke emissions is enforced.

## Engine types

The most common type of engine used in heavy vehicles is the conventional six-cylinder in-line direct-injection CI engine. Other more unconventional types have however been developed over the years and include those of a vee configuration and those of a horizontal or inclined layout, all of which are currently in use.

### In-line engines

These engines are used in most goods and passenger vehicles. The six-cylinder version is the most popular, although four-, five- and eight-cylinder units are also in use. The current trend is however to develop engines of high power output to match the increased, and the possible further increases in,

gross vehicle weights, and to comply with legislation governing power-to-weight ratios. For these and other reasons, engines with high torque and power are now being developed, the majority of which are turbocharged.

A notable exception to the turbocharged range of engines is the Gardner automotive diesel engine (Figure 47). These engines, which are very popular and fitted in many heavy goods vehicles, have a fairly high torque output at a comparatively low engine speed. The maximum engine speed of the Gardner diesel range is between 1700 and 1850 rev/min depending upon the model. An interesting engine is the Gardner eight-cylinder 13.93-litre in-line LXB model which develops 198 kW (265 bhp) at 1920 rev/min and produces 1022 Nm (752 lbf ft) maximum torque at 1000–1200 rev/min. This model is a very popular choice for goods vehicle operators even though it is of considerable overall length.

British Leyland produces a wide range of engines to power its own vehicles and the engines are also fitted in other makes of vehicle. The TL 12

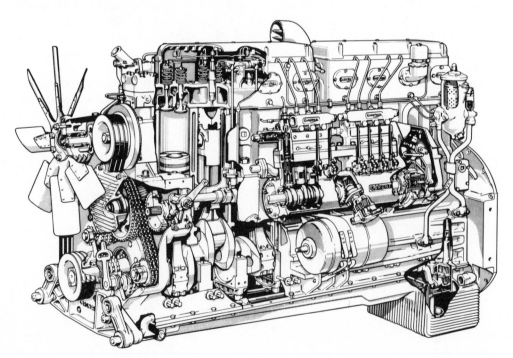

Figure 47    *Gardner 8LXB CI engine*

engine (Figure 48) is an in-line, six-cylinder turbo-charged unit with a capacity of 12.47 litres. The gross power rating is 203 kW (270 bhp) at 2000 rev/min with a maximum torque of 1100 Nm (860 lbf ft) at 1200 rev/min.

The Rolls-Royce range of engines (Figure 49) are developed with 205, 220, 265, 305, 320 and 340 bhp. The 320 and 340 engines have four valves in each cylinder and all the models have an inlet manifold designed to give inertia-ram filling of the cylinders. The normally aspirated engine operates on a 16:1 compression ratio, and the turbocharged version has a compression ratio of 13.5. The maximum torque produced by the 340 turbo-charged model is 1300 Nm (956 lbf ft) at 1300 rev/min.

The E400 Cummins engine has a power rating of 298 kW (400 bhp) which is developed at 2100 rev/min. This is a 14-litre engine fitted with a turbocharger and charge cooling system. The compression ratio is 13.9:1 and its peak torque is 1560 Nm (1150 lbf ft) at 1300 rev/min.

### Vee engines

Perkins Engines Ltd produces a 90° V8 (Model 510) (Figure 50) with a capacity of 8.4 litres and a gross power output of 134 kW (180 bhp) at 2800 rev/min. The maximum torque is 54 kg m (398 lbf ft) at 1600 rev/min and the net weight is 640 kg (1405 lb).

Another popular vee engine is the Detroit Diesel built by General Motors Corporation, USA. The six-cylinder, two-stroke version has a capacity of 6981 $cm^3$ with a power output of approximately 177 kW (238 bhp) at 210 rev/min and the maximum torque is 82 kg m (600 lbf ft) at 1600 rev/min. This engine has a compression ratio of 18.7:1 and the net weight is 889 kg (1960 lb).

An advantage of the vee configuration is that it gives a shorter and more compact power unit than an in-line unit with the same number of cylinders. This type of engine is preferred by many cab designers as it can be accommodated more easily within the cab. It is also useful in vehicles where the overall vehicle length is important.

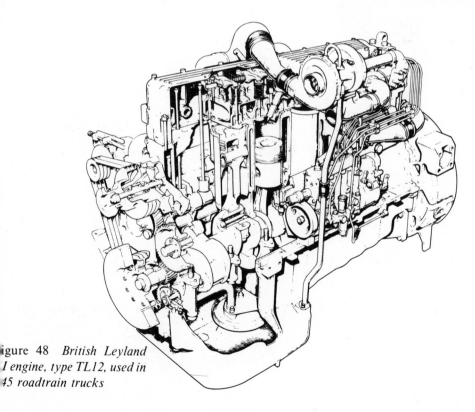

Figure 48 *British Leyland engine, type TL12, used in 45 roadtrain trucks*

Figure 49   *Rolls-Royce Eagle Mk 3*

Figure 50   *A Perkins 90° V8 (Model 510) engine*

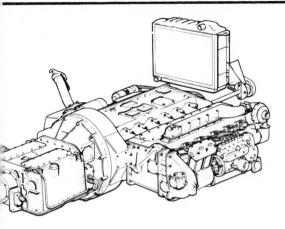

Figure 51    *Horizontal engine*

## Horizontal and inclined engines

These are sometimes fitted in vehicles and are particularly useful in passenger vehicles where a low floor level is required (Figure 51). Many of these engines are positioned amidships (central) or at the rear of passenger vehicles so that more room is available at the front of the saloon for the driver and passengers.

## Cylinder blocks and crankcases

Some engines have their cylinder block and crankcase manufactured as an integral unit, but many of the heavier engines have a separate block and crankcase which are bolted together during assembly. When the block and crankcase are separate units, the two are usually made from different metals as their functions differ considerably. The block is usually made from cast iron which has good casting and wearing qualities, and aluminium alloy is sometimes used for cylinder blocks which have wet liners. When a separate crankcase is employed it is usually made from aluminium alloy.

### Integral construction

This type is normally used for the lighter range of engines and is less costly to manufacture than separate units. The cylinder bores may be in line or an alternative configuration may be employed

within the single casting. The crankcase houses the webs which support the crankshaft and camshaft bearings, and they provide crankcase rigidity. The camshaft is usually housed in the upper crankcase and the front end of the crankcase normally houses the timing gears. The rear end of the crankcase usually contains a flange to which is attached the clutch housing.

### Separate units

Engines with a separate cylinder block (Figure 52) and crankcase are more costly to manufacture than the integral type, but this arrangement allows different materials to be used in the manufacture of each unit and it has the advantage of making possible the removal and replacement of the block with the crankcase *in situ*.

Some engines have one cylinder block containing all the cylinders, other engines have more than one block. Examples of the latter are the six-cylinder Gardner engines, some of which have two separate blocks, each containing three cylinders. This type of engine has the advantage of lower handling weights when removing and replacing the blocks, and occasionally one block may be changed while the other block is left undisturbed.

Separate cylinder blocks are usually located on the upper face of the crankcase by dowels and secured by bolts. In some engines a shim gasket is used between the block and crankcase. Engine manufacturers stress the importance of tightening

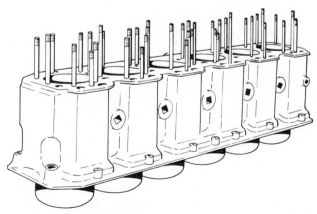

Figure 52    *Cylinder block*

down the blocks to the crankcase with the recommended torque values, otherwise the components may distort if they are over-tightened. The cylinder-head/piston-crown clearance must also be checked after assembly of blocks on the crankcase, as the height of the piston in relation to the top surface of the block is extremely important. Core plugs are used in cylinder blocks and these must be periodically checked for tightness and leaks. Inspection windows are also fitted on some blocks for checking the water jackets and cleaning out any rust which tends to accumulate within.

## Cylinder liners

Most CI engines are fitted with cylinder liners (Figure 53), the increase in initial cost of these being more than compensated for by higher mileages and reduced maintenance costs between overhauls. Liner material is usually different from that used for a cylinder block, the block material being a type suitable for intricate styling and machining. Liners are usually made from alloy cast iron or chromium-plated steel, these materials being chosen for their high resistance to wear caused by abrasive and corrosive conditions.

### Dry liners

These are usually centrifugally cast, pre-finished to very close tolerances, and are an interference fit in the cylinder block. Some are copper plated on the outer surface to make assembly and removal easier and, as copper is a good conductor of heat, heat transfer between the liner and block is improved. These liners are externally finished to about 0.05 mm (0.002 in) above bore size, and they must be lubricated on the outer surface before being pressed into the cylinder block with the use of a liner press. When liners have been fitted into a block, the top surface of the block is usually lightly machined and the inner edge of the liners are filed to remove any burrs or sharp edges. The liners require finish grinding or honing after being fitted in the block and connecting rod slots may have to be cut out at the lower end of the liners. A disadvantage of this design is the difficulty in replacing damaged or worn liners.

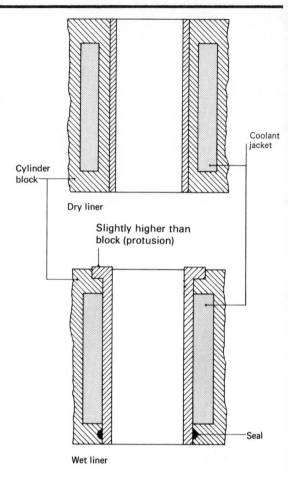

Figure 53   *Cylinder liners*

### Push-fit dry liners

A different type of dry liner from the interference-fit type is the push-fit liner which can be pushed or tapped into and out of the cylinder block. These liners are prefinished and no machining is necessary after fitting. They are located in position and held rigidly in the block by a shoulder which fits into a recess in the top of the block and the shoulder slightly protrudes above the surface of the block to form a gas-tight seal with the cylinder head gasket when assembled. No special tools are required for fitting and removing, and a further advantage when compared with interference-fit liners is that they can be removed and fitted without removing the engine from the chassis.

## Wet liners

These have much thicker walls than dry liners and are in direct contact with the coolant. They are simple to replace when damaged or worn as removal and fitting can be done without any special tools as they are a push-fit in the block. Wet liners are held in position by a shoulder, usually fitting into a recess in the top of the block, and sealing rings or gaskets are used between the liner and the block to prevent leakage of coolant into the engine sump. The top of each liner protrudes slightly above the top of the block to ensure a gas-tight seal with the cylinder head gasket when assembled. Engine cooling is better with the wet type of liner due to direct contact between the coolant and the liner.

## The camshaft

The camshaft (Figure 54) is normally located in, and supported by, the cylinder block or crankcase and contains a number of cams whose function is to control the operation of the valves in relation to the piston position in each cylinder. Alloy steel is normally used for the manufacture of the camshaft from which it is forged, or alloy iron may be used from which the camshaft is cast. The material is chosen in either case for its stiffness, which is necessary during operation, its resistance to impact shocks caused by operating the valves, and its resistance to torsional loads. Most shafts have case-hardened integral cams although some of the Gardner engines have pairs of cams manufactured separately from the shaft and secured to the shaft by locking screws which locate in countersunk drillings in the shaft. These drillings correctly position the cams on their shaft in relation to the piston position. A separate cam is contained on the camshafts of some engines to operate a mechanically driven fuel pump.

Figure 54  *Section of engine camshaft*

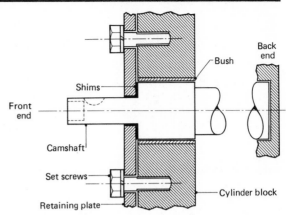

Figure 55  *Location and adjustment of camshaft in cylinder block*

## Camshaft bearings

The camshaft journals are usually supported by pre-finished bearings which are fitted into the cylinder block or crankcase. The diameter of the bearings is usually large enough to allow the cams to pass through them for assembly and removal of the camshaft. Manufacturers recommend a running clearance between the camshaft and its bearings. This clearance varies depending upon the size, load capacity and materials used for the shaft and bearings but it is usually in the region of 0.058 mm (0.0023 in). Camshaft end-float and endwise location are adjustable in most engines and attention should be paid to these during engine overhauls.

A number of materials are used for the manufacture of camshaft bearings, the most common of these being a white metal lining on a steel back, or a reticular tin–aluminium lining on a steel back; the word 'reticular' describes the micro-structure of the alloy which is aluminium containing 20% tin. Bearing lubrication is normally achieved with engine oil which is supplied under pressure through drillings in the crankcase to the bearing surfaces.

## Overhead camshaft

The British Leyland 500 Series engines have fixed heads and employ an overhead camshaft (Figure 56) with integral cams located in an aluminium

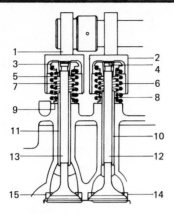

1. Camshaft
2. Tappet
3. Valve split cone
4. Tappet adjustment washer
5. Valve spring collar, upper
6. Valve spring, outer
7. Valve spring, inner
8. Inlet valve seal
9. Valve spring collar, lower
10. Valve guide, inlet
11. Valve guide, exhaust
12. Inlet valve
13. Exhaust valve
14. Valve seat inlet
15. Valve seat exhaust

Figure 56   *Overhead camshaft layout*

alloy tappet block secured to the top of the cylinder block. The cams operate directly on the tappets and their centre lines are slightly off-set to cause tappet rotation and minimize wear.

*Camshaft drives*

The camshaft is driven by the crankshaft with one or more chains (Figure 57) or by a gear train. A toothed belt (Figure 58) is used for this purpose in some of the lighter vehicle engines. If the engine is operating on the four-stroke cycle, the camshaft is driven at half the speed of the crankshaft as each valve is required to operate once every two revolutions of the crankshaft.

Gardner engines have a chain drive with a triple row chain passing round an adjusting idler gear, a fixed idler gear and an alternator drive sprocket, in addition to the camshaft and crankshaft sprockets.

Some engines have an all-gear drive (Figure 59) for the camshaft, fuel injection pump and other auxiliaries. This type of drive gives maximum reliability and long life, and no adjustment is necessary whereas chain drives periodically require adjusting to compensate for stretch and wear.

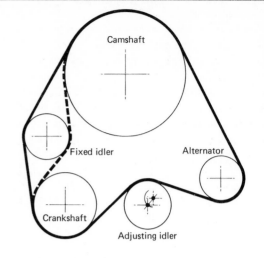

Figure 57   *Chain driven gears*

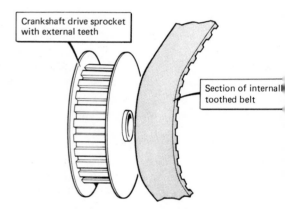

Figure 58   *The camshaft may be driven by a belt*

## Cylinder heads and gaskets

*Cylinder head*

This engine component is an intricate shape of casting made from cast iron or aluminium alloy and its main purpose is to seal the upper cylinder. Most heads are of the detachable type and are secured to the cylinder block by studs or bolts with a gasket at the joint faces. A fixed head is used with some engines where the block and head are made as a one-piece casting. Cylinder heads usually contain a water jacket, the injector recesses and

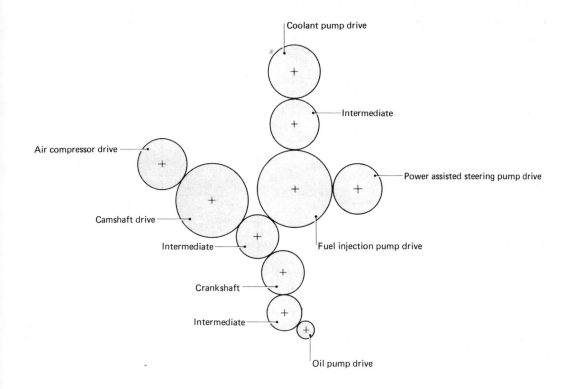

Coolant pump drive

Intermediate

Air compressor drive

Power assisted steering pump drive

Camshaft drive

Intermediate

Fuel injection pump drive

Crankshaft

Intermediate

Oil pump drive

Figure 59 *Some engines have an all-gear drive*

the valve ports with provision for housing the valves and their operating mechanisms.

*Detachable cylinder heads*
These are secured to the cylinder block (Figure 60) by studs and nuts, or bolts, and a gasket is fitted between the two to seal the joint between them. An overhead valve layout is usually employed with CI engines, and the valves are located and operated through guides by rocker gear and push rods. The injectors are usually housed in the cylinder head and the water jacket supplies cooling for the whole assembly.

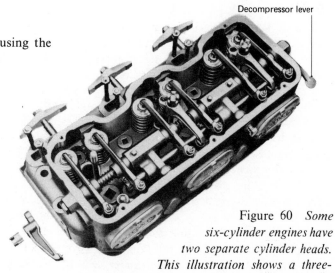

Decompressor lever

Figure 60 *Some six-cylinder engines have two separate cylinder heads. This illustration shows a three-cylinder head fitted to a six-cylinder engine*

## Cylinder head gaskets and fitting

Gaskets are used to provide a seal between the head and the block. One of the most common types is of copper–asbestos consisting of two thin sheets of copper separated by a layer of clay and asbestos. The holes have their inner edges rolled over or lined to reinforce the sealing effect at these critical edges.

Steel is also used as a gasket material. One type of steel gasket is the thin sheet steel type with reinforcement around the holes. Another type is of corrugated steel which aids sealing owing to the flexibility of the corrugations around the holes. Steel gaskets are normally used with aluminium alloy cylinder heads as the combination of the two different metals causes less corrosion than when a copper–asbestos gasket is used with these heads.

The British Leyland TL 12 engine has an asbestos–base gasket with steel fire rings, steel eyelets and a thin steel core. Gardner engines have a number of small synthetic rubber rings used in conjunction with the gasket as water joints. These rings are located on the block over the coolant holes with the use of ferrules.

If a gasket is replaced with a thicker one it will cause a slightly lower compression ratio in the cylinder due to it giving a slight increase in the clearance volume. Alternatively, a thinner gasket will increase the compression ratio. Cylinder head and cylinder block faces together with cylinder head studs and stud holes must be clean and free from rust and foreign matter before fitting a new gasket. If the old gasket shows signs of blowing, the head and block faces should be examined for distortion and, if found to be distorted, should be resurfaced by grinding (skimming). Cylinder head studs and nuts, or bolts, should also be checked for stretch and thread damage as these defects can also lead to gasket failure. A jointing compound is sometimes used on a gasket during assembly but the gasket manufacturer's recommendations on this point should be followed when in doubt.

In the absence of the engine manufacturer's nut tightening data, it is important that a correct method of tightening down the cylinder head is used (Figure 61), which means starting at the

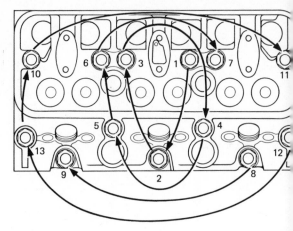

Figure 61   *An order of tightening cylinder head nuts*

centre nut and working outwards in sequence. Some manufacturers recommend that 'torqueing down' should be done in three stages, starting with a relatively low torque wrench setting and concluding with a higher one. After an engine has run for 100 miles or so, the nuts or studs should be checked again and retightened to the recommended tightness. It is important not to overtighten as this may lead to stretching or stripping of the screw threads, and also to the possibility of distortion of the components. As a general rule cast iron heads should be retightened when the engine is hot and aluminium heads when cold but the manufacturer's advice should be adhered to if it is available.

### Fixed heads

The trend to turbocharge engines with the resulting high cylinder pressures and temperatures has led to the use of a fixed cylinder head by some engine manufacturers, and the British Leyland 500 Series engines are of this design. The elimination of a cylinder head gasket makes for good cylinder sealing, improved thermal conductivity between block and head, and reduces the possibility of distortion of the structure. The absence of cylinder head studs leaves more scope in design for layout of the valve ports, coolant passages and injector holes.

A disadvantage of this design is the inaccessibility of the valve heads and seats during engine servicing and special tools are necessary for this work.

## Valves

The function of the valve is to control the flow of gas into or out of the cylinder. The usual arrangement consists of one inlet valve and one exhaust valve for each cylinder but there are some engines with two valves of each type for each cylinder.

The valve head rests on its seat in the cylinder head which has a seat angle usually cut at 45°, but in a few cases 30° is used. Valves are usually made from high-tensile alloy steel containing nickel, chromium and molybdenum. Exhaust valves, which operate at temperatures in excess of 2000°C, also include cobalt or silicon in their alloy which assists in resisting metal creep and corrosion at high temperatures.

*Adjustment of valve clearances*
The correct valve clearance (lash) is necessary for the best engine performance and economical fuel consumption. Excessive clearance causes the valve to open late and close early in the operating cycle which will also increase engine noise by 'tappet rattle'. On the other hand, too small a valve clearance causes the valve to open too soon and close late in the cycle which increases the risk of the valve and seat faces becoming burned due to the valve not properly seating under certain operating conditions.

Valves must be set to the correct clearance recommended by the engine manufacturer found in the service manual or handbook for an engine. The recommended clearance is sufficient to allow for expansion and contraction of the valve stem and related components during the varying operating temperatures of the engine. Different clearances may be recommended for inlet and exhaust valves on the same engine as exhaust valves operate at higher temperatures than inlet valves, and, therefore, tend to vary slightly more in their stem length. Some manufacturers supply two settings of clearances, one for use when the engine

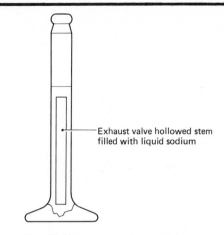

Exhaust valve hollowed stem filled with liquid sodium

Figure 62   *Hollow-stem exhaust valve*

is hot and the other for when it is cold. Setting valves to their correct clearance, sometimes known as tappet clearance, ensures that the valves are properly seated during their closed period under all operating conditions.

Adjustment of valve clearances (Figure 64) is carried out by making sure that the operating cam is not in its lifting phase, slackening the lock nut on the adjuster, turning the adjusting screw whilst holding the correct size of feeler gauge in the clearance gap until the gauge is slightly nipped, then locking the lock nut to complete the task. A second check should be made with the feeler gauge after locking up to make sure that the clearance is correct.

*Valve seat inserts*
Cast iron cylinder heads may have valve seats machined directly in the casting, but it is more common for them to be fitted with seat inserts (Figure 63) which normally provide for longer service life. When the head is made of aluminium alloy, it is usually necessary to fit valve inserts as the alloy from which the head is made is far too soft for use as a valve seat.

Materials used for the manufacture of inserts include nickel-chromium steel, phosphor bronze, Stellite steel, which includes cobalt, nickel and chromium, and cast iron. Fitting of inserts may be carried out by interference fitting, or by screwing them into the cylinder head.

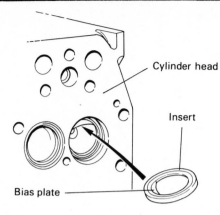

Figure 63   *Valve seat insert*

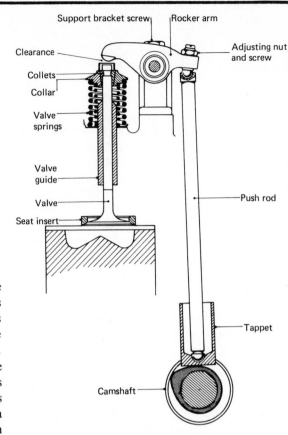

Figure 64   *Valve operating assembly*

The seat angle of 45° or 30° is chosen by the manufacturers to provide assistance for the gas flow through the open valve. The inlet valve ports are usually of a larger diameter than exhaust valve ports to permit efficient charging of the cylinder.

A feature of some of the Rolls-Royce Eagle Mark 3 engines is the bias plate on the seat inserts used in normally aspirated engines. This provides directional air flow through the open valve and a predetermined swirl rate in the combustion chamber by blanking off a small area of the port.

*Valve guides*
These support the valves (Figure 64) and they are an interference fit in the cylinder head. The clearance between the valve stem and the guide should be within the limits recommended by the engine manufacturer. Too small a clearance can cause the valves to stick during operation, while too large a clearance between the inlet valves and their guides will cause excessive oil consumption by allowing oil to be admitted into the cylinders through the large clearance.

Valve guides are normally made from cast iron, which has good wearing quality and gives long service life. Aluminium bronze is an alternative material used for valve guides and is used with aluminium alloy cylinder heads.

Some valve guides have a shoulder which limits the distance they can be pressed into the cylinder head during assembly. Other types are parallel and these should be pressed in until the specified length is left projecting outside the surface of the cylinder head.

*Valve springs*
The purpose of valve springs is to return the valve to its seat as the cam closes and to hold the valve closed, with the assistance of any cylinder gas pressure, on its seat until the cam reopens it. Springs are of the helical-coil type and are made from quality steel which has high resistance to fatigue. Some engines have two or three concentrically arranged springs for each valve and these have the following advantages:
1   The valve is held tightly closed on its seat when in its closed position which prevents gas leaks.

2 Valve bounce is reduced at higher engine speeds.
3 If one spring breaks, the valve is prevented from dropping into the cylinder by the other spring.
4 As the load is shared, the springs have longer life.

When two springs are used, one of them may be wound in the opposite direction to the other. This reduces the risk of entangling if one spring fractures. Some engines have close coil springs and these can be recognized by having their coils close together at one end. The closed end of the coils should be fitted towards the cylinder head.

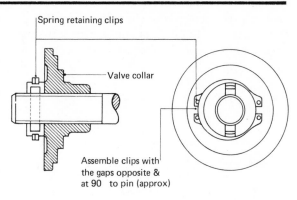

Figure 65 *Valve collar and spring clip assembly*

## Spring retainers

The spring end closest to the cylinder head is either in direct contact with the head or, in some engines, is in contact with a separate seating collar between the spring and the head.

The spring end furthest from the cylinder head is in contact with a collar or cap (Figure 65) which is retained on the valve stem by collets, or alternatively is retained by being screwed on to the end of the valve stem.

## Rocker arms

These operate on the rocker shaft which is secured to the cylinder head by support brackets. The rocker arms function as levers with the supporting brackets at their centres acting as pivots. One end of each rocker arm carries an adjusting screw with a cap or cup which is in contact with the push rod. The other end of each rocker arm contacts the valve and the valve clearance is arranged between the valve tip and the rocker arm. Bushes may be fitted in the rocker arm centre bearing hole.

## Push rod

The push rod is the link between the tappet and the rocker arm. Push rods are either of a circular solid or hollow section. They are designed to be as light as possible to minimize inertia forces and are made from steel with both ends case-hardened.

## Tappets

These are in contact with the cams and lift the push rods during operation. Some method of ensuring tappet rotation is used with some engines. This design has the advantage of evening out the wear on the tappet faces.

Some tappets include a bearing which runs on the cam. This type of tappet is prevented from rotating by the use of pegs and slots in the crankcase. Separate tappet guides secured in the crankcase are used in some engines.

## Decompressor gear

Some earlier models of heavy vehicles fitted with direct-injection CI engines were started with a starting handle, which was permanently suspended below the vehicle's front-mounted radiator. In order to obtain the necessary cranking speed for combustion in the cylinders when starting, the decompressor gear was used in conjunction with the starting handle.

The decompressor arrangement on these vehicles consisted of a small lever located at the side of the starting handle and coupled through a linkage to an operating shaft in the cylinder head. When the lever was operated, the shaft turned and opened the inlet valves by acting on their rocker arms.

The engine was started by first operating the decompressor lever into a position which would hold open the inlet valves. The starting handle was then cranked with one arm until a high cranking speed was reached, then the other arm was used to operate the decompressor lever to the normal running position while still cranking. The valves operate normally once the decompressor lever is moved to the normal running position when cylinder compression is restored for starting.

However, modern engines are fitted with an electric starter motor which eliminates the need for arm cranking, and decompressor gear is rarely used. It is, however, retained on some engines with a simple linkage and is used for engine maintenance purposes.

## Pistons

The three main functions of a piston (Figure 66) are:

1  To form a movable gas-tight plunger in the cylinder which confines the charge to the upper cylinder during its operation.
2  To transmit the force caused by the expansion of gases in the cylinder through the connecting rod to the crankshaft during power strokes.
3  To form a guide and a bearing on the cylinder wall for the small end of the connecting rod, by receiving and transmitting side-thrust caused by angularity of the connecting rod during its operation.

*Operating temperatures and pressures*
The operating temperature of a CI engine piston crown is in the region of 200°C. The pressures acting on the piston vary considerably during the different strokes and reach a maximum pressure of approximately 5000 kN/m² (725 lbf/in²). Stresses are set up in the piston during running which are caused by the changes of piston speed, the changes in working temperature, by side thrusts during power strokes and, to a lesser extent, by side thrusts during compression strokes.

*Designs and materials*
In order that fine clearances may be used without the risk of seizure, special piston designs are necessary. The top of the piston, known as the

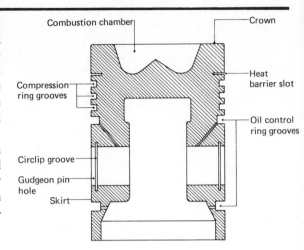

Figure 66    *CI engine piston*

crown, may be flat or have a cavity recessed for valve clearance, depending upon the shape of combustion chamber and the compression ratio required by the engine designer.

The crown and the gudgeon pin bosses are reinforced to allow them to sustain the high mechanical and thermal stresses caused by the high pressures and temperatures in the cylinder. Heat from the piston crown is transmitted through the piston rings to the cylinder bore and through the block to the coolant.

The materials commonly used for piston manufacture are:

1  Aluminium alloys.
2  Cast iron.
3  Steel alloys.

Some pistons have a combination of different metals. One example employs a cast iron groove insert in an aluminium alloy skirt. Another type has a skirt made of cast iron and a crown of heat-resistant steel. Aluminium alloy pistons are very commonly used in CI engines as they are comparatively light and have good thermal conductivity. Their principal disadvantage is the high coefficient of expansion of the material when compared with cast iron or steel, and this is taken into account by piston manufacturers who design them carefully to compensate for this disadvantage.

*Types*

The skirt of a CI engine piston is comparatively longer than that of a spark ignition engine piston, and split skirts are not normally employed as these would be too weak to withstand the onerous operating conditions of a CI engine. Solid skirt pistons are usually employed which are normally ground both oval and tapered in shape. Ovality allows for piston expansion parallel to the gudgeon pin as the engine temperature increases, and the taper is to allow expansion of the crown when heated. As the piston warms up to its normal running temperature it becomes both round and parallel in shape.

Direct-injection engine pistons usually have a deep cavity in their crown which is spheroidally shaped and forms the combustion chamber. Heat barrier slots are used in some pistons to control heat flow in the skirt and the crown. Some indirect-injection engine pistons have a shallow recess in their piston crown with their combustion chamber in the cylinder head.

## Piston rings

Piston rings (Figure 67) perform three functions:
1  Maintain a gas-tight seal between the piston and the cylinder wall to prevent blow-by of the gases.
2  Provide a path for conducting heat from the piston for the cylinder walls.
3  Control the quantity of oil reaching the piston crown and rings, allowing sufficient to ensure lubrication but limiting an excessive quantity which would cause an increase in oil consumption and carbonization.

The two basic types of piston rings used are known as compression rings and oil control (scraper) rings. Most rings are made from fine-grained cast iron which has excellent heat resistance and wearing qualities. Each ring is formed with a gap which is necessary for assembly and removal from the piston and for the ring to exert a radial pressure on the cylinder walls. Radial pressure should be high enough to allow the ring to perform its functions but not so high as to cause excessive cylinder and ring wear. Com-

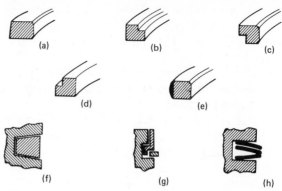

Figure 67   *Piston rings*

pression rings are constructed to give a uniform radial pressure of about 140 kN/m² (20 lbf/in²) and slotted scraper rings about 280 kN/m² (40 lbf/in²). Higher radial pressures are obtained with the use of more elastic materials and special shapes of ring section.

There should be sufficient clearance between the top and bottom of the ring and its groove to ensure that side thrusts acting on the piston are transferred to the cylinder wall through the skirt and not through the ring. This clearance should not be enough to allow the ring to float in the groove and cause a pumping action for the lubricating oil to pass into the combustion chamber. Neither should this clearance be so small as to prevent some ring movement to reduce the risk of sticking caused by carbonized oil.

The number of rings on a CI engine piston varies with the make and model of the engine, any number from two to five being in common use. A smaller number of rings enables a low-height piston to be used with a reduced skirt area, this being advantageous where the height of the engine is an important factor. Some engines have pistons carrying an empty groove which is fitted with a ring when the cylinder bore becomes worn.

*Compression rings*

The simplest type of piston ring (Figure 67a) has a plain rectangular cross section. This is sometimes modified by a slight taper of about one degree on its periphery, the purpose of the taper being to speed up the bedding-in process.

An internally stepped ring *(b)* has the effect of tilting slightly when the piston is moving up and down the bore. The tilting action serves three functions:

1  The bottom edge of the ring is pressed firmly against the cylinder wall giving a scraping action of the oil.
2  The greater pressure on the bottom edge of the ring has a similar effect to a ring with a slight taper and promotes bedding-in.
3  The possibility of ring sticking is minimized owing to tilting.

Externally stepped rings *(c)* stepped on the lower face, give a scraping action in addition to their normal functions. An upper face step *(d)* sometimes known as a 'ridge dodger' is used for fitting into the top groove of a piston in a worn engine. The cut-away step allows clearance for the cylinder ridge near the top of a worn bore. To facilitate correct assembly, stepped rings are marked 'top' and must be fitted accordingly.

Another type of ring has a barrel-shaped periphery *(e)* and is normally used in the top groove of the piston. The periphery of the ring is chromium plated and lapped for controlled and quick bedding-in.

A taper or wedge section ring *(f)* is often used in two-stroke CI engines to reduce the possibility of ring stick due to sticky carbon deposits in the piston grooves caused by the high operating temperatures. The rings may have one or both modified by a slight taper of about one degree on piston grooves. Some are internally stepped.

A 'fire' ring *(g)* is used with the Roots opposed-piston engine and provides good sealing of the cylinder when the engine is cold. Also, its good cylinder wall contact assists in heat transfer thereby reducing the operating temperature of the piston.

Laminated rings *(h)* are sometimes used in engines fitted with chromium cylinder liners. The three-segment type is used in Perkins engines.

## Oil control rings

These rings (Figure 68) are designed with a specific wall pressure. Their main purpose is to control oil

(a)                    (b)                    (c)

Figure 68   *Oil control rings*

consumption by scraping the excess oil from the cylinder walls during each stroke of the piston. One of the most common rings is the slotted type *(a)* used as a bulk oil scraper. Two scraping lands are employed, separated by a groove in the periphery which is ventilated with slots. This type of ring is fitted in a well ventilated piston groove.

The hooked and taper faced ring *(b)* is used where large amounts of oil have to be removed from the cylinder wall. The hooked relief ensures retention of the sharp scraping edge.

The slotted or drilled conformable ring *(c)* has a high degree of conformability in the cylinder bore. The radial load is imparted by the butting helical coil spring which is located in a groove on the inside of the ring. The land surfaces which are in contact with the bore are chromium plated for those rings working with a high cylinder wall pressure.

*Plating and coating*
Electro-deposited hard chromium is used on the periphery of some rings to combat corrosion and abrasive wear thus ensuring minimum ring and bore wear. One or both side faces may be chromed to increase ring and piston groove life. Scuffing can be reduced with the use of molybdenum, nickel aluminide and other metals which are inlaid in the periphery of rings by spray techniques. Copper coating is used to aid initial bedding in of chromium-plated rings, the soft copper being a good bearing material and wearing off quickly during the running-in period.

## Under-crown cooling (Figures 69 and 70)

Adequate piston cooling is necessary, particularly in turbocharged engines, for trouble-free running and long service. Oil is sometimes used as a cooling agent for this purpose and cools the

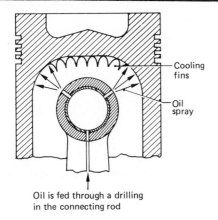

Cooling
fins

Oil
spray

Oil is fed through a drilling
in the connecting rod

Figure 69 *Undercrown cooling of a piston*

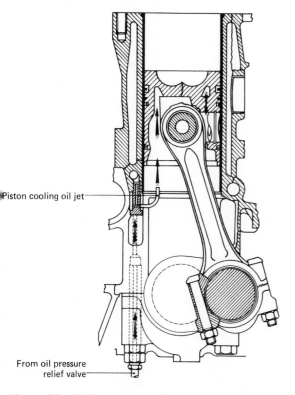

Piston cooling oil jet

From oil pressure
relief valve

Figure 70 *Undercrown cooling*

crown temperature to about 200°C during operation.

The cooling system usually consists of an oil jet which forces oil, under pressure, to the interior of

the piston, with the effect of removing heat from the underside of the crown and the ring belt area. Some engine designs have oil jets in the small end of their connecting rods, others have a separate jet which is aimed so as to direct the oil jet into the piston when the connecting rod passes through a particular angle. In the engine shown, oil is directed into passages above the gudgeon pin bosses. Cooling systems are designed to cool without causing severe temperature gradients in the piston which would inevitably lead to fatigue and cracking.

## Connecting rod

This links together the crankshaft and piston (Figure 71). The small end, which carries the gudgeon pin in either a phosphor bronze bush or a clamped eye, reciprocates with the piston, and the big end is attached to, and rotates with, the crankshaft. Its function is to transfer thrust in either direction between the piston and the crankpin.

The cross-section of a connecting rod is usually H-shaped. The rod is made from an alloy steel forging or an aluminium alloy of equal strength but lighter. The big end is split so that it can be fitted on the crankshaft and the cap is secured to the rod by bolts and nuts, or set screws, together with suitable locking devices.

Figure 71 *Exploded view of piston and connecting rod assembly*

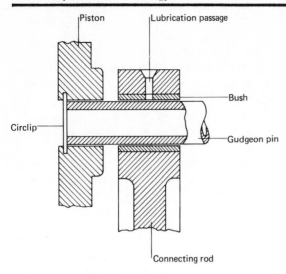

Figure 72   *Fully floating gudgeon pin assembly*

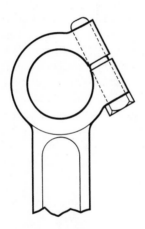

Figure 73

## Crankshafts

The principal shaft within an engine is the crankshaft. This is usually a chrome molybdenum alloy steel forging which may be surface hardened by nitriding, although a few engines have cast crankshafts. Most heavy CI engines are designed with main bearings between each crankpin which makes possible a crankshaft of reduced dimensions and weight without the danger of whip.

The crank webs are usually extended or counterbalanced to balance the crankpin and big end of the connecting rod. Crankshaft end-float is controlled by the use of thrust washers fitted on one of the main bearings. These washers are supplied in matched pairs of a particular thickness and they are not interchangeable.

To obtain good engine breathing and balance, the following firing orders are used:

Four-cylinder engine  1, 3, 4, 2
or 1, 2, 4, 3
Six-cylinder engine   1, 5, 3, 6, 2, 4
or 1, 4, 2, 6, 3, 5
Eight-cylinder engine 1, 5, 2, 6, 8, 4, 7, 3
or 1, 7, 3, 8, 4, 6, 2, 5
or other alternatives

Various attachments are mounted on the crankshaft. These include the timing gear drive sprocket, the fan belt drive pulley and the flywheel (see Figure 74).

## Bearings

Most CI engines have pre-finished bearing shells in their big end and main bearings. These consist of a pair of steel shells for each bearing lined with

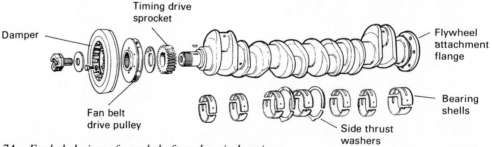

Figure 74   *Exploded view of crankshaft and main bearings*

white metal, copper–lead, aluminium–tin or other suitable bearing material.

### White metal

White metal-lined shells are used in some engines. This metal has high resistance against fatigue and has good wearing properties. The composition of white metal is about 88% tin, 8% antimony and 4% copper. These shells must be properly fitted in their recesses and are located by small lugs or projections pressed out of their backs. An important property of white metal is its low melting point of about 300 to 350°C. This is an advantage when there is a breakdown in bearing lubrication as the metal will easily melt when the frictional heat increases and the metal will be flung out of the bearing leaving enough clearance to prevent seizure.

### Copper–lead

This lining material is used on a steel back. Its composition is about 70% copper/30% lead, with a small proportion of tin or silver. The bearing surface may be plated with a thin layer of lead, lead–tin or lead–indium. This material is more suitable for heavy vehicle engines which operate with high bearing pressures under arduous running conditions.

### Lead–bronze

This material is much harder and stronger than white metal and has a longer life, although it is more expensive. Its composition is about 70% copper, 28% lead and 2% tin. In some engines only half the bearing shell is of lead–bronze, this being the half which carries the greater load. The other half is usually lined with white metal.

Expansion is usually greater with lead–bronze and copper–lead bearings than with white metal bearings, and greater running clearances are necessary to allow oil to remove the frictional heat generated during running.

### Reticular tin–aluminium

This material is used in some steel-backed bearings. 'Reticular' describes the microstructure of the alloy which is aluminium containing 20% tin.

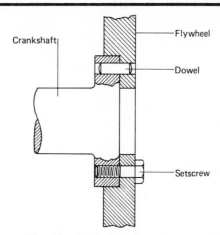

Figure 75 *Flywheel attachment to crankshaft flange*

## Flywheel

The main function of the flywheel is to absorb kinetic energy during power strokes and use this to carry the engine over its idle strokes. It is also used as a pressure face for the clutch and it is usually fitted with a toothed ring gear on its periphery for use with an electric starter motor.

The flywheel is designed with sufficient mass and is suitably shaped to reduce cyclic speed variations to a minimum. It is secured to the crankshaft by set screws and lock tabs or by self-locking bolts, and it should always be checked for running true after fitting. Engine manufacturers specify figures for this check.

A spigot bearing is carried at the centre of the flywheel and this may be a bush or a ball bearing. Some flywheels have a separate spigot bearing housing hub which is bolted at the centre of the flywheel. Dowels are usually employed between the crankshaft flange and the flywheel to aid correct fitting.

## Crankshaft damper (Figure 76)

This is attached to the crankshaft and may be within or on the outside of the engine. The purpose of the damper is to reduce torsional vibration in the crankshaft during running caused by the

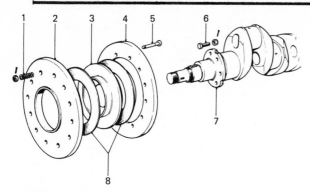

1   Torque Loading Spring and Nut
2   Damper Ring (outer)
3   Hub Plate
4   Damper Ring (inner)
5   Torque Loading Bolt
6   Hub Bolt and Nut
7   Crankshaft Flange Attachment
8   Fibre Friction Washers

Figure 76   *Crankshaft damper assembly*

winding-up and unwinding as the torsional impulses are applied at the cranks.

The damper consists of an inner hub which is secured to the crankshaft by a key or serrations, and a heavy inertia member which is used in some engines as a fan belt drive pulley. The hub and inertia member are bound together but move in relation to each other and the torsional vibrations are absorbed by a friction material, rubber or a viscous fluid.

Most dampers are not adjustable, but one exception is that fitted in Gardner engines. This type has a flanged inner hub bolted to the crankshaft. Between the two spring-loaded rings and the hub flange are two hard red fibre washers which are sandwiched between the rings and loaded to a predetermined slip torque of 175 kg m (127 lbf ft) by adjusting the torque loading bolts.

## Crankshaft pulley (Figure 77)

The front end of the crankshaft is extended from the front main bearing and carries, in addition to the timing gear, a drive pulley. The pulley, which is designed to carry one or more 'V' belts, drives the cooling fan, coolant pump and alternator. It may also be used to drive the compressor for a power braking system and the hydraulic pump for power assisted steering. The pulley is attached to the

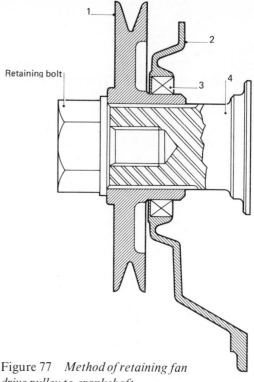

Figure 77   *Method of retaining fan drive pulley to crankshaft*

crankshaft by either splines or a key which prevent it slipping on the shaft and it is secured by a bolt or nut at the end of the crankshaft. The bolt head or nut is sometimes provided with 'claws' into which a starting handle can be engaged for use during engine maintenance.

## Sumps (Figure 78)

With the wet sump system, the sump collects lubricating oil from the engine and acts as a storage tank. Sumps are manufactured from aluminium alloy or pressed steel and some of them are finned to increase their heat-dissipating area. Their capacity varies depending upon the size of the engine and whether a separate oil cooler is fitted, but it is usually between 11 and 23 litres (2½ and 5 gal).

Some engines are fitted with a gauze filter which is located in the sump and fitted to the suction side of the oil pump. This prevents foreign particles

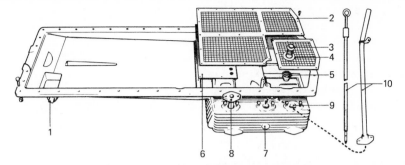

1 Scavenge sump drain plug
2 Primary gauze filter
3 Suction pipe locating collar
4 Collar retaining washer
5 Collar retaining spring
6 Dam plate (engines with transfer pump)
7 Main oil reservoir
8 Suction pipe (engines with lub. oil cooler)
9 Oil return from cooler
10 Dip rod and tube

Figure 78 *Engine lubricating oil sump*

entering the pump and being fed to the engine bearings. Other engines have a coarse gauze strainer which is fitted over the sump well and prevents foreign particles entering the well. Sumps are usually fitted with a drain plug at their lowest point.

## Crankcase breathers

These are used in engines to allow adequate ventilation of the crankcase. Gases escape from the combustion chamber via the piston rings and cylinder walls and enter the crankcase. These gases vary in quality and quantity but consist mainly of the products of combustion. Sludge would be formed quickly as these products would come into contact with the lubricating oil if there was no ventilation. Another reason for the use of a breather is to prevent the build-up of crankcase pressure. An excessive rise in pressure could cause damage to oil seals and gaskets.

Some engines are fitted with more than one breather. A common arrangement is one breather on the side of the engine cylinder block and another on the valve rocker cover. Recent legislation is leading to more sophisticated arrangements for breathers and many petrol engines are designed with a sealed system that pipes the engine's gases and fumes directly back into the induction system. Emission controls are likely to become stricter in the future.

## Exhaust system

An exhaust system normally consists of a front downpipe which is connected to the exhaust manifold, one or more silencers and a tailpipe. The pipes and silencer are usually connected together with clamps or clips and the whole assembly is attached to the vehicle with brackets or straps.

Most exhaust systems are designed to discharge gases on the offside of the vehicle where they will have least effect. This is particularly important in the case of buses which frequently halt at the kerbside for passengers to board and alight. There are also special vehicles such as fuel tankers which have their exhaust systems located in front of the front wheels so that the gases are discharged as far away from the tank as possible.

### Silencers
The main reason for using a silencer in the exhaust system is to reduce exhaust noise level. An engine produces a wide range of noises, some being simpler to quieten than others. These include mechanical noise, combustion noise, gas roar

through valve ports and resonances in the exhaust pipeline. Some of these noises are transmitted to the atmosphere via the exhaust system and can to some extent be silenced. The two most commonly used exhaust silencer systems are absorption and baffling. Each system is effective by removing some of the vibratory motion energy of the gas.

*Absorption silencer (Figure 79)* This design allows the gas to pass generally straight through a perforated steel tube. This tube is housed in an outer casing with sound-absorbent material between the two.

The vibrating exhaust gas passes through the holes in the tube and penetrates into the absorbent material, usually of wire or glass wool, where the direction of gas flow is changed. This process lowers the frequency of gas vibrations which lowers the pitch of the sound. The absorption silencer sounds different from, though it is not necessarily noisier than, the baffle type. There is little back pressure with this design of silencer and it is used on some heavy vehicles.

*Baffle type (Figure 80)* This design is rather more complex than the absorption type. The removal of the vibratory gas energy is achieved by feeding gas into an expansion chamber at its high pressure and temperature. The effect of this is to reduce the pressure and temperature of the gas as it passes through holes in the baffles and tubes where its turbulence dies out, and as the gas enters the tail-pipe it is flowing quite smoothly. The silencer chambers are normally different sizes to make silencing more effective.

*Materials*
The choice of materials for exhaust pipes and silencers depends on a number of factors, which include their initial cost, expected life, the degree of silencing required and noise emission legislation requirements. The exhaust system should be attached to the body in such a way that vibrations from the exhaust system are not transmitted to the body. This is usually achieved by the use of flexible elements between the exhaust support brackets and the body. Silencers for CI-engined vehicles accumulate a comparatively large proportion of

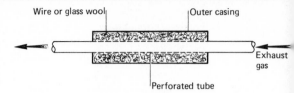

Figure 79   *Straight-through silencer – absorption type*

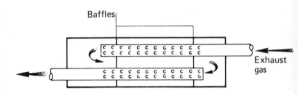

Figure 80   *Two-baffle silencer: expansion/resonator chambers are different sizes*

soot from the engine, and it is possible that cleanable silencers will be used more often in the future to overcome this drawback, despite their higher initial cost.

The most common material for the manufacture of silencers is mild steel. This has a comparatively low initial cost together with a reasonable life span. The gauge thickness is selected to suit particular requirements. Too thick a gauge will increase the weight of the silencer and exhaust system, while too thin a gauge may not be strong enough to withstand the local stressing around the attachment brackets and the inlet and outlet stub pipes. Silencer end plates are usually made from a thicker-gauge material than is used for the shell for this reason.

Any vehicle that operates on salted roads, especially motorways, will have its silencer life severely limited by the effects of corrosion from the outside. A petrol-engined vehicle operating on short journeys where the engine never reaches its optimum working temperature will give rise to rapid silencer corrosion from the inside owing to the condensation of vapour and the acidic products of combustion passing through.

To combat some of these problems, stainless steel is used as an alternative material. A stainless steel silencer is claimed to last about eleven times as long as a mild steel silencer and will therefore in many instances last for the working life of the vehicle. Though the initial cost of stainless steel is about seven times higher than mild steel on a weight comparison basis, a thinner gauge is often used to keep the cost reasonable. When this is considered together with the savings in replacement fitting costs which occur with unfailing regularity when mild steel units are used, the future of stainless steel exhaust systems is a likely proposition.

## Air cleaner and silencer unit

The main reasons for fitting this unit to an engine are to clean and silence the air which is consumed during running. The average heavy vehicle engine consumes 1280 m$^3$ (45 000 ft$^3$) of air per hour of running time, and the air inevitably carries contaminants with it which include dust, dirt and moisture. If these contaminants are allowed to enter the engine, they will act as an abrasive compound and shorten the life of the bearing surfaces, particularly the piston rings and cylinder bores.

If not silenced, air intake noise can, on some vehicle layouts, be irritating to drivers and passengers as well as contributing to environmental noise. Silencing of the intake air is achieved in the design of these units by damping the frequency of the vibrations of the air columns down to a frequency which is not audible to the human ear. This is done by the use of pipes or tubes which are part of the unit, and these are selected in the design stage to suit the particular intake system of the engine.

### *Dry type (Figure 81)*
This type basically consists of a cleaner element enclosed in the unit casing. The element filters the intake air as it passes through before entering the engine cylinders. A special pleated-paper element is normally used for air filtration which has a relatively large area for the air to pass through. The large area is necessary to avoid a high resistance to the air flow. Elements are usually of the disposable type and these should be changed

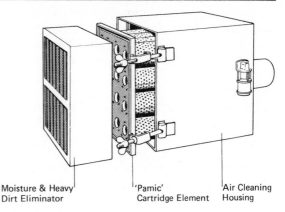

Moisture & Heavy Dirt Eliminator     'Pamic' Cartridge Element     Air Cleaning Housing

Figure 81    *Air cleaner – dry type*

periodically or cleaned according to the manufacturer's instructions. Other materials such as cloth or felt are also used for this purpose.

The Unipamic dry-type air cleaner consists essentially of two parts. Air enters the first part which consists of a metal filter media designed to eliminate large dust particles and provide engine protection against water from splashes or cleaning jets. The water is drained off through holes in the base of the casing and the assembly can be cleaned when the filter media becomes clogged with dirt. The second part of the cleaner consists of paper filter cartridges which are supported by plates. Dust particles greater than one micron in size are removed from the air by these filters.

### *Wet type (Figure 82)*
This type of unit can be fitted inside or outside the cab, and single or twin units are used with heavy vehicles. These units must be firmly supported as the oil contained within them makes them heavier than the dry type.

The principle on which they work is by causing the air path to change its direction as it passes through the unit. This has the effect of causing the contaminants to strike the surface of the oil and, in turn, settle at the bottom of the oil bath. The air then passes through wire mesh or tangled wire which is damped by oil, and dust particles are removed from the air as they pass through this material. Oil is continually splashed up and drained back during running which keeps the mesh clean. These filters should be periodically washed out, refilled with clean oil and new gaskets fitted as recommended by the manufacturers.

### Gardner oil bath filter (Figure 83)

Air enters at the intake B and is directed downwards through the annulus C. The annulus is of reduced area which causes an increase in velocity of the air as it passes through. As the air turns at the bottom of its path, particles of dust which are denser than air impinge on the oil's surface. During this process, a small quantity of oil is picked up by the air stream and is carried upwards into the filter element. The oil wets the element which attracts any remaining dust in the air stream. This dust is continually washed into the oil container as the oil drains back into the base. All dust eventually settles in the base in the form of sludge which, together with the filter element, should be periodically cleaned. The period for cleaning and replenishing the container with clean oil varies and depends upon the conditions under which the engine operates. Four hundred running hours or four thousand miles are recommended by the manufacturers as average periods for this service.

## Pressure charging

Originally, the idea of pressure charging was solely to increase the power output of a normally aspirated engine, and problems arose in the choice of suitable fuel injection equipment and in cylinder head gasket design. However, when these initial problems were overcome, pressure charging showed that it had several other advantages which include the up-rating of an engine to comply with legislation governing such factors as minimum values for power-to-weight ratios, engine noise and exhaust smoke emissions. Most engines are today designed and developed for pressure charging and usually differ from earlier normally aspirated models by their redesigned components, the most affected being the crankshaft, connecting rods, pistons, piston rings and cylinder head gasket.

Figure 82   *Air cleaner – wet type*

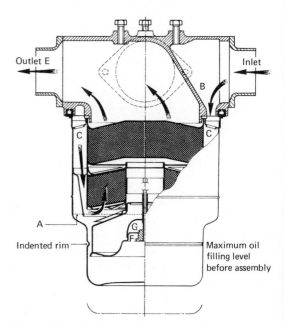

Figure 83   *Gardner universal air filter*

Two methods of pressure charging are normally used by engine manufacturers: one is by using a mechanically driven supercharger (blower), the other is by using an exhaust driven turbocharger. Either method has the same effect on an engine to which it is fitted, i.e. to increase torque and power in a given engine with as small an increase in weight, size and initial cost as is possible. The increase in engine power achieved with pressure charging above that of a normally aspirated engine of the same capacity is normally in the region of 20 to 30%, giving a substantial increase in its power-to-weight ratio. To achieve this same increase in power output from a normally aspirated engine would mean building a much larger and heavier engine which would not be acceptable to many vehicle designers or operators due to its necessary additional weight and size.

## Superchargers (blowers)

A positive displacement mechanically driven supercharger is normally used with two-stroke CI engines as it is necessary with this type of engine to provide good cylinder scavenging for a reasonable performance, and it can also be used with four-stroke engines to great advantage. The supercharger forces air, under a pressure slightly higher than atmospheric pressure, into the engine cylinders during the inlet strokes. The denser charge produced by this method of pressure charging reduces the ignition delay period and gives better control over cylinder pressure rise with little increase in specific fuel consumption.

There is some wastage of air through the exhaust system during scavenging of the cylinder when this method of pressure charging is used, but an overall advantage is gained from this system caused by the cooling effect in the cylinder which reduces the thermal loading on the engine components. About 40% of the engine power used to drive the supercharger is directly returned to the crankshaft by the increased pressure on the engine pistons during inlet stroke and the increased power output of the engine makes a supercharger invaluable.

Some of the most widely used superchargers are the Roots two-lobed and three-lobed models. These consist of their two- or three-lobed rotors mounted on ball and roller bearings enclosed in a finned aluminium alloy casing, and they are mechanically driven. This type of supercharger absorbs between 5 and 10% of engine power for driving purposes and increases the engine power output by up to about 40%.

## Turbochargers

Turbocharging, normally used with four-stroke CI engines, eliminates the need for a mechanically driven system which is used with a supercharger, and noise levels from turbocharged engines are little above those of a normally aspirated engine of a comparable size.

Basically, the turbocharger is a lightweight unit attached to the engine which interrupts the flow of both the exhaust gases from the engine and the inlet gases flowing into the engine. It consists of a housing containing two wheels secured on a common shaft mounted in bearings. The turbine wheel, driven by the outgoing exhaust gases which

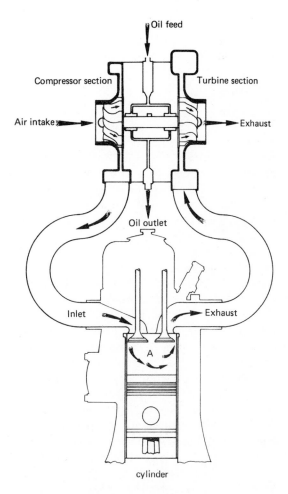

Figure 84  *Method of turbocharging*

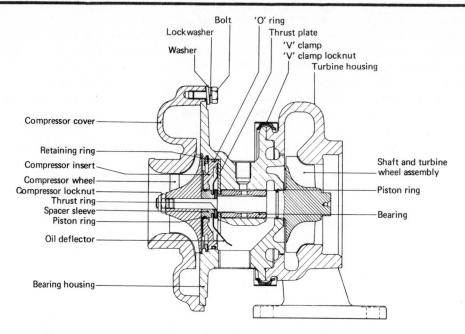

Figure 85  *Sectional view of typical Holset model 3LD turbocharger*

would otherwise largely be wasted, rotates the wheel and shaft at high speeds, thus driving the compressor wheel. The compressor wheel forces air into the engine cylinders with the effect of increasing the density of the air charge in the cylinders when compared with a normally aspirated engine.

The blades of the exhaust wheel are curved so that the exhaust gases contacting the outside of the blades will travel radially inwards towards their centre and produce an increase in output torque on the shaft. Air enters at the centre of the compressor wheel, where it is compressed and driven radially outwards through a tangential outlet port leading into the inlet manifold.

Turbochargers operate at speeds up to 40 000 rev/min. The driveshaft is usually supported in separate fully floating bearings or a single floating bearing whose contact area is reduced in the middle by an annular groove to form, in effect, two separate bearings. As the bearing is free to rotate relative to the shaft and its parent bore, the bearing will rotate in the same direction as the shaft but at a substantially reduced speed, thus

reducing the frictional surface speed of the bearing below the turbine speed causing lower frictional force with less heat generated. This design also protects the bearing from damage at high speeds provided that it is adequately lubricated. Engine oil is normally used as a lubricant and cooler for the bearing which is supplied under pressure from the engine oil gallery and passes through an additional filter unit in some applications. The oil drains back to the engine sump under the force of gravity after leaving the unit.

At low fuel deliveries, a normally aspirated engine will often return a better specific fuel consumption than the turbocharged version of the same engine, but as the fuel delivery is increased the turbocharged version returns a better specific fuel consumption than the normally aspirated unit. The reasons for this difference in performance are that, at low fuel delivery, the turbocharger adds to the total pumping losses of the engine by increasing the back pressure in the exhaust system, this being in some cases 75% of the boost pressure in the inlet manifold. As fuel delivery increases however, better performance is obtained from the turbocharged version which in some cases produces an increase of torque and power in the region of 50%. Turbocharging also reduces exhaust smoke density over the upper part of the engine speed range, though there is little difference between the two engine versions at lower engine speeds.

Some further features of engine design where a turbocharger is employed are that coolant jackets are made thicker, engine valves are of an increased diameter, and engine timing and valve tappet clearances differ from a normally aspirated engine. Both inlet and exhaust manifolds are re-designed to accommodate the turbocharger between them, and piston profile is altered to provide a closer fit in the bore (this being necessary to retain the high gas loading in the cylinder and to increase heat transfer to the coolant).

*Charge cooling*

Charge cooling systems are used with some engines to cool the air delivered to the cylinders by a turbocharger. The combination of charge cooling and pressure charging has a number of advantages, which include an increase in the density of the air charge delivered to the cylinders and an increase in available oxygen for combustion. Further, it makes that portion of the air charge used for scavenging the more effective as a coolant by lowering the thermal loading on engine components, and in addition the lower cycle temperature leads to a further increase in final charge density.

Figure 86 shows a system of air-to-air cooling consisting of an air cooler located in front of the coolant radiator and connected to the turbo-charger by a system of pipes. The boosted air from

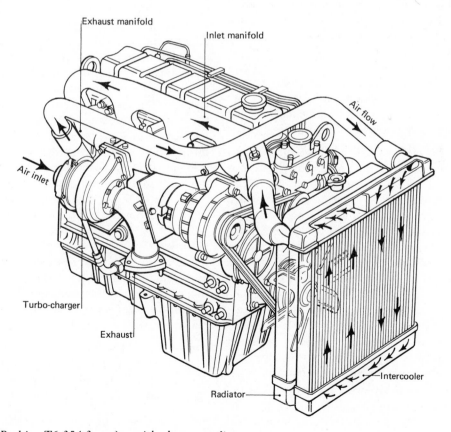

Figure 86   *Perkins T6 354.3 engine with charge cooling*

the turbocharger is directed into the air cooler (intercooler) passing down the tubes on one side of the cooler and upwards on the other side of the unit which is divided into two sections. The matrix is normally constructed in a similar way to a cooling system radiator with finned air tubes of copper and brass, and tanks made from steel.

## Engine brake

Some diesel-engined trucks and buses are fitted with an engine brake. A hydraulic attachment is fitted on top of the rocker shaft assembly and actuated by the engine push rods which is the basis of the brake assembly. The principle of its operation is to convert the engine into a power-absorbing compressor and this is achieved by the action of the assembly which opens the exhaust valves near to t.d.c. on the compression stroke. The heat generated by the operation of the engine when functioning as a brake is absorbed by the engine's cooling system in the normal way.

Originally, the brake was designed to suit the Cummins 'three-cam' engine by using the injector cam motion to transfer movement to the exhaust valves when the brake needs operating, but conventional engines with a separate fuel injection system may also be adapted for this type of brake.

*Operation*   Once the engine has warmed up, the brake mechanism can be brought into action by operating a switch which, in turn, brings an automatic accelerator switch and clutch switch into the circuit. Each time the accelerator is released the engine brake comes on automatically and provides a smooth and effective retardation of the vehicle without any operation of the normal service brakes. The force required to open the exhaust valves against cylinder compression pressure towards the end of compression stroke is supplied by oil pressure from the engine's lubrication system which, through a hydraulic circuit, operates a piston and forces open the exhaust valve releasing the compressed air.

Engine brakes may be fitted to turbocharged engines and two-stroke engines as well as normally aspirated four-strokes and the noise level during operation of the brake is no greater than that produced by an engine when working under full-load conditions. The use of engine brakes gives a reduction in brake lining wear with less servicing, lower costs and less risk of brake fade on long downhill gradients. Service buses which are operated on stop-start routes and fitted with an engine brake have considerably less brake lining wear and drivers have added confidence due to the extra independent brake which adds to greater safety and less driver fatigue.

## The rotary engine

The rotary engine operates on the same basic principles as the conventional reciprocating piston engine, but it is free from the disadvantages caused by reciprocating components. The principal components of the rotary engine are the rotor which contains three lobes, the driveshaft and the casing. As the rotor moves in the epitrochoidally shaped chamber, the three apices (tips of the rotor lobes) maintain continuous contact with the inner wall of the chamber, so forming three chambers of continuously varying volume, in each of which the processes of induction, compression, power and exhaust take place. The rotor has an internally toothed gear meshing with an inner externally toothed fixed gear, which has a hollow centre through which the driveshaft passes. The fixed gear has two-thirds the number of teeth of the internally toothed rotor gear thus providing a gear ratio of 2 to 3, causing the driveshaft to rotate three times for one complete turn of the rotor.

*Operation*

*Induction*   As the rotor rotates clockwise the inlet port is uncovered and the volume of the combustion chamber increases causing a depression, and the charge is forced into the chamber by atmospheric pressure.

*Compression*   The rotor continues turning clockwise, blanking off the inlet port and compressing the charge by the reduction of volume in the chamber as shown between B and C.

*Power*   As the centre of the side BC passes the spark plug, the charge is ignited and the resulting

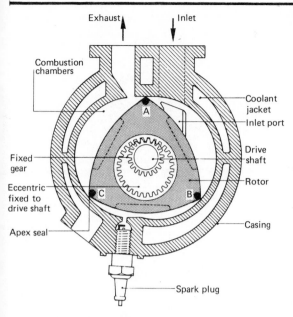

Figure 87 *Spark ignition rotary engine*

expansion of the gases forces the rotor to turn clockwise and rotate the driveshaft.

*Exhaust* As the rotor continues to turn under the pressure of the expanding gases the apex of the rotor communicates with the exhaust port shown at position CA and the gases leave the combustion chamber under their own pressure. Further rotation of the rotor reduces the volume of the combustion chambers and the gases are forced out through the exhaust port. The cycle of operation recommences as the inlet port is uncovered by the rotor.

An overlap period, comparable with that in a valved engine, is achieved by designing the inlet and exhaust ports close together so that the flank of the rotor spans both ports. The simultaneous sequence of operations is carried out in each chamber in turn resulting in three power impulses on the driveshaft for each one complete turn of the rotor.

The engine has two cooling systems. Liquid cooling is used in the casing, and this functions in a similar manner to the system used in a conventional engine. The difficulty of cooling the

inner part of the rotor and the gears is overcome by using oil which also lubricates the gears and bearings.

*Rotary CI engine*
A two-bank, two-stage rotary CI engine known as the 2-R6 has been developed by Rolls-Royce Ltd. It employs a low-pressure compressor/exhaust stage and a high-pressure combustion stage. The air enters the engine at the inlet port of the low-pressure stage and is compressed at this stage before passing through the transfer passage to the high-pressure stage, where it is further compressed to a higher ratio, after which combustion occurs. This arrangement is considered to be the best means of raising the compression ratio sufficient for diesel operation and maintaining a low surface-to-volume ratio in the chamber. The exhaust gases are transferred from the high-pressure stage through the exhaust transfer passage to the low-pressure stage where they are discharged from the engine through the exhaust port.

Some other details of this engine are its displacement which is 6500 cm³, height 835 mm, width 726 mm, length 718 mm and its estimated weight 450 kg. Its maximum power is 261 kW (350 bhp) at 4500 rev/min.

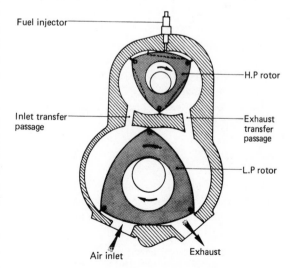

Figure 88 *A two-stage rotary CI engine*

### Three-rotor engine

This engine, the Rolls-Royce R2, consists of three rotors which are the compressor, the high-pressure rotor and the expander. The compressor and expander have two-lobe rotors and the high-pressure rotor has three lobes. Air is admitted to the engine at the compressor stage and transferred via the compressor transfer passage to the high-pressure stage where it is further compressed, and combustion takes place. The gases are then transferred from the high-pressure stage via the exhaust transfer passage to the expander chamber and leave the engine via the exhaust port. Gas flow through the engine is controlled by the size of the ports and the passages, and these are designed to give the desired performance. The mechanical efficiency of this engine is claimed to be about 66% and internal friction is fairly low.

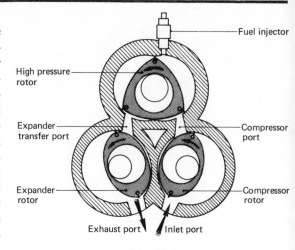

Figure 89   *A three-rotor CI engine*

### Advantages of rotary engines

The main advantages claimed for rotary engines compared with reciprocating engines are:
1  Simplicity, few moving parts.
2  The absence of reciprocating components permits high engine speeds.
3  Engine balancing and vibration problems are more easily overcome.
4  Breathing and volumetric efficiency are improved as the ports are continually open.
5  Lightness for a given swept volume giving an improvement in power-to-weight ratio.
6  The compactness of the engine aids body designing.
7  Little maintenance is required because of its simple construction.
8  Low engine noise caused by the absence of reciprocating components.

## The gas turbine

The demand for higher power outputs from conventional CI engines, and the possibility of further legislation governing the maximum limits of engine noise and exhaust smoke emissions, are causing the road transport industry to consider alternative types of power units. The gas turbine engine is a likely possibility to replace the conventional engine as its design will meet the demand for high and constant road speeds during long-distance journeys, and it has adequate power to propel vehicles with higher gross vehicle weights than are currently permitted. The present minimum value of the power-to-weight ratio is 4.4 kW/tonne (6 bhp/ton) thus making a power unit with 143 kW (192 bhp) necessary to drive a 32.5 tonne (32 ton) gross vehicle weight vehicle. As the power-to-weight ratio is likely to be increased to a higher value, power units with outputs up to 300 kW (400 bhp) are now under consideration, and the gas turbine engine can be designed to develop this power output.

### Construction

Gas turbine engines used for automobiles have their compressor turbine and power turbine mounted on separate shafts which run completely independently of each other and, for this reason, are often described as the twin shaft turbine or free turbine. Both the compressor turbine and the power turbine are housed in a common casing and their shafts rotate about the same axis. The single-stage centrifugal air compressor is mounted on the outer end of the compressor turbine shaft with the axial flow compressor turbine, designed for long life and high operating temperatures, mounted at the inner end. The power turbine is mounted on the inner end of its shaft, opposite the compressor turbine, and the outer end of the shaft contains the drive gear which is connected to the transmission through suitable reduction gears.

## Operation

The basic operation of the gas turbine engine is similar to the internal combustion engine with its processes of induction, compression, power and exhaust. However, in the internal combustion engine, these processes all take place at different times in the cycle of operation whereas they take place constantly and simultaneously in the gas turbine engine but in different parts of the engine.

Air is drawn into the compressor and delivered to the combustion chamber where it combined with atomized fuel and burns, causing an increase in gas pressure and temperature to well above 1000°C. The expanding gases release their pressure and heat energy and this is converted to mechanical energy as it passes through a series of nozzles to the compressor turbine blades, where sufficient energy to drive the compressor turbine, compressor, and compressor drive accessories is extracted. The gases are then directed through another set of nozzles and drive the power turbine producing torque to drive the vehicle through the gearbox and transmission system.

## Some details of the British Leyland engine (Figure 90)

### Combustion chamber

The combustion chamber contains a fuel sprayer and an igniter plug and is of the reverse-flow type. This means that air from the single stage compressor with a pressure ratio of 4:1 passes upwards through an annular space between the flame tube and outer casing, and enters the interior of the flame tube through a series of holes in the tube wall and its top face. The quantity of air delivered by the compressor is far in excess of that required for combustion in the chamber – a large proportion being used as dilution air to reduce gas temperature.

### Heat exchanger

The power turbine extracts much of the gas energy to propel the vehicle but before being discharged to the atmosphere the gases still have a temperature in the region of 750°C. These gases pass through the regenerative heat exchangers which reduce the temperature by approximately 500°C and increase the temperature of the inlet air charge during entry to the combustion chamber. The temperature of the exhaust gases on finally leaving the engine is in the region of 250°C.

The disadvantages of bulk and low-heat storage capacity of heat exchangers used with earlier models of gas turbine engines have been largely overcome in this engine by the use of large self-cleaning discs of glass ceramic material. These are positioned vertically one at each side of the engine, and rotate slowly about a horizontal axis at about 20 rev/min. Glass ceramic combines high operating temperature quality with low thermal expansion and it has a high heat-storage capacity. During rotation, a section of the disc is exposed first to the hot exhaust gases, then immediately to the cooler air from the compressor. By this process the inlet air acquires a substantial amount of heat before combustion heat is produced, resulting in a considerable increase in thermal efficiency and a reduction in specific fuel consumption.

### Starting and control systems

When light-up is initiated by operation of the starter switch, a high-tension spark is discharged across the igniter plug electrodes. The plug electrodes are situated adjacent to the sprayer and ignite the atomized fuel as it leaves the sprayer which then continues to burn constantly when the igniter system is cut out. An air pump, operated by electricity, is also brought into use by the starter motor switch and is used to deliver air to the combustion chamber for starting which assists in atomization of the fuel. After starting, air is supplied from the engine compressor and the pump is cut out.

The engine is controlled after light-up by the throttle pedal. The compressor turbine can be accelerated up to its full speed of approximately 38 000 rev/min by the throttle pedal while the

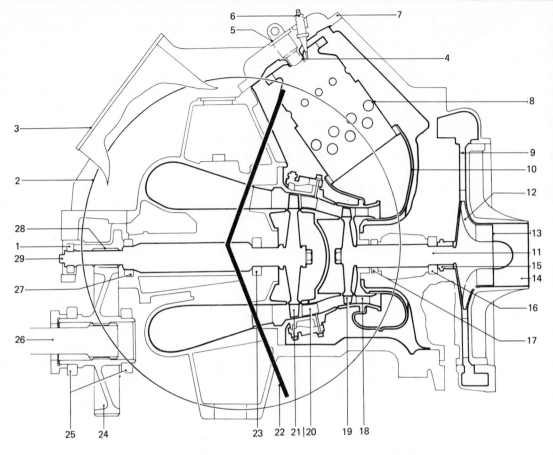

Figure 90　*British Leyland gas turbine engine*

| 1 Power turbine shaft end bearing | 11 Compressor shaft | 21 Power turbine |
|---|---|---|
| 2 Heat exchanger disc | 12 Impeller | 22 Dividing line between compressed air and |
| 3 Exhaust outlet duct | 13 Rotating guide vanes | exhaust gas seals |
| 4 Spark plug earth electrode | 14 Air intake duct | 23 Power turbine shaft forward bearing |
| 5 Sprayer | 15 Auxiliary drive pinion | 24 Large reduction gear |
| 6 Spark plug | 16 Compressor shaft forward bearing | 25 Reduction gear support bearings |
| 7 Combustion chamber cover | 17 Compressor shaft rear bearing | 26 Output shaft to gearbox |
| 8 Flame tube | 18 Fixed guide vanes | 27 Power turbine shaft rear bearing |
| 9 Volute | 19 Compressor turbine | 28 High speed reduction pinion |
| 10 Diffuser vane | 20 Variable guide vanes | 29 Power turbine shaft |

vehicle is held stationary by the brakes. When moving off, the throttle pedal is depressed, a gear is engaged, and torque is readily available to drive the power turbine and move the vehicle as the brakes are released. The speed of the power turbine ranges from approximately 4000 rev/min at idling to approximately 30 000 rev/min at maximum speed.

*Variable nozzles*

The position of the nozzle guide vanes immediately before the power turbine blades is varied by means of an electrically driven trimmer. The trimmer is responsive to temperature and speed signals causing a high turbine inlet temperature to be maintained at part load and therefore improving thermal efficiency.

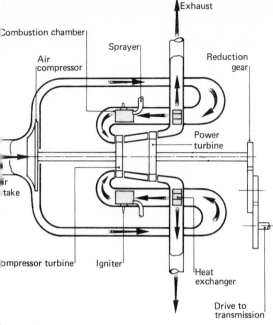

Figure 91   *Simplified view of gas turbine engine*

Labels on figure: Exhaust; Combustion chamber; Air compressor; Sprayer; Reduction gear; Power turbine; Air intake; Compressor turbine; Igniter; Heat exchanger; Drive to transmission

Variable nozzles also provide a degree of engine braking when rapid deceleration is required. This is achieved by movement of the nozzle vanes to a position in which the gas is directed into the turbine blades against the direction of rotation, and gas energy is used to reduce the speed of the turbine.

### Intake and exhaust systems

A silencer box and six replaceable paper-element filters are used to reduce intake noise and protect the engine from dirt under normal operating conditions. The interior surfaces of the silencer box are lined with a sound-damping material to reduce intake noise.

*Below:* Figure 92   *General external rear three-quarter view of the British Leyland power pack*

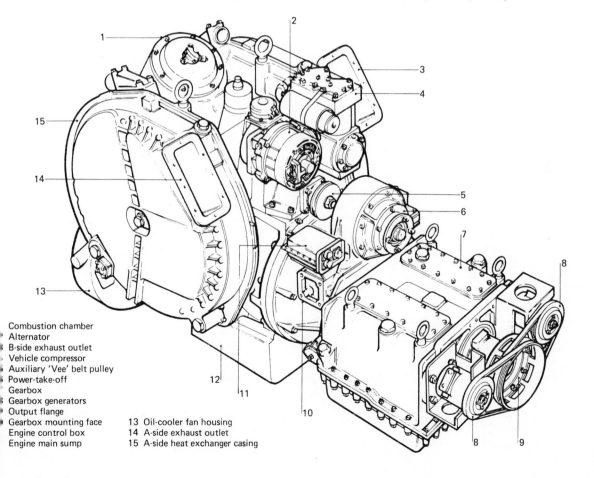

1   Combustion chamber
2   Alternator
3   B-side exhaust outlet
4   Vehicle compressor
5   Auxiliary 'Vee' belt pulley
6   Power-take-off
7   Gearbox
8   Gearbox generators
9   Output flange
10  Gearbox mounting face
11  Engine control box
12  Engine main sump
13  Oil-cooler fan housing
14  A-side exhaust outlet
15  A-side heat exchanger casing

The exhaust system consists of outlet ducts attached to the heat exchanger casing and they terminate in short vertical stub ducts. Two large circular stacks are situated at the rear of the cab which assist in emitting the exhaust gases above the cab level and provide adequate silencing.

*Conclusion*

This engine is designed for the British Leyland six-wheeled tractive unit built to operate at road speeds up to approximately 112 km/h. There are less engine vibrations and a lower noise level compared with the conventional CI engine of the same power output. Maintenance costs are expected to be exceptionally low and engine life before overhaul is estimated to be in the region of 800 000 km. Fuel economy is comparable with the CI engine over a wide power range and engine oil consumption is negligible.

# 3 Lubrication

The main reason for using a lubricant is to reduce, as much as possible, friction between two surfaces when in contact and moving relative to each other. This is done by the lubricant absorbing heat caused by friction from the surfaces in contact, and transferring it to another region where it can be dissipated more easily. If an adequate supply of the recommended lubricant is provided at the surfaces, the oil film itself will shear and the risk of excessive wear and seizure will be considerably reduced.

## Viscosity

One of the main properties of a lubricating oil is its viscosity. This is a measure of the resistance of an oil film to shear or, more simply, a measure of an oil's ability to flow. Easy engine starting and rapid oil distribution during starting-up demand an oil of low viscosity. On the other hand, high engine working temperatures and hard operating conditions demand a high viscosity oil.

All oils thin out, to some extent, and lose viscosity when heated. A good quality oil however will not change its viscosity too greatly when its temperature is raised and will retain sufficient body for efficient lubrication when hot. When the same oil is cold it will have a sufficiently low resistance for cold starting. Ideally, of course, an oil should not be affected by changes in working temperature, but so far this state has not been achieved in practice.

## Multigrade oils

A step towards this ideal state has however been made with the development of multigrade oils. These oils contain additives which reduce the extent to which they thin out when heated and thicken when cooled. They make cold starting easier and also provide adequate lubrication at high running temperature.

## Detergency

Most oils contain additives that reduce the formation of sludge on the inner walls of the engine by keeping the particles of foreign matter in suspension in the oil. The use of a detergent oil causes the oil to appear dirty fairly quickly after an oil change while the engine remains clean. The detergent additives do, however, become exhausted after a period of time and sludge deposits begin to appear in the system. Regular oil changes are therefore necessary to avoid this happening.

The action of a detergent, or dispersant, is to prevent the engine from becoming dirty. It ensures that finely divided solid contaminants are held in harmless suspension so that foreign matter is prevented from coagulating and settling out to form a sludge emulsion with the oil and water. (Water is formed from combustion of fuel.) Another reason for using an oil with a high-quality detergent additive is to combat the effects of sulphur present in varying quantities in almost all fuel oils for CI engines.

## Sump oil dilution

A small amount of fuel invariably escapes and finds its way into the engine crankcase and sump with the effect of diluting the lubricating oil, changing the viscosity and flash point. The degree of dilution can be experimentally determined by a simple distillation test which separates the fuel from the lubricating oil.

## Terms used with oils

*Oiliness and film strength*   Oiliness is the property of forming a slippery film on the surface to be lubricated. *Film strength* relates to the tenacity of that film when formed. Both can be improved with chemical additives.

*Stability*   Some oils tend to combine with oxygen to form contaminants such as carbon, lacquer, sludge and organic acids which can corrode copper and iron. Products from the incomplete combustion of fuel oil can act as catalysts and accelerate the rate of oxidation of an oil. A good oil will have high stability and resist these tendencies.

*Pour point depressants*   These lower the temperature at which an oil will cease to flow satisfactorily when cold.

*Colloidal graphite*   This is sometimes added to oils when used for running-in as it promotes film formation and it reduces friction and wear of the bearing surfaces.

*Viscosity index*   The measure of the change in an oil's viscosity when heated or cooled is the viscosity index of the oil. The index is based on an empirical scale having 100 for the good quality Pennsylvanian blends, and 0 for a poor oil of extreme variability which shows a very steep viscosity/temperature curve. However, modern oil refining techniques can achieve a viscosity index in the region of 110–120 and higher with the use of VI improver additives. The viscosity/temperature curve of these oils is relatively flat which is indicative of a good quality oil which has a suitable low viscosity for cold starting and is also suitable for providing efficient lubrication at higher working temperatures.

*Oil wedge*   During a state of full fluid film lubrication the oil in a bearing becomes a self-sustaining wedge and forces the shaft away from the bearing surface. When the bearing is working under this condition there is no metal-to-metal contact and frictional resistance depends upon the lubricant used.

## Transmission lubricants

The main function of a transmission lubricant is to provide a film of lubricant on the meshing surfaces of the gear trains and provide the bearings of supporting shafts with adequate lubrication. During operation, high tooth pressures occur between gear teeth in mesh, and efficient lubrication is essential to prevent excessive heat being generated which causes wear and noise, finally leading to seizure. Transmission components are usually housed in a casing which is small and compact to keep its weight and volume to a minimum. It is therefore important to use the correct quantity and the recommended grade and type of lubricant for the components.

*Extreme pressure (EP) lubrication*
Some oils contain an extreme pressure agent which generally reacts with the metal surfaces to form a protective film and so reduce any risk of metallic contact between mating gear teeth during operation. These oils are particularly useful where gears are subject to very high pressures under which conditions an ordinary lubricating oil would be squeezed out from between the contacting surfaces causing damage. The action of an EP additive comes into effect at high temperatures in those areas where seizure is likely to occur. Hypoid gears, in which the relative movement of the teeth is both a rolling and a sliding motion, work at extremely high pressures and temperatures and demand an oil with a very active EP agent.

*SAE numbers*
Engine and transmission oils are classified into grades depending on their viscosity. Each grade is numbered by the Society of Automotive Engineers (SAE) and defines, within specific limits, the viscosity at a given temperature. The number indicates only the viscosity of the lubricant and does not imply a particular quality or any special

additives contained in the oil. SAE numbers for engine oils range from SAE 10 which is extra light, to SAE 60 which is extra heavy. Transmission oils are numbered SAE 75, 80, 90, 140 and 250.

*Greases*

These are composed of a base oil, additives and thickeners, the latter being used to hold the oil in suspension within the structure. A commonly used thickener is metallic soap compound which has a strong natural attraction for metal surfaces. Hydrate is sometimes used as the metallic element and compounding is carried out at high temperatures and pressures in a pressure kettle, often well above 150°C.

Different thickeners in use are aluminium soap, calcium soap, sodium soap and lithium soap.

Aluminium soap-based grease has a smooth texture, has a fair resistance to water, and is satisfactory when used up to 79°C. Calcium-based grease has excellent resistance to water as it is insoluble in water. A sodium base can be used for applications up to 149°C but it has poor resistance to water (soluble). A lithium or lime-soda-based grease has good general purposes and it is often used as a chassis grease.

## Engine lubrication system (Figure 93)

The system is designed to adequately supply oil to engine components which require lubricating when in motion and working under high pressures and temperatures. Oil is delivered at pump pressure to most components; this reduces friction

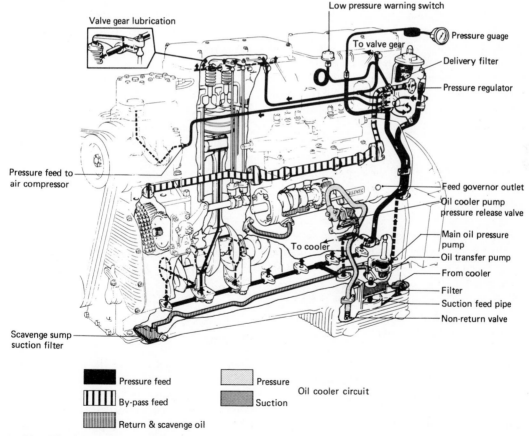

Figure 93   *The lubrication system*

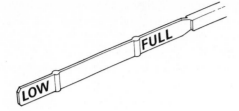

Figure 94    *Dip-stick*

and wear to a minimum and prevents the generation of heat which would otherwise develop and possibly lead to seizure of the engine. A few components are not pressure-fed but rely on spray, mist and splash for supply of the lubricant. The circulating oil in the lubrication system also assists in engine cooling.

*Oil level indicators*

The majority of engines have a dip-stick (Figure 94) which is used to determine the level of lubricating oil in the sump. The dip-stick may be rigid and straight or it may be flexible; it is marked to indicate the maximum and minimum limits for the oil level. Some vehicles are equipped with an oil level warning lamp, and this is usually mounted on the cab instrument panel.

*Oil pressure*

The operating pressure of the engine oil is very important and some device for monitoring this during running is essential. There are two common systems in use. One system consists of a warning lamp on the instrument panel which is controlled by a pressure switch in the lubrication system. When the electrical system is switched on for starting the engine, the light will be illuminated. After starting the engine, the oil pressure, if satisfactory, opens the pressure switch and the lamp goes out. When the engine is idling the lamp may flicker, but at higher engine speeds it should be out. Should the lamp remain on at higher speeds, the reason for this should be investigated. It should be remembered that the lamp, when out, indicates an adequate oil pressure and does not indicate the oil level in the sump.

An alternative type of oil pressure indicator is

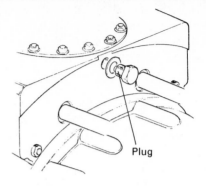

Figure 95    *Magnetic chip collection plug*

the gauge. This is usually mounted on the instrument panel and is connected to the lubricating system by a pipe which may be rigid or flexible, or be a combination of the two. The gauge is preferred to the warning lamp by most drivers as it indicates the full range of operating pressures and gives some indication of the engine's condition, particularly the degree of wear in the crankshaft bearings.

*Filter warning lamp*

Some vehicles are fitted with a filter warning lamp. This indicates, when out, that the filter is working normally. If the lamp remains on when the engine is running, this indicates that the filter is blocked with accumulated deposits which resist the flow of oil into the engine resulting in unfiltered oil being fed to the bearings.

*Magnetic chip collection plug (Figure 95)*

This is fitted in some engine sumps to collect minute metal particles which are present in the oil. The plug should be periodically examined and cleaned.

## Oil pumps

There are a number of methods used to drive the engine oil pump. Some are driven by gears from the engine crankshaft, others are driven directly from the end of the crankshaft. The design shown in Figure 96 shows how a pump is driven by the crankshaft through an intermediate gear.

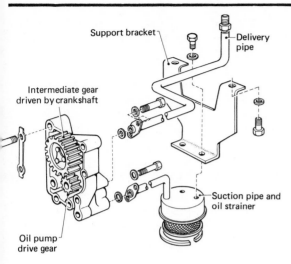

Figure 96    *Oil pump drive for Volvo engine*

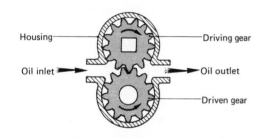

Figure 97    *Gear pump*

## Gear pump

This type is very commonly used and consists of two spur gears which rotate within a close fitting housing (see Figure 97). One gear is driven by the camshaft and drives the idling gear with which it is in constant mesh.

Oil is drawn into the sump on one side of the housing and each gear traps a small quantity of oil between its teeth and the housing during operations. The oil leaves the pump at the outlet passage under pump pressure and it is delivered to the lubrication system.

This type of pump is simple, robust and effective but it relies for its operation on close fitting gears in their housing. The pump should be periodically examined for wear on the gears and for excessive end-float of the gears in the housing,

as this wear can cause an inability to maintain oil pressure, particularly at low speeds, which can lead to engine seizure.

Some engines have two pumps, one working as a feed pump, the other as a scavenge pump. They are usually driven by a common shaft and both pumps are usually built within one housing. The scavenge pump is employed to scavenge any excess oil that may collect in the shallow portions of the sump and transfer it back into the main oil reservoir. This condition is likely to occur when an engine is operating with extreme forward or rearward inclination for long periods.

### Vane pump (Figure 98)

In this pump, oil is drawn into the inlet port and is carried between pairs of rotating vanes and the housing during operation. The oil leaves the pump at the delivery port under pump pressure.

The vanes are supported by a rotor which runs eccentrically in relation to the casing, and the vanes may be spring loaded to maintain contact with the casing, or they may rely on centrifugal force for their operation.

### Eccentric pump (Figure 99)

This pump usually consists of a multi-lobed rotor eccentrically mounted in a ring provided with internal lobes corresponding with the rotor. The ring usually has one more lobe than those on the

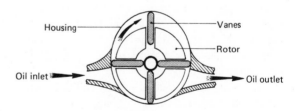

Figure 98    *Vane pump*

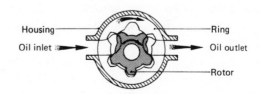

Figure 99    *Eccentric pump*

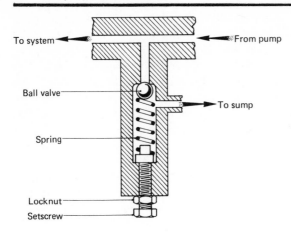

Figure 100   *Spring-loaded pressure relief valve*

rotor. The ring rotates in the circular bore of the pump housing. Pumping action is created by the progressive increase and decrease of clearance between each set of lobes as they rotate. This pump can be directly driven from the crankshaft or the camshaft and it has a much lower rate of wear than the gear type pump.

*Relief valve (Figure 100)*
Oil pumps are designed to supply an adequate quantity of oil at a pre-determined pressure during engine idling. At higher engine speeds therefore, the pump delivery pressure is excessively high, and some means of relieving some of this pressure is necessary if excessive oil consumption and damage to seals and joints is to be avoided. Pressure relief is achieved by the use of a relief valve incorporated in the system.

The valve assembly consists of a ball or plunger which is held on its seat by a spring, and the whole assembly is contained in a housing connected to the main feed from the oil pump to the gallery. Alternatively it may be connected directly into the gallery itself, or housed in the casing of a full-flow oil filter.

*Operation* When the engine is stopped, the spring keeps the valve pressed on its seat. After starting up, the valve remains closed or slightly open depending upon the oil pressure and the

spring tension. As the engine speed increases and the oil pressure increases, the valve opens further and the surplus oil passes through the bypass passage returning to the sump.

The correct spring loading is effected by an adjusting screw and a lock nut. If the screw is turned inwards, pressure on the spring will be increased and a higher oil pressure will be required to lift the valve off its seat. By turning the screw outwards, pressure on the spring will be reduced and a lower oil pressure will lift the valve off its seat. Engine manufacturers recommend settings for their valves and these are usually in the region of 2.5 kg/cm$^2$ (35 lbf/in$^2$) at an oil temperature of 43°C at about 1000 rev/min.

## Oil filters

There are two general types of filters in use and both types are fitted to the pressure side of the lubrication system.

*Bypass filter*
This type is fitted between the main oil gallery and the sump and receives only a small quantity of oil from the pump. After filtering, the oil is returned to the sump. A metering orifice is used in the oil feed pipe to the filter to control the quantity of oil flowing into the unit, this usually being about 1/10 of the pump output, and the whole quantity of sump oil is filtered about twelve times in each hour at normal running speeds. A drop in oil pressure across this type of filter is less important than with the full-flow type as the oil is

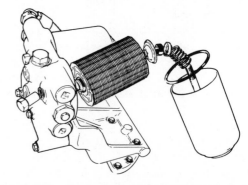

Figure 101   *Typical oil filter assembly*

drained to the sump after passing through the filter. In the full-flow type, an oil pressure drop would result in a low pressure of oil delivered to the bearings.

Some designs of bypass filter are the replaceable element type where the old element is removed and disposed of during a service and a new element is fitted. Some elements should be washed off in petrol during servicing, and the manufacturer's instructions must be followed with this type. Other designs of filter have the element sealed in the casing and the whole unit must be replaced during a service. Filter elements are of impregnated paper or other suitable filtering material.

### Full-flow filter (Figure 102)

This type of filter is fitted between the pump and gallery, and all the oil from the pump passes through the filter under normal running conditions before being fed through the gallery to the bearings. The design must be such as to give a balance between effective purification and flow quantity of the oil. Should the element become choked, a safety valve or a spring-loaded element arrangement will allow unfiltered oil to pass the gallery and bearings.

This type of filter is designed to offer little resistance to the flow of oil passing through it, as it is in the main oil feed line, and a drop in pressure across the filter will cause a lower delivery pressure at the engine bearings. Filtration of foreign matter will therefore be limited to larger particles than those which will be filtered by a bypass filter.

Where a topping-up plug is provided in a filter casing, it is advisable to top up with lubricating oil after the filter assembly has been dismantled and reassembled. This will prevent the engine from being starved of oil during starting up.

### Centrifugal filter (Figure 103)

This type of filter is usually driven by engine oil pressure or it is mechanically driven by the engine. It is normally used with the bypass system of filtration.

The filter works on the principle of centrifugal force. Oil is fed into the rotating bowl which

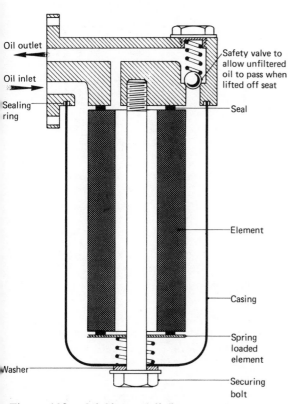

Figure 102   *Oil filter – full flow type*

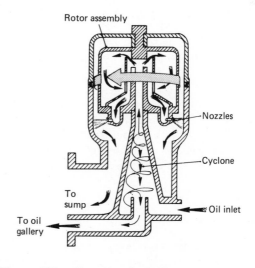

Figure 103   *Centrifugal oil filter*

rotates at a very high speed and the oil with its foreign matter is flung outwards to the inner surface of the casing.

The solid impurities (foreign matter) have the highest density and therefore stick to the casing after being flung against it under the effect of centrifugal force. Any water which may be present in the oil is also flung on to the casing with slightly less force than the solid matter and this therefore deposits on the surface of the solid matter and, in turn, is discharged at a separate outlet. The oil which has the lowest density is flung towards the inner layer on the casing and is subsequently returned back to the sump in its clean state.

Some filter designs permit the removal of solid matter while the unit is operating but a more commonly used arrangement is designed to be cleaned while stopped. This is done by partly dismantling the unit, removing the casing and scraping out the solid matter, then washing out and reassembling.

The Scania filter consists of a cyclone section and a centrifugal section. In the cyclone section, contaminated oil is separated from clean oil with the latter passing to the oil gallery. The contaminated oil is forced up the cone to the centrifuge where the impurities are separated by centrifugal force. The centrifuge consists of a rotor with two nozzles in its base. Oil is forced out through these nozzles causing the rotor to rotate at about 7000 rev/min. The clean oil is directed back into the sump after leaving the nozzles and the solid contaminants are cleaned out during servicing.

*Dry sump system*
Some horizontal engines have a separate oil well mounted on the side of the collecting sump and a scavenge pump is used to return the oil to the well. A pressure pump is used with this system to lift the oil from the well and deliver it to the engine bearings.

## Oil coolers

It is necessary to fit oil coolers on some vehicles to prevent harmful rises in oil temperature during heavy engine running conditions. The oil is cir-

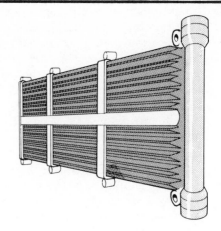

Figure 104    *Oil cooler – air type*

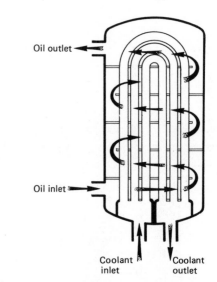

Figure 105    *Oil cooler – coolant type*

culated by a pump and passes through the cooler from which the heat is extracted on the heat exchanger principle.

*Air cooling type (Figure 104)*
The cooler is fitted at the front of the engine coolant radiator on some vehicles. Oil is pumped from the sump, through the cooler, and back to the sump after being cooled. A separate sump is normally used for this purpose and a filter and relief valve are usually incorporated in the circuit.

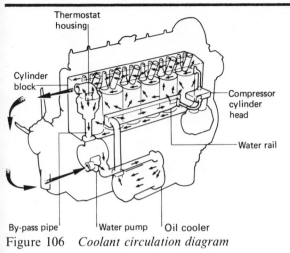

Figure 106  *Coolant circulation diagram*

Air passing over the outsides of the finned tubes of the cooler reduces the temperature of the oil.

### Coolant cooling type (Figure 105)

In this system, the oil is cooled by the coolant used in the engine cooling system which is normally taken from the delivery side of the coolant pump. This type of cooler enables the engine to reach its operating temperature quickly during warming up (see Figure 106). This shows an oil cooler (heat exchanger) incorporated in the cooling system of an engine.

## Automatic chassis lubrication (ACL)

This system of chassis lubrication is used on many passenger vehicles, and an increasing number of goods vehicle operators are having systems fitted to their vehicles. The advantages of ACL to transport operators include:

1   Less down-time for servicing and maintenance of vehicles.
2   Longer life of components.
3   The system is more satisfactory than a manual system of lubrication for operators who have vehicles running away from their base workshops for long periods.
4   Fewer staff need to be employed when compared with a manual system of lubrication resulting in fewer wages having to be paid to staff.
5   ACL is essential for those operators who do not work to a planned preventive maintenance system and who are likely to forget about lubrication.
6   There should be a reduction in driver fatigue caused by the use of well serviced vehicles and this, in turn, should lead to increased road safety.

Vehicles fitted with ACL should be regularly inspected to ensure that oil is reaching the bearings which it is intended to serve. Nylon tubes of about 6 mm diameter ($\frac{1}{4}$ in) are used in most systems to carry the oil from the lubrication pump to the metering valves which are located close to the point of discharge. These tubes should be regularly inspected for cracks and leaks as they tend to become brittle in service due to vibrations and changes of temperature.

There are a number of ACL systems ranging from those with semi-automatic operation to those which are fully automatic.

### Semi-automatic system

This type usually consists of a manually operated pump and a tank unit located in the cab or on the side of the chassis frame where it can conveniently be operated. When the hand lever is pumped, oil is fed to the points of discharge at a line pressure of approximately 280 kN/m$^2$ (40 lbf/in$^2$). It is usual to pressurize the system once daily for adequate lubrication from the discharge points. The capacity of the tank is usually about 1.12 litres (2 pints) and outputs vary from about 7 cm$^3$ to 22 cm$^3$ per stroke of the operating lever.

The normal lubricant used is SAE 90 oil, which has good retention properties within the bearing surfaces, but engine oil is used in some systems. Lubrication frequency at the points can be adjusted to suit operations and this varies from 5 to 30 minutes after the initial start and is repeated at regular intervals during running.

### Automatic system

Most automatic systems are pneumatically powered and, in most cases, electrically controlled. These systems are capable of supplying

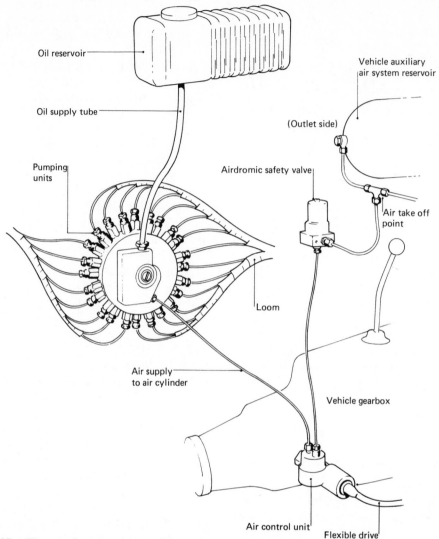

Figure 107　*The Airdromic chassis lubrication system*

100 or more points of discharge on a chassis and they are fed by a pump and oil tank. The pump is normally operated by the vehicle's air system and is controlled by an electric timer in the cab. Each time the engine is started the pump unit operates the system and a warning light on the dashboard indicates that the system is being primed. When the pressure reaches its operating pressure, usually about 560 kN/m$^2$ (80 lbf/in$^2$), all points in the system are given a shot of lubricant. The fifth wheel coupling on tractive units is normally included. Frequency of lubrication is usually adjustable and takes place every 15 to 30 minutes depending on the number of discharge points and the type of operations performed by the vehicle.

*Airdromic system (Figures 107 and 108)*
This is a mileage controlled system comprising of four major units: the pump assembly, the air control unit, the safety valve and an oil reservoir.

The pump assembly consists of a circular housing containing a driveshaft upon which are

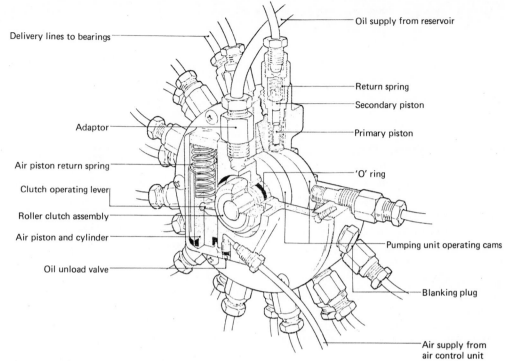

Delivery lines to bearings

Oil supply from reservoir

Adaptor

Return spring

Secondary piston

Primary piston

Air piston return spring

'O' ring

Clutch operating lever

Roller clutch assembly

Air piston and cylinder

Pumping unit operating cams

Oil unload valve

Blanking plug

Air supply from
air control unit

Figure 108   *The Airdromic system pump assembly*

mounted two, four or five single-lobed cams. Each cam operates a row of twelve pumping units which are radially arranged around the pump casing, and each unit is connected to a point of discharge on the chassis by a nylon tube.

The air control unit is mounted on the vehicle's gearbox and is driven from the speedometer take-off point. The unit consists of a worm-operated cam which operates two poppet valves, one controlling the air supply to the pump assembly and the other controlling the exhaust air from the air supply line.

The safety valve is incorporated in the air supply line to the air control unit and this isolates the system if pressure in the auxiliary air tank falls below a predetermined minimum value.

The oil reservoir may be located within, or on the back of, the cab, or alternatively it may be located on the chassis frame. It has a capacity of 6.8 litres ($1\frac{1}{2}$ gal) and incorporates a filter element. The location of the reservoir is decided upon after consideration of the following points:

1  It must be higher than the pump assembly to provide a satisfactory head of oil.
2  It must be accessible for refilling and examination of the filter.
3  The length of the pipeline between the reservoir and the pump assembly must be kept to a minimum to ensure adequate flow of oil in cold weather when the oil's viscosity will be at its highest value.

# 4 The cooling system

Heat is produced in the engine cylinders during combustion of the fuel and air causing high cylinder temperatures. The cooling system removes heat from the engine quickly and continuously to prevent overheating which would cause a reduction in engine performance and, in extreme cases, seizure and damage to engine components. Excessive cooling will also cause a reduction in engine performance by reducing combustion efficiency and will lead to excessive cylinder bore wear and dilution of sump oil caused by unburned fuel oil passing between the piston and cylinder. Control of cooling is therefore imperative if the best performance is to be obtained from an engine.

## Air cooling

Heavy vehicle engines are usually multi-cylinder in-line types which are difficult to cool uniformly by an air cooling system. For this reason, air cooling is seldom used. In the few engines where air cooling is used however, a fan and a cowling direct air to the hotter parts of the engine where cool air is most required, but this equipment is bulky and the fan is power absorbing.

The absence of a sound muffling coolant jacket causes noisy engine operation and the possibility of higher running temperatures when compared with liquid-cooled engines. This often leads to larger bearing clearances being used which further contribute to engine noise, in addition to loss of power. Variations in engine running temperature are difficult to control with air cooling and lead to temperature variation between different parts of the engine causing the possibility of distortion. Aluminium alloys are often used for the engine components as they are better heat conductors than cast iron or steel, and thin cooling fins are employed to increase the surface area of the cylinders.

The main advantages of air cooling when compared with liquid cooling are due to the absence of a coolant. Periodic checking of the coolant level and topping up is eliminated. No antifreeze, corrosion inhibitors or sealing compounds are required, and the possibility of leaks is eliminated. Engine warm-up is quicker with air cooling than with liquid cooling, and the simplicity of the system reduces maintenance and the risk of vehicle breakdowns caused by a defective cooling system.

## Liquid cooling

Liquid cooling systems are normally used for heavy vehicle engines. The coolant absorbs heat from the engine and is circulated to the radiator which transfers the heat to the cool air passing through it.

### Thermo-syphon system (Figures 109 and 110)

In this simple system, which is seldom used with modern engines, circulation of the coolant depends upon the difference in density between the hot water in the jacket and the cooler water in the radiator which produces convection currents. The coolant passages must be free from obstructions and restrictions, the connecting pipes and hoses between the engine and radiator should have a large diameter, and the jacket should be positioned low, relative to the radiator, for effective circulation of the coolant.

Successful operation of this system also depends upon the coolant level not being allowed to fall below the level of the delivery pipe to the radiator

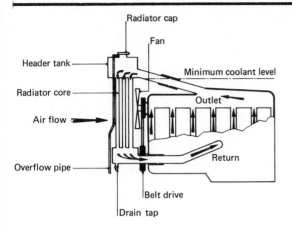

Figure 109   *Thermo-syphon cooling system*

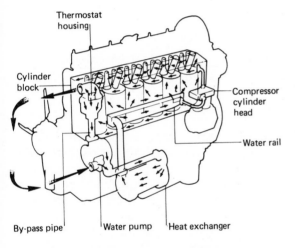

Figure 110   *Coolant circulation diagram*

header tank. A wide temperature difference between the coolant in the jacket and the coolant in the radiator is also necessary for effective circulation. This system requires a high and large radiator and a large quantity of water when compared with a pump system. Cab and coachwork designs do not usually permit a high radiator, making this system impracticable for most modern vehicles.

Most of the above disadvantages are overcome by using a pump to assist circulation of the coolant, although the thermo-syphon system is regarded as less costly to maintain and is more reliable due to its simplicity.

*Pump system*

Most modern liquid-cooled engines employ a pump. The pump ensures a more positive circulation of the coolant and is necessary for engines of high power output and complicated cylinder block and head construction which would not receive adequate cooling from a thermo-syphon system.

Many goods vehicles are fitted with tilt cabs which require a low-height coolant radiator to give adequate clearance when swivelling the cab. A pump-assisted system with a separate radiator header tank mounted on the back of the cab is normally used on these vehicles.

## Axial-flow impeller pump (Figure 111)

This type of pump has a disc-shaped impeller with widely spaced vanes on one side. The vanes are

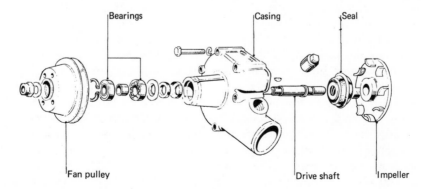

Figure 111   *Exploded view of axial-flow impeller pump*

usually, but not always, deeper at the impeller centre than at the outer edge, and they may be straight or curved. The impeller is secured to one end of its driving shaft and the drive pulley and fan assembly are secured at the other end, the shaft being mounted in bearings which are housed in the pump casing. A special grease is normally used to pre-pack the pump bearings during assembly, and they do not require any attention in service.

*Operation* When the engine is running, the impeller rotates, coolant enters the pump inlet and passes to the centre of the impeller which forces the coolant by centrifugal force along the vanes to their outer edges. It is flung off the impeller and directed to the pump outlet. If the thermostat valve is closed, the coolant leaving the pump is returned to the pump inlet via a bypass passage which may be internal or external. This type of pump does not operate with a high delivery pressure and it is not used with some of the larger heavy vehicle engines for this reason.

## Radial-flow centrifugal pump

Some larger engines have this type of pump in the cooling system. Circulation of the coolant is much faster as this pump operates with a higher delivery pressure when compared with the axial-flow pump, the higher pressure being caused by the different pump construction and the effects of centrifugal force on the coolant. This type of pump is usually driven by gears from the engine camshaft or driven from the engine timing gears.

A centrifugal pump consists of a casing which houses an impeller and drive spindle. Coolant enters the casing at the centre of the impeller and is forced radially outwards along the blades by centrifugal force into the stationary casing where it is directed to the pump outlet. The impeller spindle is carried on a self-aligning ball bearing which permits a slight misalignment between the pump and its driving member. The seal is a spring-loaded carbon gland with the carbon ring fixed in the casing, and the spherical seating rotates with the impeller shaft. In the later design of this pump, the carbon gland seal has been superseded by the unit seal shown in Figure 112.

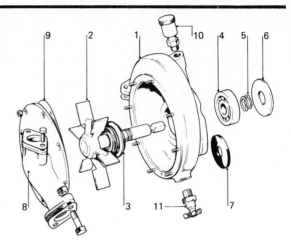

| | |
|---|---|
| 1 Pump body | 7 Synthetic rubber sealing ring |
| 2 Impeller | 8 Pump cover |
| 3 Unit seal | 9 Cover packing |
| 4 Ball bearing | 10 Greaser |
| 5 Spring clips | 11 Drain cock |
| 6 Grease retaining end-plate | |

Figure 112  *Radial-flow centrifugal pump*

## Hot spots

Extracting heat from engine hot spots has to be done without overcooling other parts of the engine or producing a variation in temperature through the cylinder block and head. Wide temperature variation could result in distorted cylinder bores causing loss of compression, increase in piston blow-by, piston drag and oil dilution which will shorten engine life, reduce reliability and may cause seizure.

If a hot spot causes the coolant to boil, heat is carried away by the steam bubbles at a higher rate than is generally possible by the normal flow of coolant, because of the latent heat of vaporization. Heat is carried away from the hot spots by the formation of minute bubbles of steam that are condensed by the coolant in the surrounding area. At exceptionally high temperatures, 'film boiling' occurs and a continuous layer of steam is formed on the hot jacket surface, which effectively insulates the coolant from the surface. As a result of this there is a rise in temperature which can lead to excessive expansion and distortion of components.

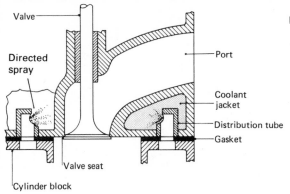

Figure 113 *Directed cooling is incorporated in some cylinder heads*

## Directed cooling (Figure 113)

The coolant can be directed to hot spots, such as those around the exhaust valve pockets in the cylinder head, to prevent local overheating and subsequent loss of engine power. The coolant is passed under pressure through holes or nozzles positioned in the cylinder head and directed on to the hot spots. This effect can also be achieved with a distribution tube consisting of drilled holes fitted into the cylinder head water jacket causing the coolant to be directed on to the hot spots before passing through the system.

## After-boiling

After-boiling can result from an engine being stopped when it has been operating under high load causing local boiling of the static coolant which is in contact with hot spots. Restarting the engine while the coolant is boiling can produce high thermal stresses which may crack the cylinder block or cylinder head. After-boiling can also lead to serious loss of coolant from the system.

## Radiators

The function of the radiator is to transfer heat from the coolant to the air stream. It is designed with a large cooling area combined with a relatively small frontal area, and it forms a container for some of the coolant in the system.

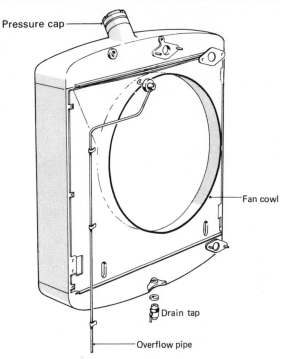

Figure 114 *Radiator with fan cowl*

Radiators usually have mounting feet or brackets, a filler cap, an overflow pipe, and a drain tap fitted to the lower tank. The radiator core, sometimes known as the matrix, may be the film or tubular type (Figure 114).

### Film core (Figure 115)
The tubes are the full width of the core and are bent to form square spaces through which air can pass, and they are sometimes crinkled to extend their length. The top and bottom tanks are secured to side plates or frames with the core located between them, and a fan cowl often completes the unit. The materials used for the radiator tanks are brass, cast iron, cast aluminium or fabricated steel.

### Tubular cores

*Tube and fin type* This consists of thin-walled copper or brass tubes of round, oval or

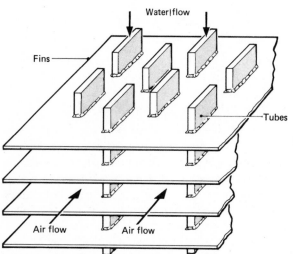

Figure 115   *Film core*

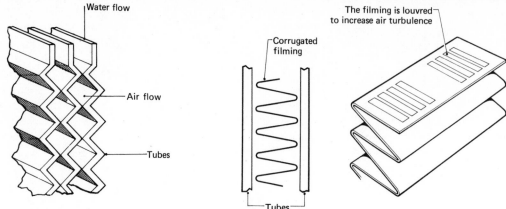

Figure 117   *Tubular core – tube and corrugation type*

Figure 116   *Tubular core – tube and fin type*

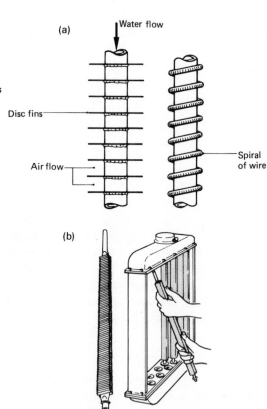

rectangular cross-section. The tubes pass through a series of thin copper fins (see Figure 116) with the top and bottom tanks attached to the upper and lower fins, respectively. The fins secure the tubes and increase the surface area from which heat can be dissipated. The tubes are placed edge-on to the air flow for minimum air resistance and they are nowadays produced from strip by lock-seaming.

Figure 118   *Separate tubes (a) and their removal and fitting (b)*

*Tube and corrugation type* These designs are sometimes used as an alternative to the tube and fin design. The corrugated separator filming (Figure 117) is made from copper and laid between the tubes to provide an airway. Each face of the filming is louvred to increase air turbulence as the air passes through it which improves the cooling efficiency in this design.

### Separate tubes (Figure 118)

Radiators with separate coolant tubes are occasionally used and they provide a stronger core than the other types but they are costly to build, heavy and time-consuming to repair. The tanks and side frames are usually bolted together and locate the thick walled tubes of rectangular or circular cross-section. The tubes are made watertight in the upper and lower tanks with rubber and metal seals, and they have bonded copper fins or a spiral of copper wire wound over their complete length to increase heat dissipation. Tube removal and refitting may be done by two methods depending on radiator construction. One method is by splitting the tanks from their side frames; the other is by springing the tubes out and in, which is usually possible due to their flexibility.

### Separate header tanks

Some vehicles are fitted with a separate header tank. This may be located above the engine or secured to the back panel of the cab, and it is connected to the cooling system by pipes. This arrangement allows a low-height radiator to be used and it is often adopted for goods vehicles with tilt cabs which require maximum clearance for the cab to tilt forward. The separate tank is usually more

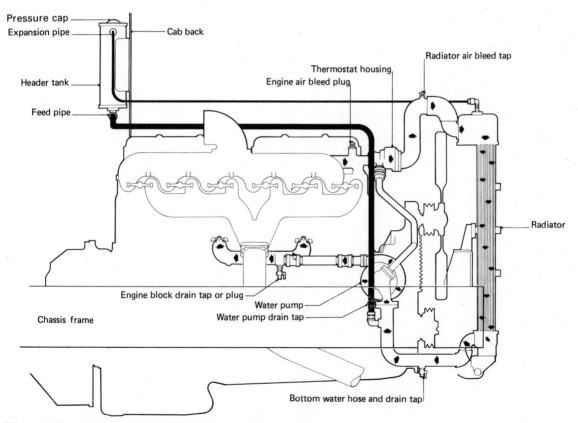

Figure 119  *Cooling system layout with Gardner engine*

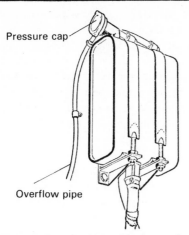

Figure 120    *Radiator header tank*

accessible for checking and refilling the coolant when compared with the location of some conventionally fixed header tanks. The tank is also used to de-aerate the coolant.

## Cooling fans

A cooling fan is usually mounted behind the radiator to draw air through the core. The fan may be mounted on a bracket attached to the engine or mounted on the end of the coolant pump spindle. In either case it is driven by a belt or belts from the engine crankshaft. Alternatively, the fan may be mounted on the end of the crankshaft or driven by an auxiliary propeller shaft from the crankshaft.

The fan has to draw sufficient air through the radiator for cooling purposes in heavy traffic on a hot day and ensure adequate cooling at engine idling speeds. Alternatively, a vehicle travelling on a motorway at a moderate speed does not require the same assistance from the fan, as the natural flow of air passing through the radiator is often sufficient to cool the air. Under the latter running conditions, the fan would be absorbing unnecessary engine power for its work.

Methods of controlling fan operation are becoming popular. Some older vehicles would satisfactorily operate in cold weather with their fans, or fan blades, removed but this is seldom done with modern vehicles. Variable-pitch fans are sometimes used which are fitted in place of the existing fan. These operate on the principle that at low engine speeds, the fan blades are at an angle to the radiator so that they draw air in the normal manner. At higher engine speeds the blade angle is reduced to zero so that no air is drawn and there is a reduction in power required to drive the fan.

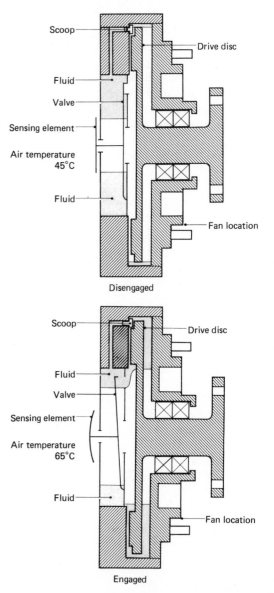

Figure 121    *Principle of operation of viscous fan drive*

These fans do not cover all operating conditions, such as climbing a long hill in a low gear with the engine speed high and a low road speed, and over-heating can occur.

*Viscous fan drives*

Many heavy vehicles are fitted with viscous fan drives that control fan speed in such a way that it only operates when required. When a vehicle is travelling at high speeds there is normally sufficient air passing through the radiator core to provide adequate cooling without the assistance of a fan. Viscous drives are designed to cut out fan operation at high road speeds and high engine speeds if it is not required which gives a saving in engine power and a reduction in fan noise. On the other hand, when the engine is working hard and requires cooling, the viscous drive acts in such a way as to provide adequate cooling.

The viscous drive operates as a shear-type fluid coupling; the drive is transmitted from the drive disc (driving member) to the housing (driven member) through a silicone fluid film (Figure 121). A bimetallic sensing element placed in the air stream senses the air temperature as the air passes through the radiator. When a predetermined temperature is reached, the sensing element opens the valve in the housing which allows the fluid to pass from the front chamber to the rear chamber where it fills the clearance between the drive disc and the housing. This causes the housing to be dragged round with the drive disc which rotates the fan and increases the air flow through the core so cooling the coolant. When the temperature of the coolant falls, so does the air temperature, and the sensing element bends back to its original shape, closing the valve between the chambers. Centrifugal force acting in the fluid forces it through the scoop into the front chamber leaving the clearance between the drive disc and the housing free of fluid so that no drive takes place between the two.

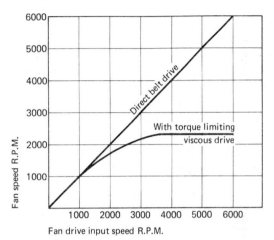

Figure 123   *Performance characteristics for a fan drive*

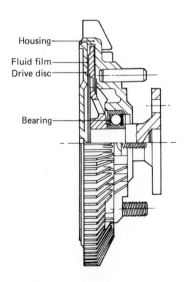

Figure 122   *Viscous fan drive unit*

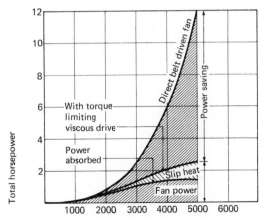

Figure 124   *Performance characteristics for a fan drive*

Control of the fan drive is therefore fully automatic depending upon the temperature of the air passing through the radiator core. The torque transmitting capacity of the unit is determined by its physical construction and the viscosity of the fluid which provides drag between the members. The torque limit of the unit is determined from the torque required to drive the fan at its desired maximum speed.

*Fan clutch*

To relieve excessive kinetic loads imposed on the fan by sudden variations in engine speed, the fan head used with some British Leyland engines incorporates a slipping clutch. This consists of a clutch centre and a clutch plate held apart by six coil springs against two friction rings which are triangular in section. The outer edges of the clutch centre and clutch plate are bevelled at an angle of 45° to give ample frictional area against the springs.

*Fan belt*

A slack fan belt will cause slipping on the drive pulleys causing inefficient cooling of the engine by not driving the fan and coolant pump at the correct speeds. A tight fan belt will overload the coolant pump bearings causing increased wear and a reduction in life. The correct tension gives

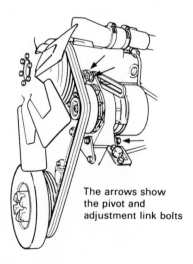

The arrows show the pivot and adjustment link bolts

Figure 125   *Adjusting the fan belts*

about 12.7 mm ($\frac{1}{2}$ in) deflection in the belt's greatest length between pulleys, and it is normally checked by pressing with the thumb. Some belts are adjusted by swivelling the generator or alternator, others are adjusted by moving the separate fan bracket adjuster (see Figure 125).

Fan belts should be regularly inspected for fraying, stretching, bottoming in the pulleys and saturation by oil. When more than one belt is used they should always be renewed as a complete set.

## Radiator shutters

Automatic shutters are fitted to some radiators to vary the flow of air through the matrix. This helps to maintain the coolant at an optimum working temperature for normal running and reduces heat loss while the vehicle is stationary, making shorter warm-up periods possible. Shutters are usually fitted in front of the radiator, but they may occasionally be fitted behind the radiator to reduce the possibility of damage by flying stones or the danger of icing.

The shutter frame is usually fabricated from heavy-gauge sheet steel and the vanes are of extruded aluminium and sufficiently robust to withstand stresses caused by a high-velocity air stream at high road speeds. Closed shutters reduce the driving power required by the fan and they reduce the possibility of over cooling the engine lubricating oil. Shutters are normally positioned over the entire radiator surface and are operated by a sensitive sensing element which responds to changes of engine temperature.

*Progressive operation type*

This system consists of a wax element incorporated into the cooling system which operates the vane mechanism above 70°C. The wax expands as the temperature rises causing the element to actuate the vanes against the tension of a spring and move the vanes towards the open position. Air will then flow through the matrix and a stable coolant temperature will be reached, the temperature depending upon engine load and ambient temperature. The coolant temperature is maintained until a change in running conditions

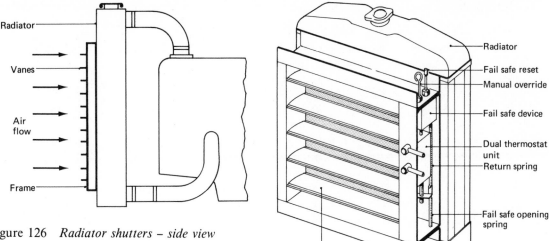

Figure 126   *Radiator shutters – side view*

Figure 127   *Thermostatic radiator shutter*

demands more or less air through the matrix when the temperature rises or falls and the vanes open or close accordingly until optimum running temperature is restored. The system contains a second wax-filled element which functions as a fail-safe device and fully opens the shutters in the event of the coolant temperature rising to a level which would cause danger to the engine.

### Snap-open/snap-shut type

This is an alternative system of operating shutters and makes use of a sensing element to actuate a power supply of an air, vacuum, hydraulic or electrical source, which is used to actuate the vanes. A spring is normally used to hold the vanes open in their fail-safe position until there is sufficient power available to overcome the spring tension.

Shutters are of particular benefit to operators of short-journey vehicles, where low-temperature operation results in excessive deterioration of pistons, piston rings and cylinders caused by the acidic products of combustion corroding their surfaces and contaminating the engine oil. Improved driver comfort and less fatigue are often obtained with the use of shutters, and, in passenger vehicles with dual heaters for the driver's compartment and the saloon, large quantities of heat can be provided.

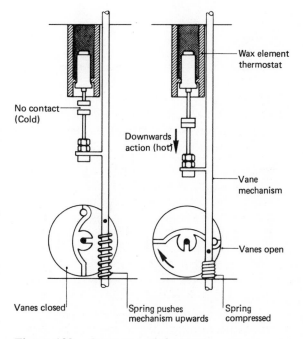

Figure 128   *Operation of shutters*

## The thermostat

A thermostat is fitted in a water cooling system to give rapid warming up of the engine from cold and maintenance of the coolant temperature during running, the operating range usually being between 77 and 85°C. The thermostat controls the flow of coolant through the radiator depending upon the engine water-jacket temperature. When the engine is cold, the thermostat prevents coolant leaving the jacket until a higher coolant temperature is reached. At this stage the thermostat valve 'cracks open' and coolant is allowed to pass from the water jacket into the radiator at a rate sufficient to maintain temperature within the normal working range.

Heavy vehicles often stand for many hours on open parks. Warming up of the engine may take several minutes in winter months and this period is critical in terms of engine life, fuel consumption and performance. By controlling the flow of coolant, the engine and lubricating oil warm up quickly which reduces frictional losses, cylinder and piston ring wear, gumming up of piston rings, excessive carbon deposits in combustion chambers and fuel consumption.

*Bellows type (Figure 129)*
The thermostat is usually housed in the cylinder head below the top coolant outlet hose. Some vee engines used in heavy vehicles have two thermostats, one at each coolant outlet passage on the cylinder heads and some in-line engines are fitted with two or three thermostats in the cooling system.

*Operation* When the engine is cold, the thermostat valve is held closed on its seat by the contraction of the bellows and no coolant can pass from the cylinder head to the radiator. As the engine warms up, the coolant in the jacket is heated which converts the volatile liquid, usually acetone or methyl alcohol, in the bellows into a vapour. This causes the partially evacuated bellows to expand and lift the valve off its seat. The coolant is then free to flow through the open valve and circulate through the radiator to be cooled, finally passing from the radiator through the

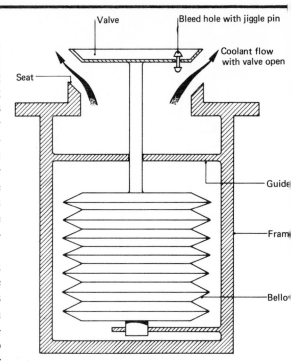

Figure 129   *Thermostat – bellows type*

bottom hose into the water jacket where it is reheated.

When the engine cools, shortly after being stopped, the valve is pulled down to its seat by contraction of the bellows as the vaporized substance is converted into a liquid by the lower temperature.

A radiator bypass passage is usually fitted to allow some circulation of coolant around the cylinder block and head when the valve is closed. This prevents localized overheating of hot-spots in the cylinder head. The bypass passage usually runs from the engine side of the thermostat to the coolant pump inlet and may take the form of a permanent bleed, or be closed by an annular valve when the thermostat valve reaches its fully open position.

The thermostat valve contains a small bleed hole which provides some coolant circulation when it is closed and prevents air locks occurring when the cooling system is filled. A *jiggle pin* is sometimes used in the bleed hole which seals the

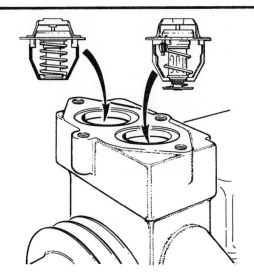

Figure 130  *Two different designs of thermostats as used in the Perkins 6.372 engine*

system under coolant pump pressure, thus preventing bleed when the engine is cold.

The thermostat will fail to operate if the bellows are punctured. Under this condition the bellows will expand to their free length when air enters them and destroys the partial vacuum which normally exists within. This action places the thermostat valve in the open position and prevents overheating of the engine. It is known as the 'fail-safe' system.

*Wax pellet type*

This type of thermostat is insensitive to normal coolant pressures and is particularly suitable for cooling systems that operate at pressures in excess of 48 $kN/m^2$ (7 $lbf/in^2$). The thermostat has a copper capsule lined with a sleeve of heavy paraffin wax impregnated with copper dust to improve thermal conductivity. The capsule is fixed to the thermostat valve seat and contains a stainless steel needle which is fixed to the valve.

*Operation*  When the capsule is heated the wax changes from a solid to a plastic state and expands, squeezing the rubber sleeve, pushing out the needle, and opening the valve. The taper end of the needle assists in giving smoother operation

although a taper is not essential. When the capsule is cool, contraction of the wax pellet releases the thrust on the piston and the spring assists in closing the valve.

Most manufacturers of wax-type thermostats claim that their thermostats will not normally fail to operate in service and they are not normally built to fail-safe. In the unlikely event of failure at elevated temperature above 130°C at which temperature engine damage is liable to occur anyway, some manufacturers incorporate a latching mechanism to hold the thermostat valve open if 130°C is exceeded. This proves, when examined, that the thermostat was doing its job at the time of overheating.

Figure 131 shows the reverse-opening thermostat in which the needle is clamped to the frame and expansion of the wax drives the capsule downwards taking the valve with it. This type cannot be forced open by coolant pump pressure and it gives a better coolant flow than the normal opening type.

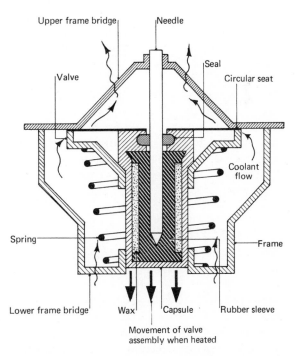

Figure 131  *Thermostat – wax-pellet type with reverse opening*

Figure 132   *Thermostat testing*

### Thermostat testing (Figure 132)

Thermostats cannot be overhauled; they must be renewed if they become inoperative. They can be tested by placing in a vessel filled with water and gradually heated. A thermometer is used to check the water temperature, and the thermostat valve should 'crack open' when the temperature marked on the valve or the frame is reached. An increase of 10 to 20 deg C will elapse before the valve is fully open.

### Choice of opening temperature

A thermostat with a higher opening temperature can be used to improve cooling efficiency and cab heating in winter months. This should of course be replaced with the normal thermostat in the following spring, otherwise overheating of the engine may result.

## Pressurized cooling system

The complicated design of the cylinder head water jacket carries with it the danger of local steam pockets being formed at critical positions such as around the exhaust valve seats, particularly when the engine is working hard. Steam is a poor conductor of heat and should therefore be removed from the pockets as efficiently as possible to allow rapid extraction of heat from the metal surface to prevent local overheating.

A pressurized or closed system allows an engine to operate at a higher and more efficient running temperature with less risk of local overheating than an open cooling system working under existing atmospheric pressure, as cooling efficiency is increased by the higher operating pressure and temperature. This is due to the heat dissipation capacity from the radiator surface being proportional to the difference in temperatures of the coolant and the ambient air. The boiling point of water is raised approximately 2.5 deg C for every 10 kN/m$^2$ increase in pressure, so a pressurized system working at 40 kN/m$^2$ raises the boiling point of water by approximately 10 deg C.

A pressurized system is necessary and is invariably used for vehicles which operate at high altitudes. At an altitude of 2134 m (7000 ft) above sea level the boiling point of water is reduced to about 95°C as a result of a reduction in atmospheric pressure from about 101 kN/m$^2$ abs. (14.7 lbf/in$^2$ abs.) to approximately 83 kN/m$^2$ abs. (12 lbf/in$^2$ abs.). Water losses under these operating conditions would be very great with an open system, and it would very likely be necessary to stop the vehicle and allow the engine to cool off after an arduous hill climb. A pressurized system has a further advantage of maintaining cooling pump efficiency by operating at its full pumping capacity whatever the temperature.

### Radiator cap

The radiator pressure cap fits into the header tank neck and is used to close and seal the system. The cap incorporates a pressure relief valve and a vacuum relief valve. The pressure relief valve is spring loaded and is designed to operate at a predetermined pressure. The usual operating pressures are between 28 and 104 kN/m$^2$ (4 and 15 lbf/in$^2$) depending upon the type of vehicle to which they are fitted. On no account should a different cap be used on a vehicle as an alternative to that recommended by the vehicle manufacturer. Systems operating under a higher pressure are sometimes preferred by vehicle designers as the gain in cooling efficiency achieved by using the higher pressure is partly offset by employing an economic size of radiator which aids the design of tilt cabs. The vacuum relief valve is the small lightly loaded valve operating in the reverse direction to the pressure valve.

Radiator caps are usually marked on the top surface with their operating pressure. If a cap is used that operates at too high a pressure for the system to which it is fitted, the radiator hoses and core may not be strong enough to withstand the higher internal pressure and damage may result. If a cap which operates at too low a pressure is used, coolant will be lost through the overflow pipe.

*Operation*  As the temperature of the coolant rises, evaporation and expansion take place and, as the pressure cap normally seals the system, the internal pressure builds up within the system. The coolant pressure fluctuates between zero and the rated pressure marked on the cap. The pressure relief is held on its seat by its spring until the coolant pressure rises above the rated pressure of the spring. The higher pressure causes the valve to lift off its seat against the action of the spring and the excess pressure together with some steam or water are relieved through the overflow pipe.

The vacuum relief valve is provided to prevent any vacuum building up in the system during

cooling off as a result of the small losses. This valve prevents the collapse or damage of the radiator and the hoses.

There are basically two types of radiator cap used for heavy vehicle cooling systems, these being known as the open valve type and the enclosed valve type. The open valve type is most commonly used although the enclosed type with its fully enclosed spring and valves is occasionally used. Most of the radiator caps used on heavy vehicles have a 76.2 mm (3 in) diameter circular top compared with a 57.2 mm (2¼ in) diameter top normally used for light vehicle cooling systems. When removing the cap, provision is made to release any pressure in the system of a hot engine by a part turn which will release the pressure through the overflow pipe, before the cap is fully turned to remove it from the neck of the tank completely. This should be done slowly and carefully by part turning the cap and waiting until the hissing noise of the escaping pressure has ceased before turning the cap the complete distance for its removal. This action should eliminate the possibility of an accident caused by the boiling coolant being blown up into the face of the person removing the cap.

### The sealed system

An efficient pressurized system only needs occasional topping up with coolant but the sealed system does away completely with this service requirement.

The sealed system in its simplest form consists of immersing the end of the radiator overflow pipe in a quantity of coolant contained in a small vessel or expansion chamber. As the engine reaches its normal running temperature, the pressure and expansion of the coolant force a small quantity of coolant into the expansion chamber through the pressure relief valve. As the engine cools, the temperature and pressure of the coolant fall, and atmospheric pressure, acting on the water in the expansion chamber, forces the coolant back into the system until the pressures equalize and the vacuum relief valve closes. These systems are normally filled with a coolant solution containing antifreeze and a corrosion inhibitor.

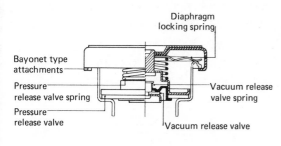
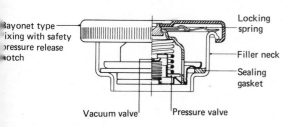

Figure  133  *Open  valve  and  enclosed  valve pressure caps*

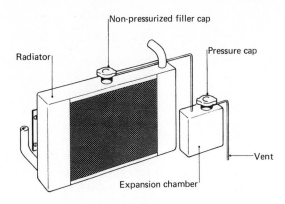

Figure 134   *Semi-sealed cooling system*

## Overcooling and underheating

Difficulties in the prevention of overcooling are sometimes created for engine designers by the paramount need to prevent undercooling in all operating conditions. If overcooling is not prevented, oxidation of the engine lubricating oil is likely to occur at a low coolant temperature which may produce sludge with a tendency to block oilways.

Overcooling can also be a disadvantage from an operator's and driver's point of view, particularly in colder weather when the cooling system is used to supply heat to the driver's cab and the saloon of passenger vehicles. For these purposes, sufficient heat must be available and an overcooled engine would not supply enough.

## Special coolant

Water is normally used as the coolant although other liquids are occasionally used. Ethylene glycol which boils at 195°C is sometimes used as this allows a smaller radiator and a reduction in weight. Other coolants are available which prevent corrosion and protect from overheating, and contain an effective antifreeze with a leak-detecting fluoresence.

## Undercooling and overheating

It is extremely important that an engine is working at its correct running temperature to develop its maximum thermal efficiency, and coolant temperature gauges or buzzers are fitted in the cab to enable the driver to read, at a glance, the engine temperature. The most obvious reasons for undercooling are lack of coolant caused by evaporation or leakage. Other reasons include a slack fan belt which slips on its drive pulleys, a defective thermostat, and an incorrectly adjusted fuel injection pump with a retarded setting. A partly choked radiator will restrict the flow of coolant passing through its tubes and cause undercooling, and choked radiator fins which prevent the air passing over them will also have the same effect. A worn or damaged coolant pump can cause undercooling, particularly when the impeller drive shaft is designed to shear when ice has formed in the pump.

## Coolant temperature gauges

It is most important that drivers are aware of the engine temperature when the vehicle is in use. A high temperature reading may indicate that the vehicle is being driven too hard or the radiator is too well blanked off. Mechanical defects such as a broken or slipping fan belt, incorrect engine timing or worn exhaust valves can also cause overheating and a high temperature reading. Too low a temperature reading is usually due to overcooling caused by a faulty thermostat.

*Mechanical type (Figure 135)*   The gauge is mounted on the instrument panel in the cab and is connected by a capillary (fine-bore) tube to a

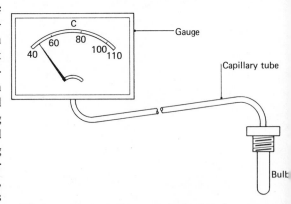

Figure   135   *Coolant   temperature   gauge –   mechanical type*

temperature-sensitive metal bulb located in the cylinder head. As the coolant temperature increases, the volatile liquid in the bulb vaporizes and increases the pressure in the system which is transmitted through the tube to the Bourdon tube in the gauge, causing the Bourdon tube to unwind and move the indicator needle towards a higher reading. When the coolant temperature decreases, the vapour is converted into a liquid, the pressure is reduced, and the Bourdon tube rewinds moving the indicator needle towards a lower gauge reading.

*Electrical type*  This type of gauge consists of a panel-mounted gauge and a transmitter unit screwed into the cylinder head, connected together by electrical cables. A small electrical current is passed from the battery to the gauge system which changes the internal resistance of the transmitter unit. The changes of resistance affect the operating voltage of the gauge and, in turn, control the position of the indicator needle.

*Coolant level alarm (Figure 136)*
This instrument is used in the cooling system for protection purposes. It consists of an electronic

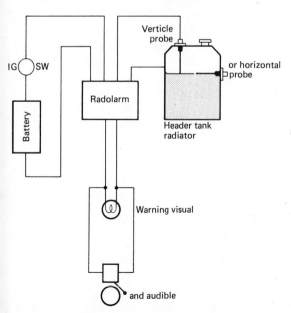

Figure 136  *Coolant level alarm circuit*

unit which sets off a visual or audible warning signal when the coolant in the radiator falls to a predetermined level. Figure 136 shows the circuit which includes a vertical or horizontal probe situated in the radiator header tank and the battery and ignition switch which supply and control the current for operation of the electronic unit.

The visual warning signal is a continuous or flashing signal from a lamp mounted on the instrument panel and the audible warning is made by a buzzer which gives an intermittent or continuous sound.

This device gives a protection against overheating and risk of damage to the engine. It differs from the temperature gauge by indicating the change in coolant level, not the change in coolant temperature.

## Anti-freeze solutions

Adequate protection must be given to the engine during winter months to prevent damage to the engine which may occur owing to the effects of frost. Water expands as its temperature falls from 4 to 0°C and can cause the cylinder block and cylinder head, usually made of cast iron, to crack. Radiator tubes often split if the water contained in them freezes. This damage is often difficult and costly to repair.

One method of overcoming freezing up in winter months is to drain off the coolant from the system. This necessitates opening all the drain taps in the cooling system and allowing all the coolant to drain off. Many cooling systems of heavy vehicle engines are too complex to drain off completely and the responsibility of performing this task may often rest with the driver of the vehicle. The use of an antifreeze solution is very often used as an alternative form of protection, this being far more simple and convenient but a little more costly.

Antifreeze is often defined as any substance which, when mixed with water, has the effect of lowering the freezing point of the mixture. There are many chemicals which produce this effect, but when considering their application to cooling systems only two are in common use, these are ethylene glycol and methyl alcohol (methanol). Methanol produces the most frost protection relative to its percentage volume with water, but it is least favoured because of its lower boiling point (82°C) which causes it to evaporate readily at normal running engine temperature. Its vapour is inflammable, which increases the risk of fire, and it is highly toxic and could cause dangerous fumes to enter the cab of the vehicle through the interior heater in the case of a leak from a loose hose joint.

Ethylene glycol is used as a base for the majority of antifreezes. It has an important advantage in that it does not form solid ice immediately when it reaches its freezing point but only produces very small ice crystals, known as 'ice mush'. In the United Kingdom a commonly recommended antifreeze ratio to use in the coolant is 25% of the cooling system capacity. This ratio remains completely liquid, and therefore free flowing, down to a temperature of –12°C. Manufacturer's recommendations should, however, always be observed when mixing antifreeze solutions.

Some cooling-system liquids have more of a searching action than others. When ethylene glycol based antifreeze is added to water, the resulting solution becomes more searching than water and may seep through a joint which would normally prevent water seepage. The searching action of an antifreeze solution can also dislodge loose particles of corrosion from the walls of the water jacket. This is due to the coolant penetrating beneath the corrosion products and lifting them from the surface. When this happens, the corrosion particles circulate with the coolant causing discoloration and blockage in the narrow coolant tubes of the radiator. A good quality antifreeze solution contains corrosion inhibitors, these being chemicals which have the effect of reacting in the cooling system, preventing corrosive attacks on metals.

## Corrosion inhibitors

Types of corrosive attack in a liquid cooling system may be summarized under four main headings:

1  Rust production due to the action of water on iron and steel parts.
2  Destruction of iron and steel surfaces caused by acid in the coolant resulting from combustion products blowing past the cylinder head gasket.
3  Corrosion of light alloy surfaces due to excessive alkalinity in the coolant. This can be brought about by salts contained in certain tap waters.
4  Electrolytic corrosion due to dissimilar metals running at dissimilar temperatures within the engine, external electrical circuits such as battery charging circuits, or straight chemical reactions, in a similar way as electricity is produced by a dry battery.

A good quality antifreeze will give protection against these forms of corrosive attack. Various selected chemicals are added which combine with the dangerous salts produced in the coolant and cancel them out. The chemicals also form a hard thin film over the water-jacket surfaces which provides a protective barrier between the surface and coolant and provides an alkaline buffer which neutralizes acids in the system. When a cooling system is completely of aluminium, a different type of antifreeze is normally recommended to give the best protection from corrosion. It is difficult to estimate the precise life of corrosion inhibitors, but six to eight months is usual. Most antifreeze manufacturers therefore recommend that the cooling system is drained, flushed and refilled each autumn ready for the following winter.

## Corrosion resistor

Some heavy vehicle engines are fitted with a corrosion resistor. This is a unit which bypasses a small amount of coolant from the system through a filtering and treating device.

Scale formation on water-jacket surfaces is reduced by treating the coolant with a chromate compound corrosion resistor. This is an advantage in areas where water causes excessive scaling. Chemicals in the resistor unit resist electrolytic attack on surfaces and are assisted by 'sacrificial plates' which attract the electrolytic action, resulting in the plates dissipating themselves. These plates are easily and cheaply replaced and prevent electrolytic attack from corroding important components such as wet cylinder liners and radiator cores.

The corrosion resistor releases a substance into the coolant which forms a soft fur on the water side of the wet liners. This protects the liners against corrosion but, providing the unit is serviced regularly, the fur is replaced as rapidly as the water attack removes it.

The unit contains a filter to collect rust and sludge which prevents blockage of the smaller passage ways in the cooling system. It is strongly recommended that the corrosion resistor unit is changed at regular intervals and, additionally, when the cooling system is completely drained and refilled.

## Cab heating and ventilating

Heating and ventilating systems are nowadays an integral part of cab design and affect the driver's environment by controlling cab temperatures and providing air conditioning. The heating system usually consists of a small heat exchange radiator

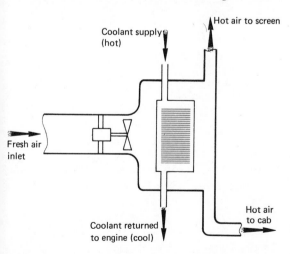

**Figure 137** *Cab heating and ventilating is usually achieved by transferring some heat from the cooling system*

mounted in the cab and supplied with hot coolant from the cooling system of the running engine. The supply of coolant to the heating system is normally taken from the cylinder head and, after passing through the heat exchange radiator, is returned to the engine. Additional radiators are used in buses and coaches for saloon heating.

The flow of coolant through the heat exchange radiator is controlled by valves which regulate the heat output and an electrically driven fan or blower is usually employed to force the hot air out of the radiator when required. The fan, sometimes driven by a multispeed motor, is controlled by a switch. The heated air is usually distributed to the footwells on either side of the cab of a goods vehicle which ensures even air distribution within. Most systems recirculate air within the cab, provide a flow of fresh warm air when required, or provide fresh cool air for operating in warm climates. The system also provides for the removal of humid and stale air which can cause the driver to become drowsy on long journeys.

Hot air can be directed to the windscreen and sidescreens in most goods vehicle cabs for demisting and defrosting, and a similar arrangement is used for the screens of buses and coaches.

### Independent system

A system of heating and ventilating that works independently of the engine cooling system is used for heating some buses, coaches, containers, vans and other special vehicles. The system may use diesel oil, paraffin or petrol as a fuel to supply heat.

Briefly, the heater unit consists of a housing containing a fresh air inlet port and a hot air outlet port connected to the vehicle's heating system. There are also two other ports for the combustion air inlet and exhaust gas outlet. To operate the unit a glow plug positioned in a combustion chamber is energized by an electric current. Atomized fuel, supplied by a pump, is injected on to the coils of the glow plug, which ignites the air–fuel mixture. Air is supplied via the combustion air inlet port to the combustion chamber under pressure from a blower. After combustion, the exhaust gas leaves the unit by the exhaust gas outlet port.

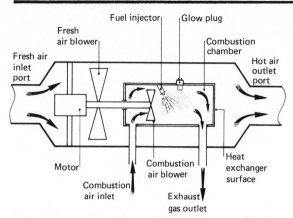

**Figure 138** *Layout of combustion-type heating unit*

Fresh air forced by a blower through the inlet port is heated by the combustion chamber heat via a heat exchanger and directed to the heating system through the hot air outlet port. The two air passages are insulated from each other and the high-pressure blowers are driven by one electric motor thus making the heating process continuous.

This type of system has the advantage of being able to supply heat independently of the engine cooling system and is useful to warm up and heat a vehicle which is parked. It is particularly useful for executive buses and coaches which are designed for a variety of uses when stationary in addition to their normal mobile operations.

## Future developments

In our opinion vehicle noise legislation during the next 10 to 15 years will be met by using a conventional CI engine modified to incorporate a number of noise-reduction features. These have been found to be effective without too great an increase in initial cost and operating costs, or a lessening in reliability and accessibility. Vehicle manufacturers and engine suppliers will no doubt work closely together and develop vehicles that satisfy legal requirements for noise emissions by providing adequate sound insulation for the engine. The driver will benefit from such developments by having a more comfortable environment in which to work, and the public will benefit by the reduction in noise made by vehicle engines.

Enclosing the engine in a soundproof compartment with an under-shield and utilizing a cooling pack above or behind the vehicle cab is a likely change in vehicle layout to meet future noise legislation. Engine noise, heat and exhaust gases would be directed upwards by fans housed in a ducting, the ducting being lined with sound-absorbing material. Exhaust gases, discharged together with the cooling air from the radiator, would benefit from rapid dilution with the warm air.

Arrangements of this type would eliminate the need for a radiator opening and grille at the front of the vehicle and for escape routes for hot air leaving the engine compartment. The enclosed engine would be ventilated by a fan with sound-insulated ducting and the hot engine exhaust manifold would be water-cooled.

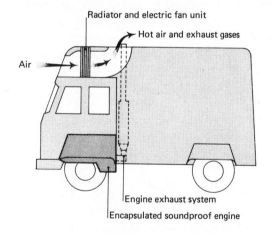

**Figure 139** *Future vehicle design may incorporate a fully encapsulated engine to reduce noise but this presents cooling problems. One method which may be used to overcome this is to locate the radiator and fan well away from the engine and use an alternative form of power to drive the fan*

# 5 Fuel injection equipment

## The fuel system

This includes fuel storage tank, low-pressure pipe lines, fuel lift pump, filter, fuel injector pump, high-pressure pipe lines, fuel injectors and leak-off pipes.

Storage tanks are usually of large cylindrical or rectangular section which will hold 225–270 litres (50–60 gallons) of fuel. Electrical fuel gauge units can be fitted, or a gauge unit mounted directly into the side of the tank to indicate level of fuel. Baffles fitted inside the tank prevent surge of fuel and a wire mesh gauze fitted to the filler neck prevents large objects of dirt from entering the tank. A pick-up and leak-off connection are usually connected into the top of the tank.

Fuel feed pipe varies in size between 10 and 15 mm (0.4 and 0.6 in) with a wall thickness of 1 mm. The pipe run should be formed without sharp bends – not less than 50 mm (2 in), and securely clamped; flared ends provide seals at any joints.

Any high-pressure piping between the fuel injection pump and fuel injector must be steel with a wall thickness of 2–3 mm depending upon pressure carried. This pipe has a bore size of approximately 1 mm and usually has brazed or shaped nipples to ensure a good seal at each end. The pipe run of the high-pressure pipes should ideally be clamped to prevent vibration which may lead to fractures and consequent misfiring. The length of these pipes should also be the same to each injector to ensure correct injection of fuel to each injector.

### Fuel filters

Dirty fuel which is fed to the fuel injector pump and injector nozzles causes very high wear rates on

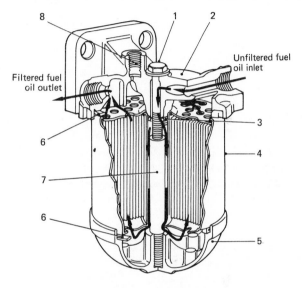

| | | | |
|---|---|---|---|
| 1 | Centre bolt | 5 | Filter base |
| 2 | Filter body | 6 | Sealing ring |
| 3 | Seal | 7 | Centre stud |
| 4 | Filter element | 8 | Venting orifice |

Figure 140 *Conventional filter – fuel flows upwards through filter element*

closely machined parts within these units. This would very soon upset their efficiency and cause loss of power and black smoke from the exhaust. Because of these very fine machining limits – clearance is approximately 1 μm (0.00004 in) – the efficiency of the filters must be such that particles of dirt approximately 3 μm in size and upwards should be removed. Tests have shown that as little as 3 g – less than half a teaspoonful – can wear out a fuel injector pump which may be expected to cope with 45 000 litres (10 000 gallons) of fuel during its lifetime.

Many different types of filter have been used, including felt, cotton and paper element. Modern heavy vehicles often use more than one filter in the fuel system and if a large engine is fitted or a vehicle is operating in very dirty conditions three or four filters may be used. A further problem is that diesel fuel can contain dissolved water in quantities up to 0.05%, which may precipitate as free droplets of water and be increased by condensation. This may cause corrosion, pitting or sticking of moving parts and consequently damage to the fuel injection equipment, particularly if the vehicle is not used for some time.

The paper element filter is the most common in use and can be in the form of a replaceable element or a replaceable cartridge type. The paper is resin-treated for high wet strength and is formed from strips of paper round a metal core to form a series of continuous vee-shaped coils. This gives a very large filter area (3550 cm$^2$) and therefore ensures a long life – a single filter element has an expected life of approximately 6750 litres (1500 gallons) of diesel fuel. A system of water separa-

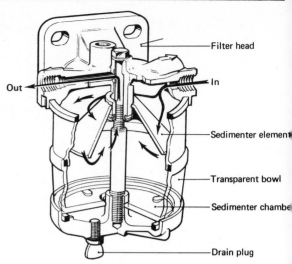

Figure 142    *Sedimenter – large droplets of water and dirt fall to the bottom of the chamber. These can be easily seen and cleaned out as necessary*

tion is often used in conjunction with a paper element filter. If the fuel oil is passed through a very fine filter element, any droplets of water will join together (agglomerate) to form larger droplets which can then be removed by sedimentation. The fuel must pass down through the filter and the water is collected in a chamber fitted below the main filter element from where it can be seen and drained off. The paper-element filter is usually fitted between the fuel lift pump and the fuel injector pump.

A primary filter is fitted between the fuel tank and fuel lift pump which is used to separate out large particles of dirt and water by sedimentation. This is really a settling vessel through which the fuel passes and any dirt and water – which is heavier than fuel – falls to the bottom of the vessel from where it can be easily seen and drained off. When this unit is fitted, the main filter will tend to have a longer life before becoming choked because the larger particles of dirt will have been removed.

Combined together, both these units will form an efficient filtration system which would be able to cope with normal amounts of dirt and water found in the fuel system.

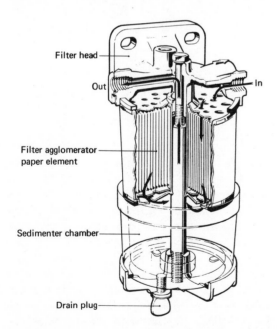

Figure 141    *Agglomerator filter – fuel flows down through filter, water is collected in sedimenter chamber*

*Fuel lift pumps*

When an in-line fuel injection pump is used, it is possible to mount the lift pump on the side of the injection pump. An eccentric on the injection pump camshaft operates this pump in the normal manner. On other fuel systems, the lift pump may be mounted on the side of the engine and be operated by an eccentric on the camshaft of the engine.

Basically the pump consists of a diaphragm, which is held between two halves of the pump body, an operating linkage and inlet/outlet valves. This diaphragm is capable of developing pressures up to 31 kN/m² (4.5 lbf/in²), by its return spring, but where higher pressures are required, a plunger is fitted on the end of the diaphragm spindle. In this case the diaphragm acts as a seal only and the plunger provides fuel pressures up to 103–124 kN/m² (15–28 lbf/in²).

All fuel lift pumps must also be fitted with some means of priming the fuel system by hand. This is important because most CI engines will not run if any air is trapped in the system. When hand priming is carried out, the priming lever operates the diaphragm in place of the eccentric on the cam. Fuel is then pumped through the system and any air is expelled through 'bleed' screws which are usually positioned on the main filter body and on the injection pump. It is important that all air is expelled through these bleed points otherwise any air which is trapped in the high-pressure side of the injection pump will be compressed and prevent injection of fuel through the injectors.

Operation of the diaphragm-type feed pump is effected by the eccentric on the cam operating the diaphragm through a bell-crank lever. As this rotates, the lever is pushed down, and a fork at the opposite end pulls the diaphragm to the right against spring pressure. A depression to the left side of the diaphragm by this movement lifts the inlet disc valve off its seat against spring pressure (outlet ball valve is closed by its own weight). When sufficient depression is built up in the fuel lines, fuel from the tank enters the pumping chamber through the open inlet valve. The return stroke of the diaphragm is controlled by the main spring which pushes the diaphragm to the left as

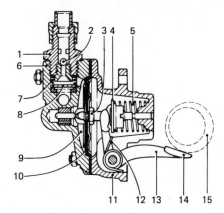

| | |
|---|---|
| 1 Union | 8 Inlet valve disc |
| 2 Outlet ball valve | 9 Pumping chamber |
| 3 Lock nut | 10 Diaphragm |
| 4 Spring plate | 11 Inner housing |
| 5 Diaphragm spring | 12 Anti-rattle spring |
| 6 Outer housing | 13 Bellcrank lever |
| 7 Inlet valve spring | 14 Hardened pad |
| | 15 Camshaft eccentric |

Figure 143(a)  *Diaphragm feed pump – low pressure*

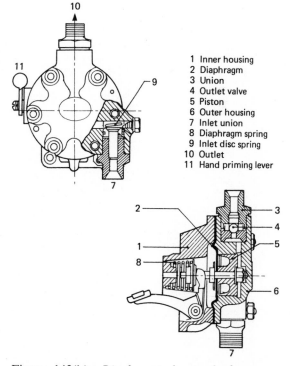

| |
|---|
| 1 Inner housing |
| 2 Diaphragm |
| 3 Union |
| 4 Outlet valve |
| 5 Piston |
| 6 Outer housing |
| 7 Inlet union |
| 8 Diaphragm spring |
| 9 Inlet disc spring |
| 10 Outlet |
| 11 Hand priming lever |

Figure 143(b)  *Diaphragm-plunger feed pump – high pressure* the operating lever moves off its eccentric. Fuel in the pumping chamber is then pushed out to lift the ball valve off its seat (inlet valve closed by its spring) and into the fuel filters and injection pump. When the system is full of fuel, the diaphragm return spring cannot fully return the diaphragm and therefore a pressure is built up corresponding to the strength of this spring. As more fuel is used, the diaphragm moves further to the left until it can be operated once again by the bell-crank lever. When the diaphragm is held away from the bell-crank lever, a light anti-rattle spring maintains the lever in close contact with the eccentric, thereby eliminating noise and excessive wear due to hammering against the cam.

Operation of the plunger-type feed pump is very similar to the diaphragm type. The stronger main spring acting against the steel plunger provides the higher operating pressures. The diaphragm provides an extra seal only.

### In-line fuel-injection pumps

The pump is usually mounted on the side of the engine and driven directly from the timing gears. Incorporated with the injection pump is the governor mechanism, excess fuel device for easy starting, stop control and sometimes an automatic advance device. Later type pumps are lubricated from the engine lubrication system via drillings in the mounting flange. A common type of in-line pump in present day use is a Minimec high-speed fuel-injection pump, which is very compact and lightweight. The main pump housing is split into

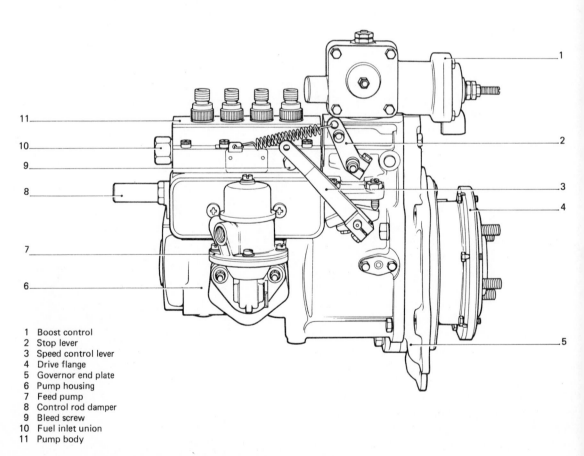

1  Boost control
2  Stop lever
3  Speed control lever
4  Drive flange
5  Governor end plate
6  Pump housing
7  Feed pump
8  Control rod damper
9  Bleed screw
10  Fuel inlet union
11  Pump body

Figure 144  *Typical four-cylinder Minimec pump*

two halves, the upper half containing the fuel passages and pumping elements. The lower half, manufactured in a light alloy, holds the camshaft, tappets and control rod.

A complete pumping element – one required for each cylinder – consists of the operating cam which is driven by the engine, cam follower or tappet, plunger and barrel, return spring and delivery valve. The plunger is rotated within the barrel by a control fork which is clamped to the control rod which in turn is operated by the governor. This movement varies the position of the inclined groove or helix in the plunger in

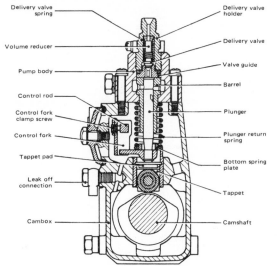

Figure 145  *Cross-section of Simms Minimec in-line pump*

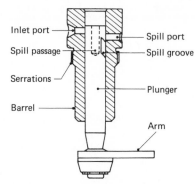

Figure 146(a)  *Pump element*

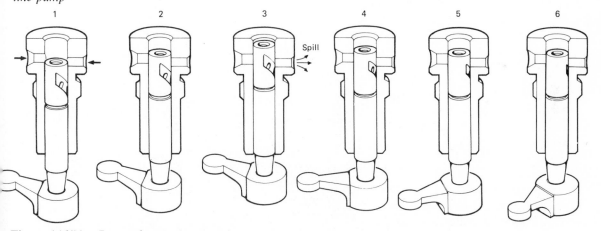

Figure 146(b)  *Pump element in operation*
*(1)  Bottom of stroke – fuel fills barrel through ports*
*(2)  Plunger moves up to close ports. This is commencement of injection or spill cut-off*
*(3)  Helix on plunger uncovers spill port. As plunger continues its upward travel, fuel flows down centre hole and back into fuel gallery – fuel delivery to injector ceases (plunger shown in maximum delivery position)*
*(4) and (5)  Plunger is rotated to a new position, spill cut-off is in the same position but the helix uncovers the spill port earlier to end delivery of fuel earlier. A smaller amount of fuel is injected, therefore the engine runs slower*
*(6)  When the plunger is rotated fully to the right, no fuel is delivered – spill port is always open and engine stops*

relation to the spill port in the barrel. On the upward stroke of the plunger, fuel is pushed back out through the inlet port until the top edge of the plunger covers the port. As the plunger moves further up, fuel trapped in the barrel is pushed out through the delivery valve to the injector. This stops when the helix uncovers the control or spill port when fuel can again be pushed back into the fuel gallery. By rotating the plunger from side to side the effective stroke is varied whilst the actual stroke remains the same. The quantity of fuel injected is therefore varied by varying the end of the delivery.

*Delivery valve*

The delivery valve has a conical seat and a fluted stem which accurately locates it in its guide. Just below the conical seat, an accurately machined cylindrical band forms a piston in the bore. The return spring holds the valve firmly on its seat until sufficient fuel pressure forces it to move upwards to clear the cylindrical band and allow fuel to flow into the injector pipe. At the end of injection, fuel pressure together with spring pressure rapidly returns the valve to its seat. This takes place in two distinct stages:

1   The cylindrical band or piston enters its guide and causes a slight but sharp reduction in the pressure of fuel in the injector pipe until
2   the conical faces meet to make a complete seal. The first contact of the piston also prevents further passage of fuel through the valve and the distance it has to travel, before the conical seat meets, represents the reduction in volume of fuel and, therefore, pressure at the injector; this helps to reduce the possibility of 'dribble'. The volume reducer limits the amount of fuel under pressure in the delivery valve holder ensuring that the next delivery of fuel from the plunger is immediately felt at the injector, and, therefore, gives an immediate action.

Pumping efficiency tends to fall as the engine speed decreases – the injection pump has time to allow leakage to occur between the plunger and barrel. At higher speeds, all fuel that is metered is pushed through to the injector as there is no time to lose any due to back-leakage. To overcome this leakage, a small 'flat' on the cylindrical band will allow fuel to escape past the piston and exert a greater pressure on the underside of the conical face to ease the opening of the delivery valve. The size of the flat will determine how much fuel can escape to match the loss of pumping efficiency.

Two types of governor are used with this type of injector pump, a pneumatic type or a mechanical type. Hydraulic governors may be used where more precise control is required, e.g. public service vehicles.

### Pneumatic governor

This is an all-speed type of governor which automatically controls the whole speed range of an

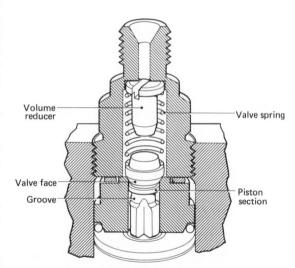

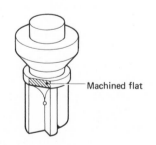

Figure 147   *Delivery valve*

engine from idling to maximum speeds. It is controlled by air flow in the inlet manifold and consists of two main parts – a venturi control unit and a diaphragm unit (see Figure 148).

The venturi control unit is fitted in the inlet manifold and contains a butterfly valve which is connected to the driver's accelerator pedal. This controls the engine speed by varying the vacuum experienced at the control unit which in turn acts against the diaphragm unit (Figure 149).

The diaphragm unit is mounted at one end of the injection pump and is connected to the end of the rack. When the engine is stationary, the governor spring pushes against the diaphragm unit which in turn pushes the rack into maximum fuel position. When the engine is running, the position of the diaphragm, and therefore the position of the rack, is determined by the vacuum acting against the diaphragm. Atmospheric pressure pushes against the other side of the

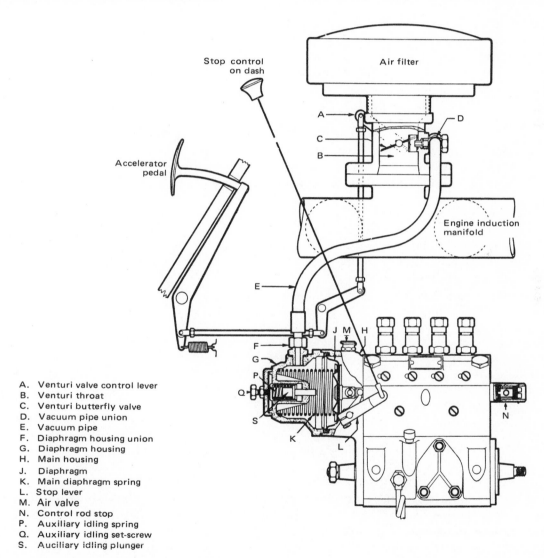

A. Venturi valve control lever
B. Venturi throat
C. Venturi butterfly valve
D. Vacuum pipe union
E. Vacuum pipe
F. Diaphragm housing union
G. Diaphragm housing
H. Main housing
J. Diaphragm
K. Main diaphragm spring
L. Stop lever
M. Air valve
N. Control rod stop
P. Auxiliary idling spring
Q. Auxiliary idling set-screw
S. Auciliary idling plunger

Figure 148 *Layout of pneumatic governor*

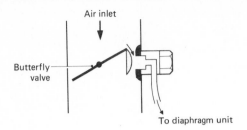

Figure 149   *Control unit*

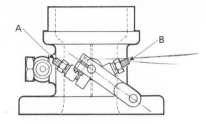

A — Adjustable screw for maximum speed
B — Adjustable screw for idling

Figure 150   *Speed control screws*

diaphragm to compress the spring according to the amount of depression.

The vacuum required for governing is created by the flow of air through the venturi in the control unit – the faster the flow of air, the greater the depression created. This flow of air is controlled by the position of a butterfly valve. When this valve is closed, most of the air required by the engine must flow through the control unit which in turn creates a high vacuum. The depression allows atmospheric pressure to push the diaphragm against the governor spring towards minimum fuel position, i.e. tickover speed.

The main governor spring is comparatively 'soft', and a stronger idling spring is usually fitted to prevent bouncing and therefore surge or hunting at engine tickover speeds.

The stop control lever, when operated from the driver's cab, pushes the control rod and diaphragm against the main governor spring and compresses the idling spring beyond normal idling position to a 'no fuel' position which stops the engine.

Figure 150 shows the speed stops which limit the position of the butterfly valve. The idling screw is usually set in conjunction with the auxiliary idling screw on the diaphragm housing. This gives a balance between the vacuum created through the venturi against idling spring tension. If this is unbalanced the engine tends to 'hunt' or 'surge'.

Excess fuel and maximum fuel can be controlled by an adaptor screwed into the end of the pump body at the opposite end to the governor. Figure 151 shows the control rod in normal maximum fuel position. The stop is pre-set to manufacturer's specifications and locked under a sealed end cap.

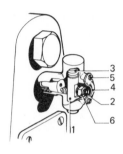

1   Spring loaded plunger
2   Maximum fuel stop screw
3   Return spring
4   End-cap
5   Retaining screw
6   Lock-nut

Figure 151   *Maximum and excess fuel*

When the end of the spring-loaded plunger is depressed, the end of the stop screw aligns with a hole in the centre of the control rod which allows the control rod to move beyond its normal maximum position – the main governor spring will push the control rod to this position when the engine is stopped. When the engine starts, the control rod moves towards idling position and the spring-loaded plunger returns to normal operating position.

A second control pipe may be used which is connected to a damping valve incorporated with the idling control spring. The effect of this is to make governing less sensitive to changes in engine speed and it is particularly effective in damping under idling conditions.

## Leaf spring governor

A leaf spring governor (Figure 152) is commonly fitted to an in-line pump and is used in conjunction with roller weights or fly weights. This is an all-speed governor which controls all speeds from idling to maximum speed. The governor spring is a variable rate spring which consists of two slotted leaf springs, the lower end of this spring is in contact with a thrust pad which is part of the weight assembly. A control lever – connected to the accelerator pedal – has a forked end inside the governor housing in contact with a roller assembly. Movement of the accelerator pedal to increase speed pushes the roller assembly down the ramp (Figure 153). As the rollers are in contact with the ramp and the leaf spring, this movement will bend or load the spring more heavily so that it can cope with the higher centrifugal forces as engine speed increases. At any speed or engine loading, this variation in spring tension can balance the centrifugal forces created by engine speed through the governor weights. This position of balance gives a governed engine speed.

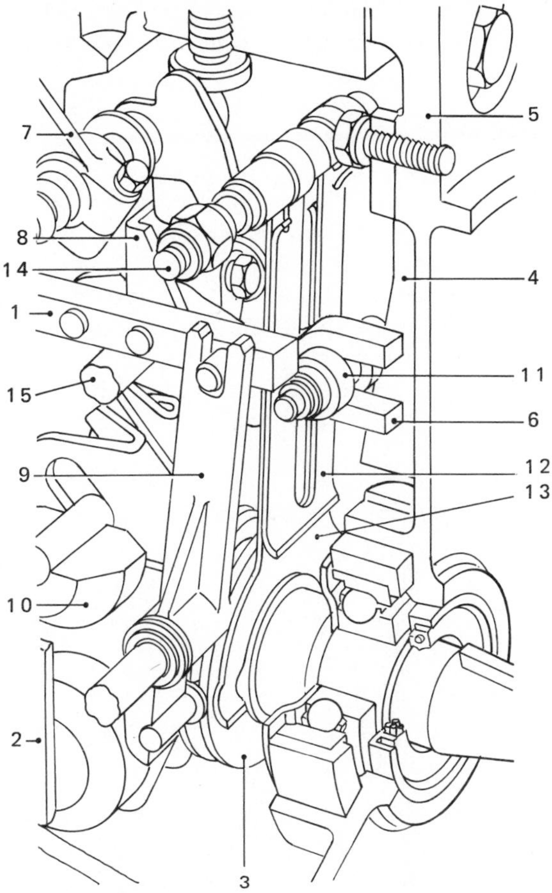

| | |
|---|---|
| 1 | Control rod |
| 2 | Backplate |
| 3 | Thrust pad |
| 4 | Ramp |
| 5 | Governor cover |
| 6 | Roller control lever |
| 7 | Stop control lever |
| 8 | Max. stop fork |
| 9 | Rocking lever |
| 10 | Governor weight assy. |
| 11 | Spring roller assy. |
| 12 | Governor primary spring |
| 13 | Governor secondary spring |
| 14 | Fulcrum pin |
| 15 | Speed control shaft |

Figure 152   *Governor details*

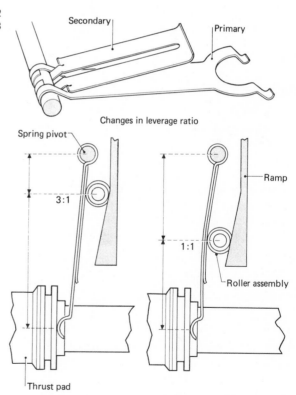

Figure 153   *Variable loading of leaf spring*

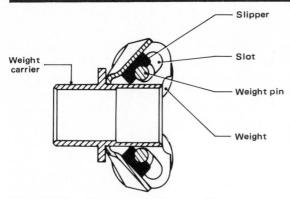

Figure 154   *Governor weight assembly*

On the roller-weight type of governor each pair of weights is held in a slipper which is free to slide along an inclined face in the centre of the carrier (Figure 154). Movement of the weights alters the position of the control rod through the rocking lever to give more or less fuel delivery. The governor spring is loaded by a roller assembly which is located in a forked lever fitted to the accelerator shaft. This roller assembly is able to move on a ramp on the governor cover so that, when the accelerator is operated, the spring load on the thrust pad moves the rocking lever which in turn moves the control rod towards maximum fuel position (Figure 155).

*Operation*

From a stable engine speed, determined by the position of the accelerator linkage, an increase in speed will make the weights move outwards owing to centrifugal force which in turn will apply a thrust through the slippers to the inclined faces of the weight carrier. Speed will increase until a stage is reached when the centrifugal force acting through the weights is greater than the force exerted by the leaf spring on the thrust pad. The

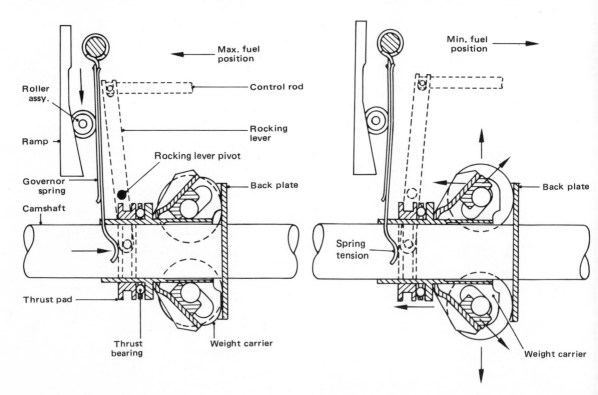

Figure 155   *Weight carrier position relative to backplate (no centrifugal force)*

Figure 156   *Weight carrier position due to centrifugal force*

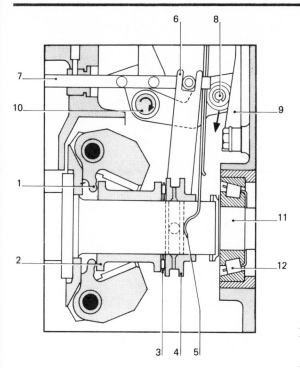

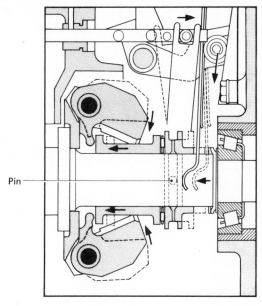

Figure 159 *Movement when accelerator is pressed*

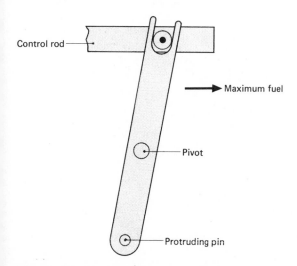

| | | | |
|---|---|---|---|
| 1 | Toe | 7 | Control rod |
| 2 | Thrust sleeve | 8 | Roller assembly |
| 3 | Thrust bearing | 9 | Ramp |
| 4 | Thrust pad | 10 | Shaft – connected to accelerator linkage |
| 5 | Leaf spring | 11 | Camshaft |
| 6 | Rocking lever | 12 | Roller bearing |

Figure 157 *Flyweight governor*

Figure 158 *Rocking lever*

weight carrier is therefore pushed away from the back plate by the thrust applied through the slippers. The control rod is then moved towards minimum fuel position to reduce fuel delivery and therefore engine speed.

## Flyweight governor operation

In this type of governor, centrifugal force acting through the rotating weights rotates the weights about their pivot. This action causes the toe (1) (Figure 157) of the weights to push the thrust sleeve, bearing and pad against the pressure of the leaf spring. At the same time, the rocking lever (Figure 158) moves the control rod towards minimum fuel and the engine speed begins to fall until the centrifugal force exerted by the flyweights is balanced by the spring force exerted by the leaf spring. If the driver now pushes his accelerator pedal down, the effect will be to rotate the shaft (10) (Figure 157) in the direction shown. This moves the roller assembly (8) down the ramp (9) and increases the force of the leaf spring against the thrust pad (4). The result of this movement is to

1  Push the sleeve against the toe of the governor weights and move the weights closer together.

2  Move the rocking lever – a protruding pin (Figure 158) located in the annular groove of the thrust pad – and control rod towards maximum fuel position.

The resulting increase in fuel will increase engine speed until the centrifugal force acting through the flyweights assumes a new balance position against the new spring loading (Figure 159). When the accelerator is released, the roller is moved in the opposite direction, reducing leaf spring tension. The governor weights can now expand and move the sliding sleeve along the camshaft and at the same time move the control rod towards minimum fuel or idling. The engine speed will be governed again when engine speed and therefore centrifugal force from the flyweights match the leaf spring tension and hold the control rod steady.

## Maximum fuel

Under full-load running conditions, the maximum stop fork attached to the control rod strikes the maximum fuel plate. The top end of this plate abuts against the lower end of the maximum fuel adjusting screw. This screw is set at the factory, or by an approved pump overhaul centre, and sealed with wire and a lead seal. Any alteration to this setting to try and improve engine power will only lead to excessive smoke.

## Excess fuel and engine stop control

Under cold start conditions, the excess fuel shaft (Figure 161) can be pushed from outside the governor housing to move the maximum stop plate away from the maximum stop fork. This allows the control rod to move beyond the normal maximum fuel position, from pressure exerted by the leaf spring, to allow the pump to deliver excess fuel. When the engine starts, governor action moves the control rod back towards minimum fuel. The stop plate is then able to be returned to its normal action by a return spring fitted to the end of the excess shaft.

When the engine has to be stopped, the driver pulls the stop cable which is connected to the stop plate by a splined shaft and lever (Figure 161). The stop plate pushes against the stop fork and moves the control rod to rotate the plungers to the no-fuel position.

## Boost control unit

When a turbocharger is fitted to a CI engine, the amount of air pushed into the cylinders is reduced

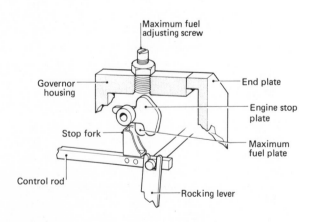

Figure 160   *Maximum fuel stop*

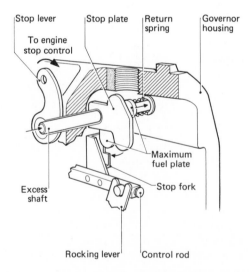

Figure 161   *Excess fuel and stop control*

as the speed of the turbocharger falls due to low engine speeds. Normally when this happens an enriched mixture and therefore black smoke from the exhaust results. In order to overcome this, a smaller quantity of fuel must be injected into the cylinder. The boost control unit provides automatic control of maximum fuel delivered at these low engine speeds. A diaphragm-operated sensor unit is connected to the inlet manifold and mounted on top of the governor housing on the injection pump. The normal maximum fuel adjusting screw is replaced by a plunger and cam arrangement.

The unit operates when boost pressure, entering the unit at (2) (Figure 162) moves the diaphragm against its spring tension. This movement causes the spindle rod to pivot the cam which in turn moves the maximum fuel rod to a new position and gives a new limit to the maximum fuel plate in the pump housing. Opposing this movement of the diaphragm, the coil spring is compressed until boost pressure is balanced. Any decrease in boost pressure will allow the diaphragm spring to push the diaphragm and spindle rod until both forces are balanced again. In order to match turbo-charger pressures with engine specifications, the adjusting spring and sleeve (4) is set according to test specifications and stop screw (3) is adjusted to give the lowest possible restriction of maximum fuel setting.

## Phasing and calibrating

The successful operation of a fuel-injection pump depends upon its ability to measure a quantity of fuel accurately and inject this fuel into the combustion chamber at the correct time.

Phasing is the procedure for checking and adjusting the interval or phase angle between each injection of fuel from the pumping elements. This is necessary when the elements or tappets have been changed or removed. A plunger clearance gauge (Figure 163) complete with a dial indicator is fitted in place of the delivery valve. With the pump mounted on a testing machine, the clearance gauge reading indicates the distance travelled by No. 1 plunger from the bottom of its

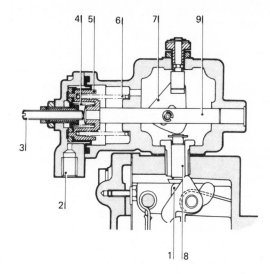

1  Maximum fuel plate on control rod of pump
2  Boost pressure inlet
3  Stop screw
4  Adjusting spring and sleeve
5  Piston and diaphragm assembly
6  Diaphragm spring
7  Cam
8  Maximum fuel rod
9  Spindle rod

Figure 162  *Boost control unit*

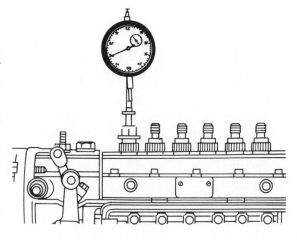

Figure 163  *Plunger clearance gauge*

stroke to the closing of the inlet port, i.e. when fuel just ceases to flow past the stem of the clearance gauge. This is also the point when the timing mark on the pump coupling should align with the mark on the timing indicator on the governor cover, and it is also used as a timing mark when coupling the pump to the engine (spill timing).

If the plunger head clearance is incorrect it can be adjusted by changing the tappet spacers which are supplied in graded thicknesses. When this adjustment is correct, a spill pipe (Figure 164) is fitted to the next element in firing order sequence after removing the delivery valve. From the zero position established in No. 1 element the pump is rotated until the inlet port is just closing on the element fitted with the spill pipe – when fuel just ceases to flow from the spill pipe. This is commencement of injection of this element and should be at an angle of 90° (4 cyl.) or 60° (6 cyl.) ± ½° after No. 1 element. If incorrect, earlier or later closing of the inlet port can be adjusted by fitting larger or smaller spacing washers. This phase angle should then be checked and adjusted for all pumping elements.

Calibration is the procedure for adjusting the quantity of fuel delivered from each element so that each element delivers the same quantity of fuel under different control rod settings. This adjustment is carried out on a testing machine with specified control rod settings and the fuel delivery from each element measured in specially calibrated test tubes. Adjustment is by moving the control forks along the control rod until each element produces equal amounts of fuel (Figure 166). Maximum fuel delivery is also checked against manufacturer's specifications and the maximum fuel stop screw adjusted and sealed. Operation of the excess fuel device is also checked whilst the pump is mounted on the testing machine.

Figure 167 shows the arrangement for coupling of the pump to the engine. This allows easy coupling with some adjustment on the drive flange (elongated slots) to ensure accurate 'timing'. The pump is connected to the engine when No. 1 piston is approximately 27° before t.d.c. – usually marked on the flywheel – on compression stroke.

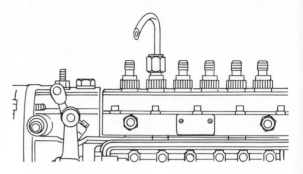

Figure 164   *Spill pipe*

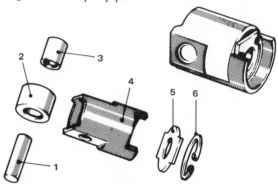

1. Roller pin        4. Tappet
2. Roller            5. Spacer
3. Bush              6. Circlip

Figure 165   *Assembly of tappet and adjusting spacer*

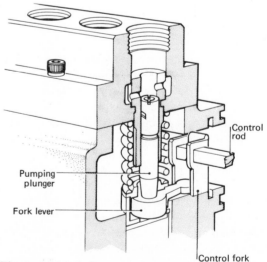

Control rod

Pumping plunger

Fork lever

Control fork

Figure 166   *Calibration adjustment*

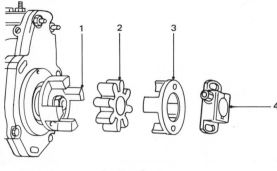

1. Pump flange
2. Rubber insert
3. Dog flange
4. Driving flange
   (adjustable)

Figure 167   *Assembly of drive*

The pump should also be set or 'spill-timed' to No. 1 and the drive coupling bolted to the drive flange. This illustration is a guide only and for any pump settings, reference should be made to the manufacturer's specifications. This type of pump drive does not allow any variation or advance at speed which may be up to 6° of advance between engine starting and maximum speed, but an automatic advance arrangement, using centrifugal force, can be fitted into the drive coupling.

## DPA distributor-type fuel injection pump

This pump is usually mounted on the side of the engine and driven by the timing gear. It is flange mounted directly on to the engine with no externally shown drive arrangement. The whole pump is lubricated by fuel oil under pressure and no additional lubrication system is required. Hydraulic or mechanical governors can be used and additional features to the basic design include automatic advance or retard, pressure damper and an excess fuel device with external minimum fuel adjustment.

All designs and sizes of pump have a common type of single element which creates the fuel pressure necessary for injection. This element consists of two opposing plungers, held in a transverse bore in a central rotor, which are actuated by lobes on an internal cam-ring. The rotor revolves in a stationary member called the

hydraulic head and also acts as a fuel inlet from the metering valve, and the high-pressure charges are distributed to the injectors at the required timing intervals through further parts in the rotor and the hydraulic head. For a four-cylinder engine there is one inlet and four outlet ports in the hydraulic head and four inlet and one outlet port in the rotor.

*Principle of operation*

The correct operation of this pump relies upon an accurately controlled fuel pressure. An eccentric vane type transfer pump is built into the end of each pump and this, together with the pressure-regulating valve, supplies this pressure. From the transfer pump fuel passes to the metering valve which controls the quantity of fuel passing to the pumping element, thus controlling engine speed and power. This quantity of fuel is controlled by two factors – fuel pressure in the metering port and the time allowed for fuel to flow into the pumping element when the inlet port in the rotor and the metering port in the hydraulic head are aligned. The effective area of the metering port is controlled by movement of the metering valve which in turn is connected to the accelerator pedal via the governor. Fuel entering the rotor, at metering pressure, forces the plungers apart – maximum fuel adjustment is effected by limiting the outward travel of the plungers.

As the rotor turns (Figure 170), the inlet port is closed and the distributor port is lined up with an outlet port in the hydraulic head. At the same time the plungers are forced together by the cam lobes and fuel under high pressure is passed to the injector. The cam lobes are specially shaped to give a reduction of pressure in the injector pipes at the end of injection to give a quick cut-off of fuel to prevent 'dribble' at the injector nozzle.

## Pressure-regulating valve

This is fastened on to the end of the transfer pump housing and performs two separate functions:
1  It controls the fuel pressure within the pump by maintaining a relationship between transfer pressure and speed of rotation.

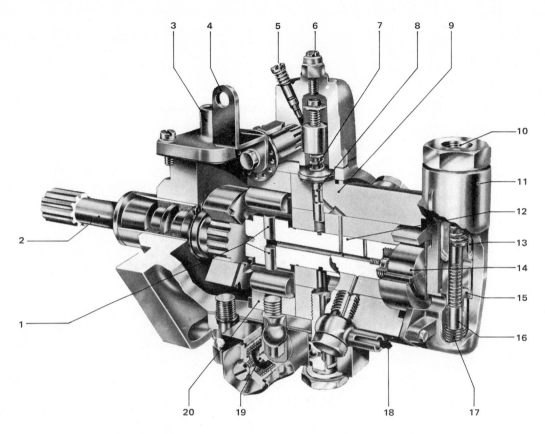

1. Plungers
2. Drive shaft
3. Back leak connection
4. Control lever
5. Idling stop
6. Vent screw
7. Governor spring
8. Metering valve
9. Hydraulic head
10. Fuel inlet

11. End plate assembly
12. Rotor
13. Nylon filter
14. Transfer pump
15. Regulating valve sleeve
16. Regulating piston
17. Priming spring
18. To injector
19. Advance device
20. Cam ring

Figure 168   *Sectioned distributor-type pump with hydraulic governor*

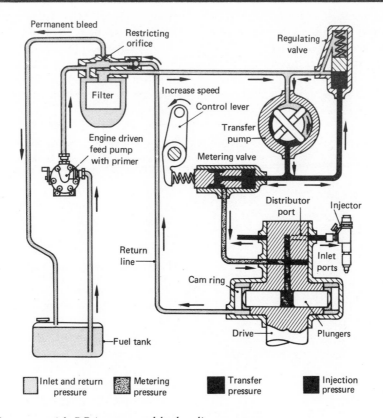

Figure 169   *Fuel system with DPA pump and hydraulic governor*

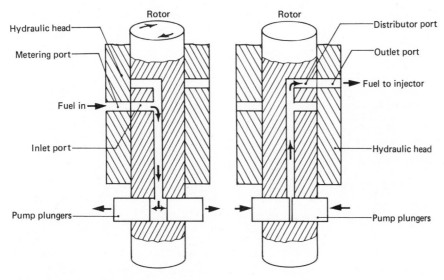

Figure 170   *Pressurizing and distribution of fuel*

2   It provides a means of bypassing the transfer pump when the pump is stationary to enable the hydraulic head to be primed.

When 'bleeding' or priming is being carried out, fuel under pressure from the hand priming pump enters the inlet connection as shown. Fuel cannot pass into the transfer pump and out through the drilled passages the normal way. Fuel pressure then pushes the piston down against the priming spring and uncovers the fuel passage to the

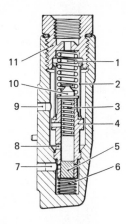

1  Retaining spring
2  Nylon filter
3  Regulating spring
4  Valve sleeve
5  Piston
6  Priming spring
7  Fuel passage to transfer pump outlet
8  Regulating port
9  Fuel passage to transfer pump inlet
10  Spring guide
11  Fuel inlet connection

Figure 171   *Pressure regulating valve – section*

transfer pump outlet. This means that the fuel can now bypass the transfer pump and pass directly into the hydraulic head.

When regulating, transfer pressure is able to lift the piston up against the regulating spring by emerging from the lower passage as shown. As transfer pressure increases with increasing engine speed, the piston is forced further upwards to progressively uncover the regulating port. This allows a quantity of fuel to leak back into the transfer pump inlet and be pumped around again. The effective area of the regulating port increases and decreases with engine speed to give the correct pressure required in the metering process.

## Hydraulic governor (Figure 174)

After leaving the transfer pump at a pre-determined pressure, fuel passes through internal passages to the base of the metering valve. Governing takes place when this pressure acting against the metering valve is balanced by the governing spring. In the hydraulic governor the accelerator pedal is connected to a rack which is free to slide on the metering valve stem between the main governor spring and idling spring. Up and down movement of the metering valve varies the area of the metering port. The amount of fuel passing into the hydraulic head through the metering port therefore depends upon the position of the metering valve.

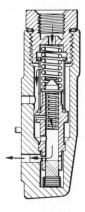

Figure 172   *Pressure regulating valve – priming*

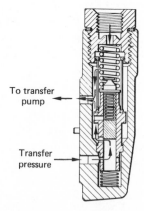

To transfer pump

Transfer pressure

Figure 173   *Pressure regulating valve – regulating*

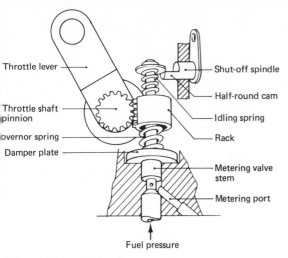

Throttle lever
Throttle shaft pinnion
Governor spring
Damper plate
Shut-off spindle
Half-round cam
Idling spring
Rack
Metering valve stem
Metering port
Fuel pressure

Figure 174   *Hydraulic governor*

As the accelerator pedal is depressed, the metering valve is pushed down by the main governor spring. This increases the area of the metering port and more fuel passes to the hydraulic head. Engine speed increases with this increase in fuel and also transfer pressure is increased. This pressure pushes the valve up against the governor spring to reduce the area of the metering port and so tend to reduce engine speed. When fuel pressure is balanced by the governor spring pressure, engine speed is governed.

When the accelerator is moved towards the idling position, the idling spring is compressed and tension on the mainspring is reduced. As engine speed decreases, transfer pressure decreases and the metering valve is pushed down its bore to increase the area of the metering port. Governing again is effected when fuel pressure and spring pressures are in equilibrium.

When the driver operates the stop control, the shut-off spindle is rotated which lifts the metering valve to completely close off the metering port. This cuts off any fuel to the hydraulic head and the engine therefore stops.

The damper plate is immersed in fuel oil and prevents violent metering valve movement by dashpot action.

## Mechanical governor

This is a flyweight-type which controls the position of the metering valve by changes in centrifugal force acting through a number of flyweights. The metering valve in this case is rotated by the governor linkage, a small slot which is cut in the valve varies the effective area of the metering port as the valve is rotated. This regulates the supply of fuel to the hydraulic head and therefore controls engine speed.

A governed speed is obtained when centrifugal force – controlled by engine speed – is balanced against a governor spring – whose tension is controlled by the position of the accelerator pedal. The governor weights move the thrust sleeve which is a sliding fit on the drive shaft. This in turn moves the pivoted governor control arm, against spring tension, and rotates the metering valve via the spring-loaded linkage. As engine speed increases because of a reduced load, the flyweights begin to move outwards due to increased centrifugal force. This movement rotates the metering valve towards the closed position and

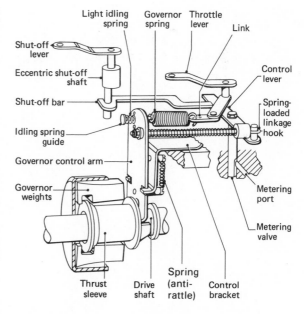

Light idling spring
Governor spring
Throttle lever
Link
Shut-off lever
Eccentric shut-off shaft
Shut-off bar
Control lever
Spring-loaded linkage hook
Idling spring guide
Governor control arm
Governor weights
Metering port
Metering valve
Thrust sleeve
Drive shaft
Spring (anti-rattle)
Control bracket

Figure 175   *Control mechanism of mechanical governor*

engine speed begins to fall. As engine speed falls, the flyweights move inwards pulling the thrust sleeve and governor control arm to rotate the metering valve and increase fuel supply to the hydraulic head. This increases speed until the centrifugal force is balanced by the spring tension.

At idling speeds, the accelerator linkage relieves tension on the main governor spring and the lighter idling spring gives a more sensitive control of engine speed.

When the driver operates the stop control, the shut-off lever rotates on the eccentric shaft. This moves the shut-off bar to rotate the metering valve to a no fuel position. This can be done at any engine speed because the control lever moves the spring-loaded linkage against its spring tension.

## Hydraulic head

When the fuel has passed through the metering valve it is at a reduced pressure depending upon the position of the metering valve. It then passes through the metering port to the hydraulic head (Figure 176). As the rotor turns, a charging port in the rotor is aligned with this metering port and fuel flows into the central passage in the rotor and forces the plungers apart. The distance moved by the plungers is determined by the amount of fuel which can flow into the element whilst the ports are aligned. Further rotation of the rotor closes the inlet port, and the single distributor port further along the rotor is aligned with an outlet port in the hydraulic head. At the same time the plungers are forced inwards by the rollers contacting the cam ring lobes, and fuel under injection pressure passes up the central bore of the rotor through the aligned ports to one of the injectors (Figure 177). The rotor normally has as many inlet ports as the engine has cylinders with a similar number of outlet ports in the hydraulic head.

A controlled back-leakage of fuel passes between the rotor and hydraulic head, between plungers and their bore for lubricating purposes. This fills the whole of the pump body and then returns to the filter body.

## Automatic advance mechanism (Figure 178)

This is a small unit which can be fitted below the main body of the pump. A simple advance with engine speed can be obtained or any combination of load and speed advance or start retard conditions can be achieved. All systems use fuel at transfer pressure to move the cam ring. In the advance with speed mechanism as shown, the spring pushes the cam ring into a retarded position for starting conditions. When the engine is

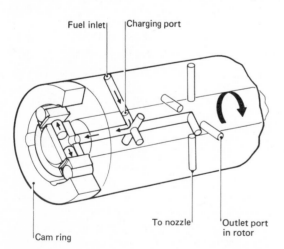

Figure 176  *Hydraulic head – fuel in (metering pressure)*

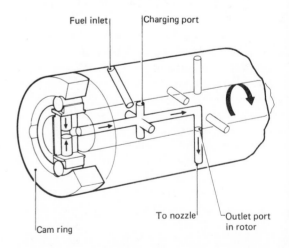

Figure 177  *Hydraulic head – fuel out (injection pressure)*

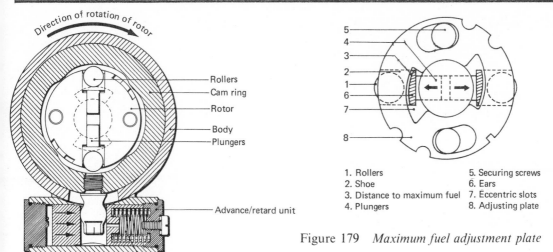

Figure 178  *Automatic advance mechanism*

Figure 179  *Maximum fuel adjustment plate*

running, fuel at transfer pressure enters the unit through internal drillings and exerts a pressure behind the piston to move the cam ring against spring pressure. As speed increases, transfer pressure increases and pushes the piston and cam ring to advance the point of injection. The cam ring moves in the opposite direction to the rotation of the rotor, which means that the plungers are forced together earlier and therefore inject the fuel into the combustion chamber earlier. As engine speed decreases, transfer pressure decreases and the spring returns the piston and cam ring towards the retarded position. Because the impact of the rollers acting against the cam lobes at the commencement of the injection stroke tends to move the cam ring towards the retard position, a non-return valve in the fuel inlet passage is fitted to prevent this movement. The amount of advance is controlled by the strength of the control spring – the stronger the spring, the higher the engine speed at which maximum advance is reached. Maximum advance is usually 12–14°.

## Maximum fuel adjustment

This is the only adjustment to the quantity of fuel injected in this type of pump. On some later type pumps this can be an external adjustment, but on the basic distributor pump, adjustment is provided within the pump, and an inspection cover on the side of the pump must be removed before carrying out this adjustment. In this case, maximum fuel setting is controlled by limiting the effective stroke of the plungers. The rollers which actuate the plungers are positioned inside a shoe which in turn is located in adjusting plates. Ears projecting from the shoes are positioned in eccentric slots in the adjusting plate so that, as the adjusting plates are moved, these ears can travel a greater or lesser distance according to its position. Figure 179 shows the adjusting plates set to give the lowest maximum fuel, as the adjusting plate is turned in a clockwise direction maximum travel of the plungers is increased to give higher maximum fuel.

## Starting aids

On many CI engines it is sufficient to provide excess fuel for cold start conditions. Some fuel injection pumps however do not have this facility and other means of starting under cold conditions are required. When starting under extreme cold conditions it may not be sufficient to provide an excess of fuel as the air temperature cannot be raised sufficiently to provide the self-ignition characteristics required by the CI engine.

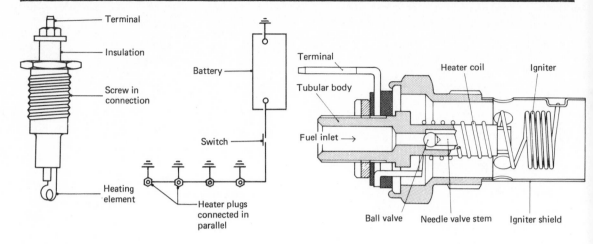

Figure 180    *Heater plug*

Figure 181    *CAV thermostart starting aid*

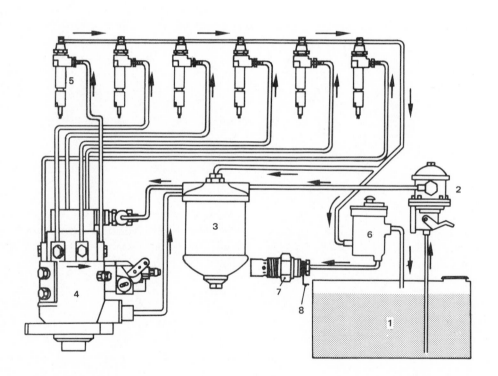

1. Fuel tank
2. Fuel lift pump
3. Fuel filter
4. Fuel injection pump
5. Atomisers
6. Cold start aid fuel reservoir
7. Thermostat
8. Electrical connection to switch

Figure 182    *Layout of fuel system incorporating thermostart*

A simple system that is usually used in conjunction with an indirect combustion chamber is an electrically operated heater plug (Figure 180) which is positioned within the pre-combustion chamber. Prior to turning the engine, a separate push button is operated which switches on the heater plugs. Each plug consists of a small element which glows and heats up the air in the combustion chamber. This pre-heated air should be sufficiently warm to enable air at temperatures of down to –10°C to be drawn into the combustion chamber from outside and yet start the engine. A larger version of this may be fitted as a single unit in the induction manifold to serve the same purpose.

Another system (Figure 182) operates by heating the incoming air by burning fuel in the induction manifold. The fuel used is stored in a small reservoir which is kept topped up by a leak-off pipe from the main fuel system, and an electrically operated igniter coil supplies the heat to ignite this fuel. The whole assembly is screwed into the manifold and the valve body is surrounded by a heater coil which extends to form the igniter coil. Inside the valve body is a needle valve which holds a ball valve against a seat to prevent the flow of fuel when the unit is not in use.

When switched on, the heater coil heats the valve body which expands and allows fuel to push the ball valve off its seat. The fuel is then vaporized by the heat of the valve body which in turn is ignited by the glowing igniter coil. When the engine is then turned to start, a quantity of very hot air is drawn into the combustion chamber. This can continue to burn fuel as the engine is being turned and give an easy starting condition even under very cold conditions. As soon as the unit is switched off the flow of air in the manifold cools the valve body which pushes the needle against the ball to cut off the fuel supply.

A different type of cold start system uses a very volatile liquid introduced into the main air flow as the engine is being cranked. Ether is usually used because of its low boiling point and ignition qualities. A very simple method of introducing this into the air flow is by means of an aerosol-type spray (Figure 183). A more satisfactory method is

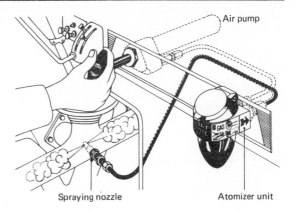

Figure 183  *Start pilot starting aid*

to use this type of fluid in conjunction with a separate air pump and mixer valve. When the hand pump is operated, air is fed to the mixer unit where the starting fluid is atomized. It is then fed to a spraying nozzle which is fitted into the induction manifold to mix with the incoming air as the engine is cranked.

## Fuel injectors

Many different types of fuel injector are used for the CI engine. The main purpose of the injector is to break down the measured quantity of fuel from the injector pump and atomize it into such a condition that it will readily mix with the air in the combustion chamber, and inject it into the compressed air in the combustion chamber. In order to do this the fuel is subjected to a high pressure and then forced through one or several small holes.

A complete injector consists of a nozzle, body and spring. The nozzle consists of a body and valve or needle, the two being ground and lapped together to form a close fit. Operation of the nozzle is controlled by fuel pressure from the injector pump. As soon as this pressure exceeds the tension of the spring, it acts against the taper face of the needle which lifts it off its seat and allows fuel to escape past the valve seat and is forced into the combustion chamber through the injection hole or holes. Because of the high fuel

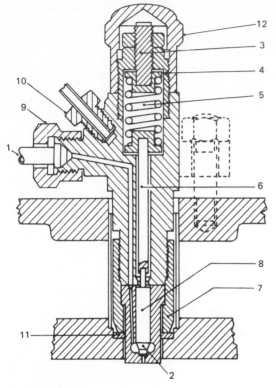

1   Fuel inlet
2   Taper face
3   Adjusting (compression) screw
4   Spring cap nut
5   Valve spring
6   Valve spindle
7   Nozzle cap nut
8   Needle valve
9   Fuel inlet connection
10  Leak-off connection
11  Special copper washer
12  Protecting cap

Figure 184   *Section through injector*

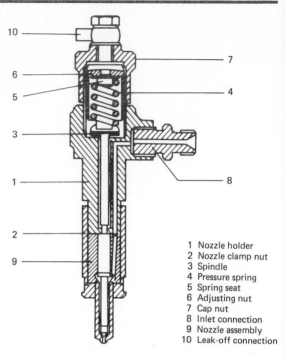

Figure 185   *Typical Leyland injector*

1   Nozzle holder
2   Nozzle clamp nut
3   Spindle
4   Pressure spring
5   Spring seat
6   Adjusting nut
7   Cap nut
8   Inlet connection
9   Nozzle assembly
10  Leak-off connection

pressure required to lift the needle, it is possible that some fuel may escape between the needle and the nozzle body. This is collected in the main injector body and fed back into the fuel filter or back to the fuel tank by a leak-off pipe connected to each injector.

Different types of nozzle are used according to the design of the combustion chamber.

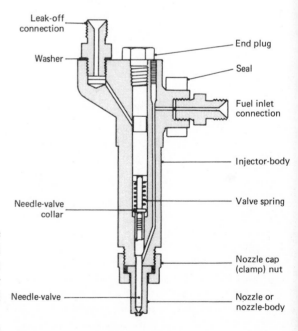

Figure 186   *Simms fuel injector*

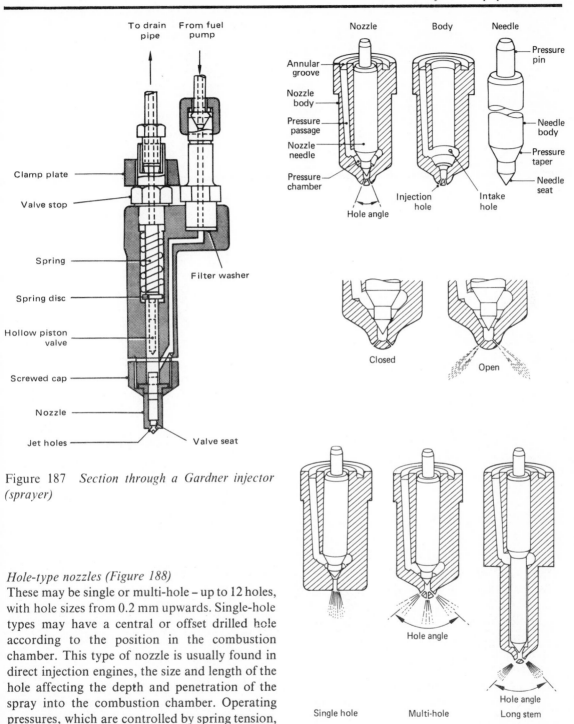

Figure 187   *Section through a Gardner injector (sprayer)*

Figure 188   *Hole-type nozzles*

*Hole-type nozzles (Figure 188)*

These may be single or multi-hole – up to 12 holes, with hole sizes from 0.2 mm upwards. Single-hole types may have a central or offset drilled hole according to the position in the combustion chamber. This type of nozzle is usually found in direct injection engines, the size and length of the hole affecting the depth and penetration of the spray into the combustion chamber. Operating pressures, which are controlled by spring tension, are usually adjustable and vary between 15 000 and 20 000 kN/m² (2100 and 3500 lbf/in²).

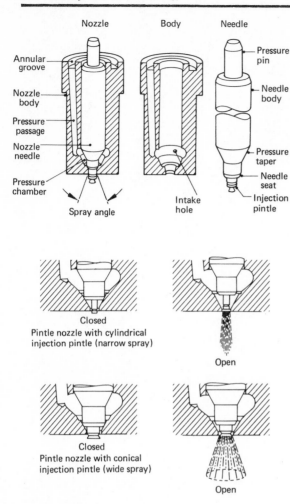

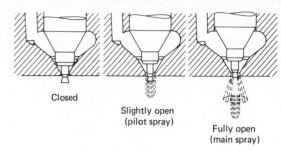

Closed     Slightly open
(pilot spray)     Fully open
(main spray)

Figure 190   *Delay nozzle*

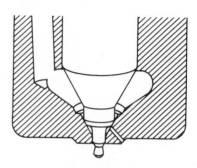

Figure 189   *Pintle-type nozzles*

Figure 191   *CAV Pintaux fuel injection nozzle*

*Delay nozzle (Figure 190)*

This is a pintle nozzle with a specially shaped pintle to give a pilot spray just prior to the main injection of fuel. In some pre-combustion engines, this reduced initial injection of fuel diminishes 'diesel knock' and gives quieter running at idling speeds.

*Pintle nozzles (Figure 189)*

This is a single-hole nozzle with the end of the needle extended to form a pin or pintle which protrudes through the hole in the nozzle body. By varying the size and shape of the pintle, the spray formation can be varied to suit different engine requirements. This type of nozzle is usually found in pre-combustion chamber or indirect-injection engines where high air turbulence gives an efficient mixing of fuel at lower operating pressures – between 8000 and 12 500 kN/m$^2$ (1150 and 1800 lbf/in$^2$).

*Pintaux nozzle (Figure 191)*

This is also a pintle nozzle but is modified by having an auxiliary spray hole at the side of the main discharge hole. When the engine is being turned over by the starter motor, the needle is not lifted far enough to clear the pintle hole and fuel is discharged through the auxiliary spray hole. This gives better atomization of the fuel and therefore easier starting under cold conditions. When running normally, the higher fuel pressures lift the needle completely so that the main part of the fuel is discharged as in a normal pintle nozzle.

## Nozzle holders

In order to locate the nozzle correctly in the combustion chamber, a holder is provided which clamps or screws into the cylinder head. Inside the nozzle holder is a spring and spindle which provides the tension against the needle valve to determine the opening pressure. The spring pressure is often adjustable by an external screw and locknut or steel shims inserted under the spring. The nozzle is held by a screw cap on to a surface-ground face of the holder and an annular groove aligns with a drilling in the holder to supply fuel from the injector pipe through to the nozzle.

## Nozzle testing

Incorrect functioning of the injector may lead to bad starting, poor idling of engine, diesel knock or black smoke from the exhaust. The main points to check are

1   *Back leakage* – wear between the needle valve and its holder will allow fuel to leak back into the injector body instead of being injected into the combustion chamber.

2   *Pressure setting* – correct atomization of the fuel will be achieved only when the spring tension is correct.

3   *Spray form* – mixing of the atomized fuel with the compressed air in the combustion chamber can be achieved efficiently only when the hole or holes in the tip of the nozzle give the correct spray patterns. Holes may be blocked with carbon or dirt.

4   *Seat tightness* – an important function of the injector which prevents the emission of black smoke from the exhaust is that the needle returns quickly back to its seat to maintain an efficient seal. Because the injector pipes are maintained at a pressure just below opening pressure, any 'dribbling' of fuel into the combustion chamber will quickly form carbon deposits and emit black smoke from the exhaust.

## Cummins fuel system

In this system the fuel metering is based on a pressure time principle. The whole system includes

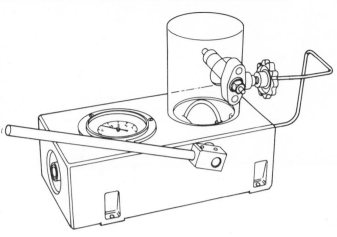

Figure 192   *Hand-operated nozzle testing kit*

a filter, a fuel pump which incorporates a governor, throttle control and fuel cut-off valve and the injectors. Fuel is drawn from the tank to the lift pump where it is pressure regulated by a governor and throttle control. It then passes at low pressure to the injectors where its pressure is increased and fed into the cylinder in an atomized form. Any fuel not used by the injector is returned back to the fuel tank. Each injector is mechanically actuated by a camshaft-driven push-rod and rocker arrangement which creates the pressure required for injection of the fuel.

The pressure time principle is derived from the method of fuel metering.

1   Pressure in the fuel system is controlled by the combined lift pump/governor. This variable pressure together with a fixed size opening in the injector meters the fuel to be injected.

2   The time interval during which this fixed size metering orifice is uncovered is determined by the camshaft and engine speeds.

It follows then that a low fuel pressure with a small orifice time will allow only a small amount of fuel to be injected, and the longer time the fuel has to enter the nozzle the more fuel will be injected. A higher fuel pressure will also increase the amount of fuel entering the injector nozzle.

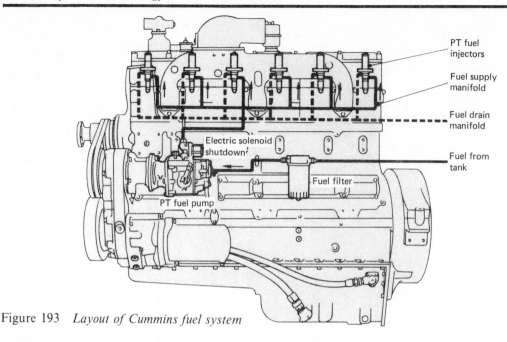

Figure 193    *Layout of Cummins fuel system*

**(a) Start-up stroke**
The piston would now be close to BDC intake stroke. The plunger has been lifted by the spring following the camshaft. The groove has now indexed, allowing fuel to pass through the injector, out of the drain orifice to the fuel tank. As yet the metering orifice is not open.

**(b) Metering**
The plunger has continued to rise following the cam lobe position. The groove is still indexed with the inlet drilling. Now, however, the metering orifice is also open. Fuel, therefore, enters into the cup, the quantity dependant upon:
1 Fuel pump pressure (pressure)
2 Engine speed (time)
3 The diameter of the metering orifice

**(c) Injection**
As the piston rises toward TDC on the compression stroke, the camshaft pushes the injector mechanism, which in turn forces down the injector plunger. The metering orifice closes, thereby holding the metered quantity of fuel in the cup. (The metering orifice actually closes at 0–2032" BTC). The plunger continues down displacing the fuel from the cup through the spray holes into the cylinder. This is of course at very high pressure. When the plunger is bottomed, then injection is complete.

**(d) Injection complete**
The injector is in this position a few degrees after TDC compression stroke, until about half way through the intake stroke.

Fuel enters the injector at the inlet orifice, flows down the injector but cannot proceed further as the plunger index groove is too far down.

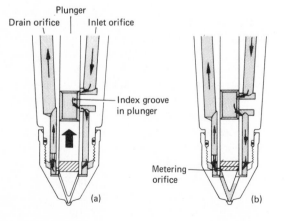
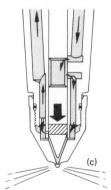
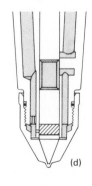

Figure 194    *Sequence of operation of Cummins injectors*

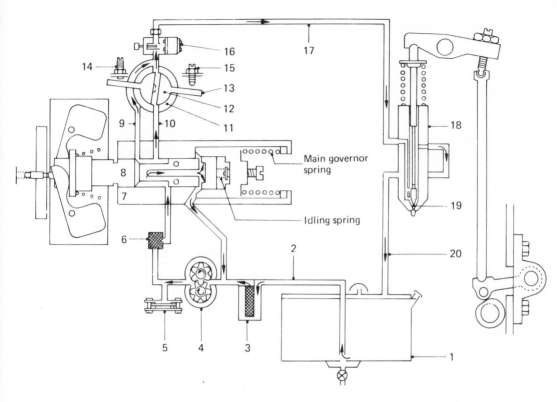

Main governor spring

Idling spring

| | | |
|---|---|---|
| 1 Diesel oil tank | 8 Gov. plunger | 15 Rear throttle screw |
| 2 Suction pipe | 9 Idle press. | 16 Shut down valve |
| 3 Fuel filter | 10 fuel press. | 17 Fuel manifold press. |
| 4 Gear pump | 11 Throttle sleeve | 18 Injector |
| 5 Pulsation damper | 12 Throttle shaft | 19 Metering orifice |
| 6 Filter screen | 13 Throttle stop pin | 20 Injector return |
| 7 Gov. barrel | 14 Front throttle screw | |

Figure 195   *Schematic design of PTG fuel system. Governing is achieved by controlling the fuel pressure. At idling speeds, the main fuel passage (10) is closed by the throttle shaft and fuel pressure is controlled by the position of the governor plunger in relation to the idling passage (9) in the governor barrel. The positioning of the governor plunger is dependent upon centrifugal force acting through the flyweights and the idling spring tension. At higher engine speeds, the main fuel passage is opened by the throttle shaft, the flyweights push the governor plunger to the right and close the idling passage*

## Detroit diesel

This engine uses another type of fuel injection system. The complete fuel system is relatively simple and comprises fuel filters, fuel lift pump and the fuel injector. The injector unit itself is more complex than normal because it meters and injects the fuel into the combustion chamber. An engine-driven mechanical governor controls engine speed by varying the amount of fuel injected into the cylinders by a rack arrangement to control the position of the plungers inside the injector. Fuel under low pressure is fed via internal drillings in the cylinder head to each injector and any fuel not used is returned to the tank.

### Fuel pump

The basic function of the fuel pump is to draw fuel from the tank and deliver it to the injectors at a suitably low pressure. A gear type of pump is used which passes fuel through a governor and throttle valve before passing it to the injectors. In this way fuel pressure and flow is controlled for the whole fuel system. Movement of the governor shaft opens or closes fuel passages to regulate fuel flow to the throttle shaft. Movement of the throttle lever varies the area available for fuel flow and therefore changes the fuel pressure in the manifold to the injectors.

### Fuel injectors (Figure 196)

In this type of fuel system, the injectors may be fed with fuel through external pipes from the fuel pump or via drillings which form fuel galleries in the cylinder head. The design of these injectors varies but the principle of operation is the same. The injector plunger is operated by the engine camshaft and a return spring lifts the plunger back to the top of its stroke. The controlled pressure at the metering orifice together with the time it is uncovered by the injector plunger accurately meter the fuel into a metering cup. As the plunger is moved down its stroke a high injection pressure is developed which atomizes the fuel as it is forced through holes in the top of the injector cup. It is important that the clearances in the push-rod and rocker assembly are maintained because this

would upset injection timing and therefore engine performance.

Fuel injection – this type of injector:

1. Meters a quantity of fuel depending upon engine speed and load.
2. Creates the high pressure suitable for injecting into the combustion chamber.
3. Atomizes the fuel as it is injected.
4. Allows fuel to flow through the injector which helps in cooling.

Fuel enters the injector through a filter element and passes through internal drillings to a port in

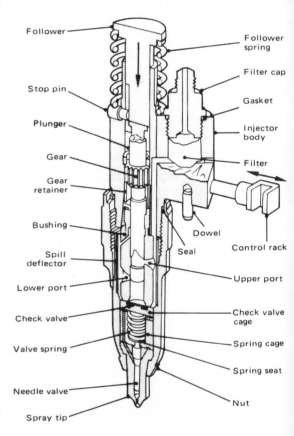

Figure 196  *Fuel injector operated by engine camshaft and rocker assembly which pushes the follower down against the plunger. The control rack from each injector is connected to a common control tube which in turn is connected to the governor. This rack turns the plunger to vary the fuel injected*

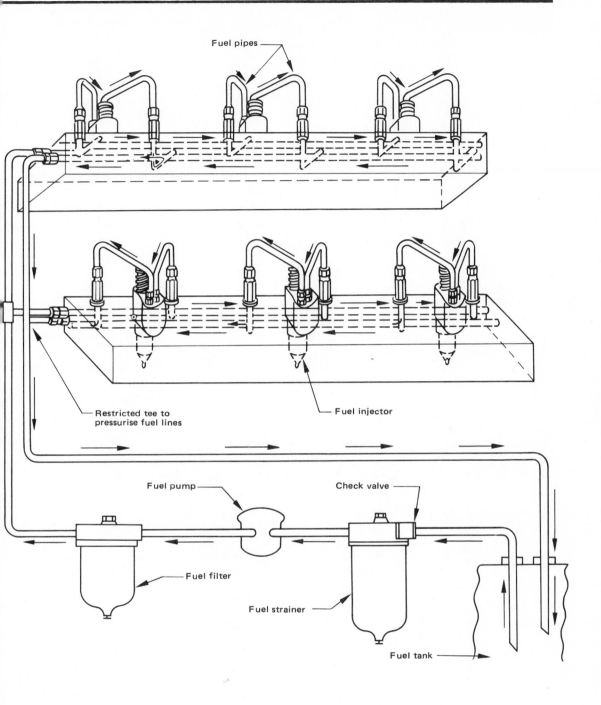

Fuel pipes

Restricted tee to
pressurise fuel lines

Fuel injector

Fuel pump

Check valve

Fuel filter

Fuel strainer

Fuel tank

Figure 197   *Layout of a typical fuel systme for a V6 Detroit diesel*

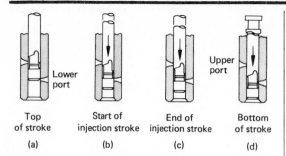

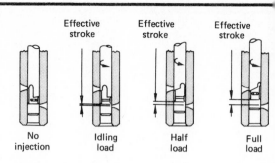

Figure 198   *Phases of injection:*
*(a)   When the plunger is at the top of its stroke, fuel fills the area below and surrounding the plunger*
*(b)   As the plunger is pushed downwards, the lower end closes the lowest port, but fuel can escape through the central drilling in the plunger and out through the upper port. When this upper port is closed, injection commences*
*(c)   Further downward movement of the plunger uncovers the lower part by the lower helix. This allows fuel to escape back into the supply chamber and injection ceases*
*(d)   When the plunger reaches the bottom of its stroke, the return spring lifts it ready for the next injection*

Figure 199   *Fuel metering from stop position to full load*
*Changing the position of the helices in relation to the upper and lower ports by rotating the plunger advances or retards the commencement and ending of injection. This also increases or decreases the amount of fuel injected. When the control rack is pulled fully out, the upper port is not closed by the helix until after the lower port is uncovered, this therefore gives no injection of fuel. When the rack is pushed fully in, the upper port is closed which produced a maximum effective stroke and therefore maximum fuel injected. Between these two positions the effective length of stroke is varied by rotating the plunger to give varying amounts of fuel injection*

the plunger bushing. When the plunger is at the top of its stroke, fuel enters the area under the plunger, through a central drilling in the plunger and then passes through a second port to return to the fuel tank. This continuous flow of fuel through the injector prevents air pockets forming and also allows corner bleeding of the fuel system when any part is disturbed. Metering of the fuel is achieved by a machined helix on the plunger. As the plunger is rotated by the governor, the position of the helix in relation to the ports in the plunger bushing controls the amount of fuel passed to the injector nozzle. The nozzle part of the injector acts as a conventional injector, i.e. fuel pressure lifts the needle against spring pressure (see Figures 198, 199 and 200).

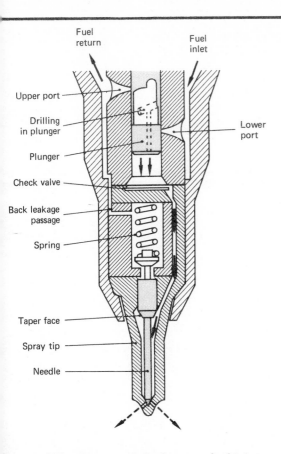

Figure 200   *Section of the lower end of injector*
*showing commencement of injection*
*When sufficient pressure is built up, the flat, non-*
*return valve is opened and fuel passes into the*
*sprayer tip. Pressure acting against the taper face of*
*the needle valve lifts it off its seat and fuel is forced*
*through the small orifices in the spray tip and*
*atomized into the combustion chamber*

# 6 Transmission system

A heavy vehicle is designed to carry a load. This load may vary from large bulky objects with little weight to smaller denser items that are very heavy. The roads which carry these loads also vary from long straight motorway-type highways to narrow steep roads leading to a quarry. This means that the torque developed by an engine needs to be adapted according to the nature of the load a vehicle carries and the road conditions before being allowed to drive the rear wheels.

This means that the transmission system varies according to the conditions that the heavy vehicle is likely to meet. It also means that many various combinations of clutch, gearbox and rear axle are used to provide the specific requirements of a vehicle.

## Clutch

A clutch has to transmit torque from the engine to the gearbox and yet be easily disengaged. One of the most vigorous tasks which a clutch has to perform is to apply the high torque and speed from the engine to the gearbox when the vehicle is moving away from rest. On a heavy vehicle which is fully laden this is a tremendous force to be transmitted, and can only be achieved by a clamping pressure of up to 2 tonnes.

### Single-plate clutch (Figures 201 and 202)

The most common type of clutch used is a single-plate, coil spring dry clutch; this varies in size and number of springs according to torque requirements. It consists of a single driven plate clamped between the flywheel and the pressure plate by a ring of coil springs which are held in the compressed state by the clutch cover.

A further development which reduces friction and maintains better balance is to drive the pressure plate by four groups of laminated spring steel straps. One end of this strap is bolted to the pressure plate and the other end is riveted to the clutch cover.

### Multi-plate clutch (Figure 203)

These usually have two driven plates lined on each side to give four friction faces. A second driven plate between these two driven plates is driven by the clutch cover. The increase in the number of friction faces increases the torque-carrying capacity of the clutch assembly.

### Diaphragm spring clutch (Figures 204)

This is becoming increasingly popular in light commercial vehicles where its characteristics and advantages are more suitable. The clamping pressure of this type of clutch is obtained by compressing the spring – shaped like a saucer without its middle – between the pressure plate and clutch cover. When assembled to the flywheel this normal shape is flattened out. As the clutch pedal is depressed, the spring is pushed towards the flywheel which withdraws the pressure plate and the spring assumes the shape shown in Figure 204b.

Advantages of diaphragm spring clutch over coil spring type are:

1 It is more compact – no long coil springs to accommodate.
2 The clamping load against driven plate increases as lining wears.
3 Easily balanced – flat spring requires no separate release levers.
4 Lower pedal force needed.

Figure 201 *Single-plate clutch*

1 CAST IRON PRESSURE PLATE. Constructed of massive proportions to aid in heat dissipation and where weight is a virtue. It is located and carried in slots formed in the clutch cover.

2 RELEASE LEVER STRUTS. Fitted between the release levers and the pressure plate, they operate on the knife-edge principle, thus reducing friction to a minimum.

3 EYE BOLT FULCRUM PINS. This pin is a rolling fit in the eye bolt and release lever - again reducing friction to an absolute minimum.

4 ADJUSTABLE EYE BOLTS. The original setting of the release levers is made by this means and they are then permanently locked in position.

5 RELEASE LEVERS. Manufactured from steel pressings for extra strength and lightness. A feature which reduces centrifugal loading.

6 RELEASE LEVER PLATE. Carried on the inner ends of the release levers and retained in position by specially formed springs.

7 THRUST SPRINGS. Carried on raised platforms on the back of the pressure plate for heat insulation.

8 PRESSED STEEL COVER. Of great strength and rigidity combined with light weight. The bolting lands and holes provide ample ventilation. Suitable for the flat faced flywheel which lends itself to volume production methods.

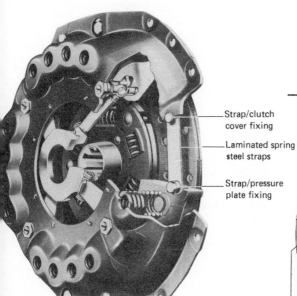

Strap/clutch cover fixing

Laminated spring steel straps

Strap/pressure plate fixing

Figure 202 *Single-plate clutch with laminated spring steel straps*

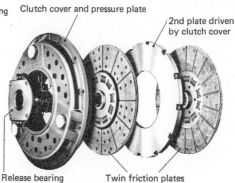

Clutch cover and pressure plate

2nd plate driven by clutch cover

Release bearing

Twin friction plates

Figure 203 *Multi-plate clutch*

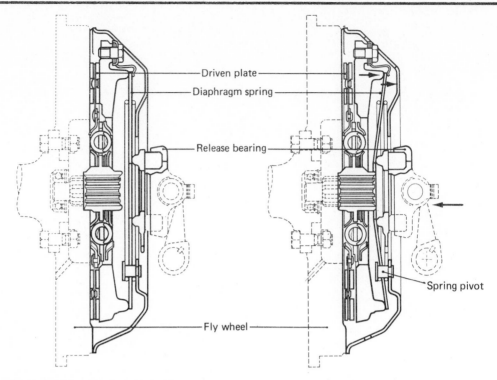

Figure 204   *Diaphragm spring clutch:* (a) *engaged position;* (b) *released position*

### Driven plates

These are clamped between the flywheel and the pressure plate with friction faces to allow gradual engagement to be achieved. The centre or hub is splined and free to move along the splined primary shaft to the gearbox.

To enable a smoother 'take-up' of drive and to allow the friction faces to bed in satisfactorily, a series of cushion springs are fitted between the friction linings. These also allow the clutch to be taken up at lower engine speeds and therefore increase the life of the linings.

The damper springs, fitted between the hub and friction faces, also help to transmit torque more smoothly during take-up and help to eliminate torsional vibrations from the flywheel. These springs are working whilst the vehicle is being driven and therefore help to relieve the rest of the transmission line from these torsional shocks. A driven plate is shown in Figure 205.

### Clutch brakes or stops (Figure 206)

When a clutch is disengaged with the engine running, the driven plate tends to keep revolving and therefore make gear engagement difficult. With heavy goods vehicle clutches, the size and weight of the driven plate may make gear changes impossible. To overcome this problem a small disc brake is often incorporated between the release bearing and the primary shaft. This does not contact when the clutch is only just disengaged because when changing down a ratio the driven plate needs to be speeded up to match the speed of the gears in the gearbox.

### Friction material

Because of tremendous heat and pressures that a driven plate has to withstand, the friction linings must be capable of working under these arduous conditions. Woven asbestos with a small amount of brass or zinc and specially sintered ceramic materials are used (see Figure 207).

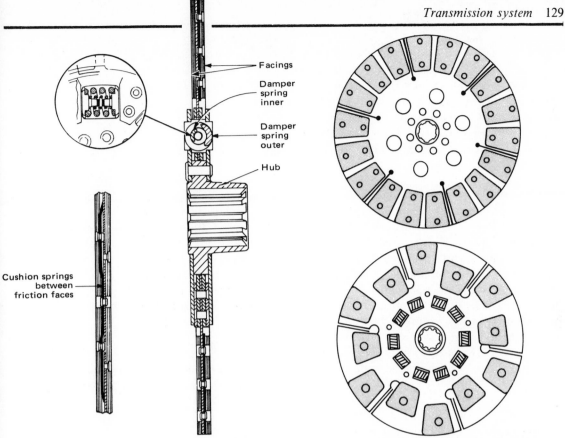

Facings

Damper spring inner

Damper spring outer

Hub

Cushion springs between friction faces

Figure 205    *A driven plate*

Figure 207    *Ceramic or sintered metal pads used as friction material on heavy duty clutches*

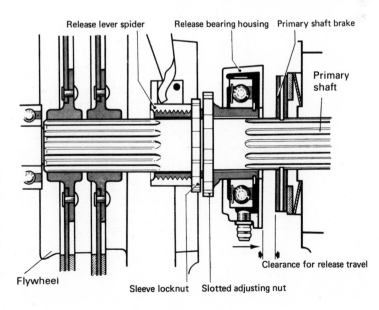

Release lever spider    Release bearing housing    Primary shaft brake

Primary shaft

Flywheel

Sleeve locknut    Slotted adjusting nut

Clearance for release travel

Figure 206    *A multi-plate clutch with a pull-type release bearing – when the clutch pedal is depressed, release bearing is pulled towards transmission. Pedal clearance is adjusted by a screwed adjusting nut. A fibre disc mounted on the transmission acts as a clutch brake by reducing the speed of the primary shaft when the brake pedal is fully depressed*

*Clutch release mechanisms*

Mechanical or hydraulic withdrawal mechanisms are often used with air assistance. The mechanical layout usually comprises a series of rods and levers connected to the release bearing in such a manner as to give an acceptable degree of leverage.

The hydraulic layout consists of a master cylinder and slave cylinder which also may be air-assisted.

*Clutch servo*

This is controlled from the normal type of master cylinder by hydraulic pressure created when the driver operates the clutch pedal. This pressure enters the inlet port to act against the hydraulic piston and the reaction plunger. This causes the plunger to move to the right which closes the air exhaust valve and opens the air inlet valve. Compressed air then passes through the inlet valve, along internal passages to the left-hand side of the air cylinder. Air pressure acts against the air pistons and pushes the push-rod to disengage the clutch.

When the driver holds the clutch pedal depressed, air pressure acting on the reaction plunger overcomes the hydraulic pressure behind the plunger causing the inlet valve to rest and stop any air supply to the cylinder. When the driver releases the clutch pedal, fluid pressure behind the

reaction plunger falls and the plunger return spring moves the plunger to unseat the exhaust valve. This operation releases air from the cylinder to atmosphere and allows the clutch springs to return the push rod to the position shown in Figure 208.

## Manual gearbox

This type of gearbox is probably by far the most common type of gearbox in use in heavy vehicles. The range of gearboxes and combinations of auxiliary or 'splitter' gearboxes make the range of ratios available suitable for any type of vehicle. The simplest – four forward speed with reverse – is still used in light commercial vehicles, but the heavy vehicle is likely to use a 5, 6, 9, 10 or 12 speed gearbox, with range change or splitter facilities.

## Constant mesh gearbox

In this type of gearbox, all the gears are in mesh all the time. The gearbox contains three shafts:
1   Primary shaft.
2   Mainshaft.
3   Layshaft or counter-shaft.

The primary shaft is splined to engage with the clutch centre plate and has one gear which engages with the first gear on the layshaft. The layshaft has

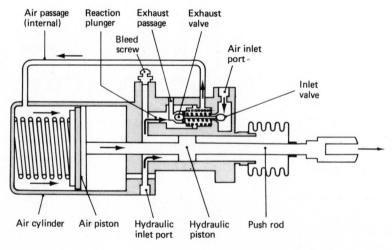

Figure 208   *Clutch servo*

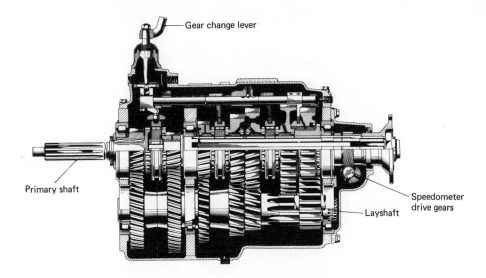

Figure 209    *Constant mesh gearbox with dog-clutch engagement on all six gears*

1  Mainshaft
2  Roller bearing between gear and mainshaft
3  Helical gear meshing with layshaft
4  Splined mainshaft
5  Clutch hub free to slide on splines

6  Sliding sleeve with groove on outside for selector fork, internal teeth mesh with dog teeth (7) to lock gear engaged to mainshaft.
7  Dog teeth which form part of main shaft gear

Figure 210    *Dog-clutch gears*

fixed gears – the number depending upon number of ratios – with a large gear engaged with the primary shaft and diminishing in size down to first and reverse gear at the other end.

The mainshaft has gears in ascending size, to mesh with corresponding gears on the layshaft, but these gears are free to rotate on a bearing on the mainshaft. Between pairs of gears on the mainshaft is a dog clutch which is splined to the mainshaft. The purpose of this dog clutch is to lock the freely rotating mainshaft gear to the clutch hub, and therefore to the mainshaft when a gear ratio is required (Figure 210).

When driving a vehicle fitted with this type of gearbox, the driver – when changing gear – has to match as near as possible, the speed of the gear to be engaged (engine speed) with the dog-clutch gear which is rotating at road wheel speed. To do this, the gear lever is moved to neutral with the clutch depressed, then with the clutch released, the engine speed is increased, the clutch is depressed and the gear engaged. The action is usually referred to as double declutching.

## Synchromesh gears

The layout of this box is very similar to the constant mesh gearbox, but the dog-clutch arrangement is replaced by a synchronizer unit. In a constant mesh gearbox with the dog-clutch arrangement, the driver has to match the speeds of the gears to be engaged by double declutching. In a synchromesh gearbox, this matching of gears is carried out automatically by the synchronizing unit.

*Operation of a lock synchronizer*
Figure 211 shows the synchronizer body splined on to the mainshaft with the gears free to rotate on roller bearings. If top gear were engaged, the path the power would take would be as shown in Figure 212.

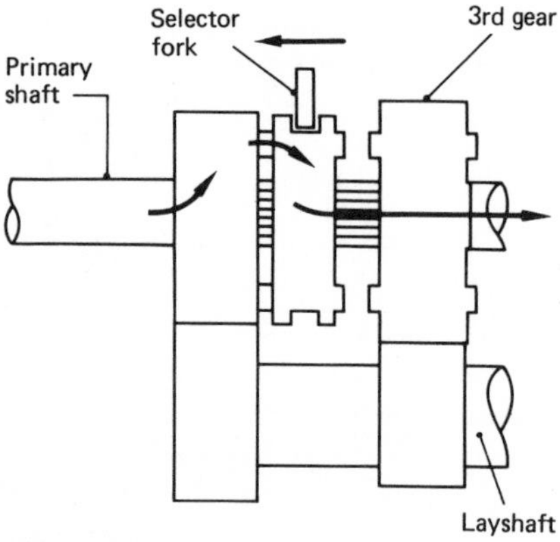

Figure 212   *Lock synchronizer*

1 Synchronizer ring
2 Pressure piece
3 Clutch body
4 Synchronizer body
5 Sliding sleeve

Figure 211   *Synchromesh gear*

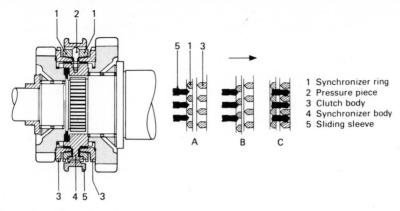

Figure 213 *Operation of synchronizer*

When changing to a lower gear (third), the selector fork moves the sliding sleeve of the synchronizer to the neutral position. At this point, the clutch is already depressed, so that the layshaft – driven by the primary shaft – is turning relatively slowly therefore third gear is also turning relatively slowly. The synchronizer unit, however, is splined to the mainshaft and therefore is being driven by the rear wheels. This means that a positively driven gear has to be meshed with a slowly revolving or stationary gear. The purpose of the synchronizer is to bring the speed of this slow gear to the speed of itself so that a silent meshing can be obtained.

When the sliding sleeve (5) in Figure 213 is moved to the right, the synchronizer ring (1) is pushed over the spring-loaded pressure piece (2) against the friction core of the clutch body (3). Because of the difference in speeds between the clutch body (3), which is connected to the stationary gear, and the synchronizer ring (1) which is part of the synchromesh unit driven by the propeller shaft, the synchronizer ring is moved around radially to assume the position shown at B. As soon as both of these parts have reached the same speed, by the action of the cone clutch, pressure acting against the sliding sleeve (5) by the selector fork allows the chamfered teeth to slide past the synchronizer ring and engage with teeth on the clutch body (3) shown in position C. The freewheeling gear is now locked to the mainshaft to provide third gear ratio.

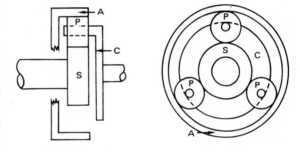

Figure 214 *Epicyclic gear train*

## Automatic gearbox

An automatic gearbox is generally used in specialist vehicles, e.g. fire engines, dumpers and (especially) public service vehicles. To assist the smooth operation of the gearbox, a torque converter is used in place of the friction clutch. Power take-off and transfer gearboxes can be attached as in a mechanical gearbox, and the use of an integral retarder makes the modern automatic gearbox a useful replacement for the mechanical gearbox, particularly in short start–stop working conditions.

The unit consists of planetary gears with hydraulic clutches and brakes to control their action when changing ratios. All the gears in this system are always in mesh and arranged in 'trains' (Figure 214). Each 'train' is built up from three elements:

1   A sun wheel, S.
2   Planet wheels, P, held together by a planet carrier C.
3   Annulus A with gear teeth on the inner circumference.

In a simple gear train, separate ratios can be obtained simply by holding or braking one of the elements (Figure 215):

*a*   If the sun wheel is driven and the annulus is braked, the effect is to drive the planet gears around the annulus and the planet carrier provides an output.
*b*   If the sun wheel is braked and the annulus driven, the planet carrier is again driven but this time around the sun gear to give a different ratio.

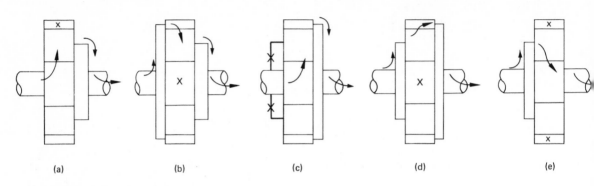

X denotes gears which are held

Figure 215   *A simple gear train*

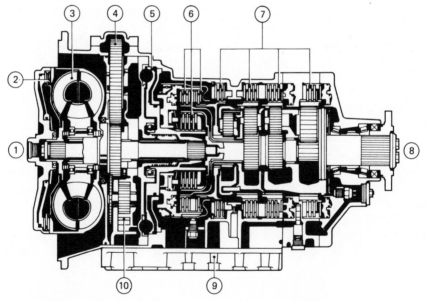

| 1 | Input | 6 | Clutches |
|---|-------|---|----------|
| 2 | Direct drive clutch | 7 | Brakes |
| 3 | Torque converter | 8 | Output |
| 4 | Drive gears for engine driven auxiliary power take-off | 9 | Oil pan and control unit |
| 5 | Retarder | 10 | Oil pump |

Figure 216   *Layout of automatic gearbox with torque converter and hydraulic retarder*

*c* If the planet carrier is braked and the sun wheel driven, the annulus is driven in a reverse direction – the planet wheels being idler wheels only – and reverse ratio is obtained.

*d* If the planet carrier is driven and the sun wheel held, a further output ratio is obtained.

*e* A final ratio is obtained when the planet carrier is driven with the annulus held.

### *Fluid flywheel*

This is a unit that replaces the clutch and operates automatically according to speed of rotation. In its simplest form the fluid flywheel consists of two members, one driven by the engine and the other splined to the primary shaft to drive the gearbox. Both halves are very similar in construction – the driving member consists of several carefully shaped chambers and the driven member is made up of many 'vanes'.

The whole unit is submerged in oil which provides the driving force. When the driving member rotates, i.e. engine running, oil is moved by centrifugal force in the direction shown in Figure 217. This is then directed across the vanes of the driven member at a pre-determined angle to strike the side of each vane. This second member is then moved according to the force applied by the oil. At low engine speeds the force is insufficient to move the second member, which, via the transmission, is indirectly connected to the rear wheels.

This therefore has the same effect as a conventional clutch with the pedal depressed.

As engine speed increases, centrifugal force within the moving oil increases, and therefore the second member has an increasing force applied to its various 'vanes'. This then begins to turn with a comparable effect to a conventional clutch slipping when the pedal is gradually released.

At engine speeds above 800–1000 rev/min, the force of the oil between the driving and driven members is so great that both are revolving at almost the same speed, and the oil is moving so very quickly between them that it would appear as an almost solid mass which is very difficult to shear, and therefore slip between the two halves is almost eliminated.

This type of fluid coupling provides a simple connection between the engine and gearbox with little maintenance apart from topping up with oil and very little to wear out apart from oil seals and bearings. A more efficient type of hydraulic coupling is usually used on automatic gearboxes because of its ability to increase the torque output of an engine at low speeds. This is a very similar type of hydraulic coupling but incorporates a converter which has the ability to increase engine torque.

### *Single-stage torque converter*

This comprises three main items as shown in

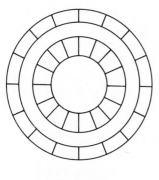

Driving member
or impeller

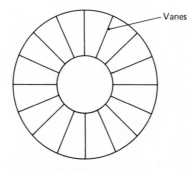

Vanes

Driven member
or turbine

1 Oil gains momentum from rotating engine

2 Oil force through narrow throat at high speed

3 Oil hits vanes of turbine and drives it in same direction. Returns to be picked up at 1. again

Figure 217 *Simple fluid flywheel*

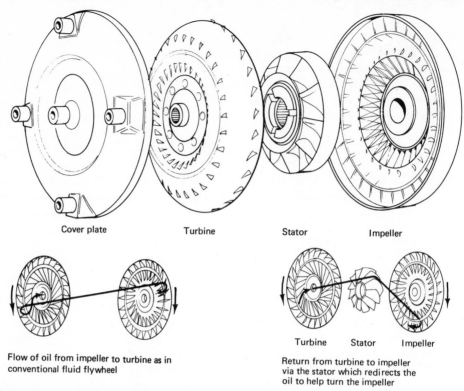

Cover plate          Turbine          Stator          Impeller

Flow of oil from impeller to turbine as in
conventional fluid flywheel

Turbine     Stator     Impeller

Return from turbine to impeller
via the stator which redirects the
oil to help turn the impeller

Figure 218    *Flow of oil from impeller to turbine*

Figure 218. The impeller which is driven by the engine consists of several chambers as in a simple fluid flywheel which acts as a pump to throw the oil against the turbine whose blades are pushed by the force of oil and therefore transmit torque to the gearbox. Between these two units is fitted the stator which consists of a further set of blades which are positioned to redirect the oil from the turbine on to the back of the impeller vanes which make up the chambers. It is this action which gives the increase in torque to the engine.

At low engine speeds the velocity of the oil is insufficient to move the turbine. As engine speed increases, the velocity of the oil increases which begins to move the turbine. As it is leaving the turbine it still has considerable velocity therefore the stator, which is stationary, redirects the oil so that it hits the back of the impeller which pushes it in the same direction of rotation as the engine and therefore increases the torque. It is then re-energized by the impeller and passes around the circuit again. Maximum torque multiplication is achieved when the turbine is stationary with a relatively high engine speed. As the speed of the impeller and the turbine become similar, the oil leaving the turbine hits the stator at a different angle and moves it in the same direction as the impeller and turbine so that the torque converter is now acting like a simple fluid flywheel.

Torque multiplication at low speeds can be in the ratio of $2\frac{1}{2}$:1. A further increase in torque can be achieved by using a multi-storage converter which operates in a similar way but with more stators to give added torque in two or three stages.

If the turbine section is being driven, because this is splined to the gearbox input shaft (an over-run condition would tend to do this), a free wheel is provided in the centre of the stator which is operated by a series of sprags located between two concentric tracks (Figure 219).

Figure 219 *Sprag clutch used as a free wheel*

available to a larger range of speeds with closer ratios.

In the type shown in Figure 220a, the arrangement allows the normal operation of the gearbox, i.e. the primary shaft gear in constant mesh with the countershaft gear. When the 'split' is operating, the synchronizer releases the primary gear in the main gearbox and locks the floating primary gear (Figure 220b) to the reduction gear and drives the countershaft at higher speeds.

## Splitter gearbox

A splitter box is a conventional four- or five-speed gearbox – constant mesh or synchromesh – with additional gearing which doubles (splits) the number of speeds of the main gearbox. This will allow maximum engine torque, which is normally limited to a small range of engine speeds and where fuel consumption is at a minimum, to be

### Selection

The selection of the locking synchromesh mechanism is usually carried out by a two-position compressed air cylinder. Each splitter change is preselected by the selector valve on the gear lever and a release valve, attached to the clutch release mechanism, releases the compressed

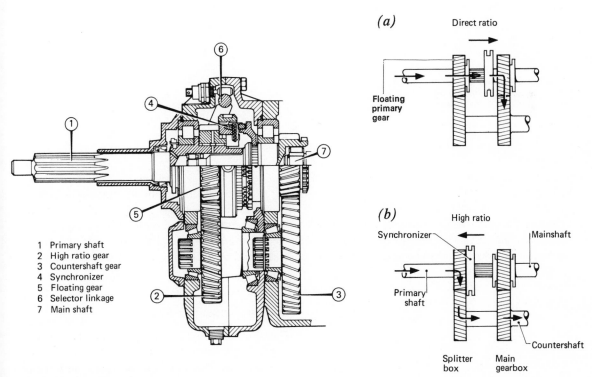

1  Primary shaft
2  High ratio gear
3  Countershaft gear
4  Synchronizer
5  Floating gear
6  Selector linkage
7  Main shaft

Figure 220　*Splitter gearbox*

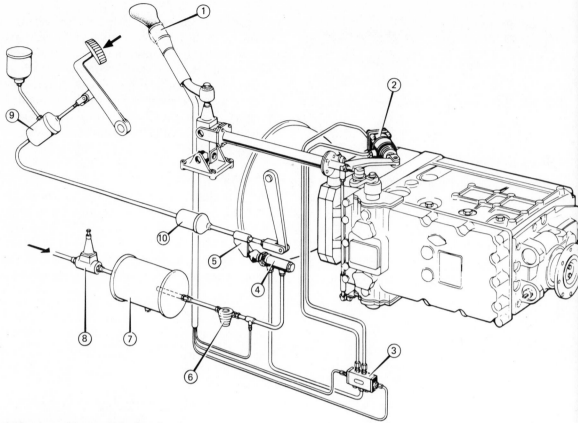

1   Gear lever with control valve for splitter box
2   Two position air cylinder for splitter selection
3   Relay valve
4   Release valve for splitter selection
5   Actuator on clutch release linkage
6   Air cleaner and water separator
7   Air storage tank
8   Relief valve
9   Clutch master cylinder
10  Clutch slave cylinder

Figure 221   *Clutch operation, gear and splitter selection. The gear lever operates the gearbox in the normal way. The actuator (5) on the clutch release lever operates the release valve (4) for a preselected 'split' change when the clutch pedal is fully depressed*

air to the selector cylinder, but not before the clutch is fully disengaged (Figure 221). This means that the clutch pedal should be fully depressed and held until both the splitter box and the normal gearbox controls have carried out a 'clean' gear change.

## Range change gearbox

An alternative to the splitter arrangement is to use a planetary auxiliary unit, attached to the rear of the gearbox, that doubles the speeds of the main gearbox. The range of speeds in the main gearbox is used twice – the first time with the auxiliary unit in low range. The ratio of the auxiliary unit is then changed and the speeds of the main gearbox are used again.

*Operation*

The main gearbox drives the sun wheel of the planetary unit and the shaft connected to the planet wheel carrier is the output shaft (Figure 223).

On starting and in the low range, the sun wheel drives the planet gears with the annulus locked to the gear case by a multi-plate clutch. This will make the planet gears rotate around the inside of the stationary annulus and give a speed reduction to the output shaft (planet carrier). Changing the planetary unit to the high range unlocks the annulus from the gear case. It is then locked to the planet wheel carrier. This makes the whole unit rotate together without any change in speed.

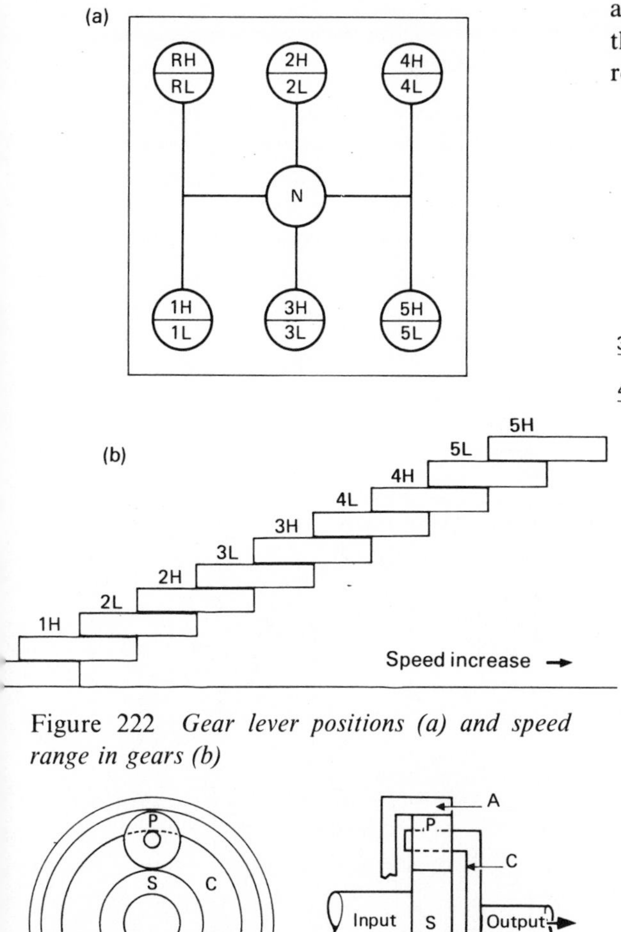

(a)

(b)

Speed increase →

Figure 222  *Gear lever positions (a) and speed range in gears (b)*

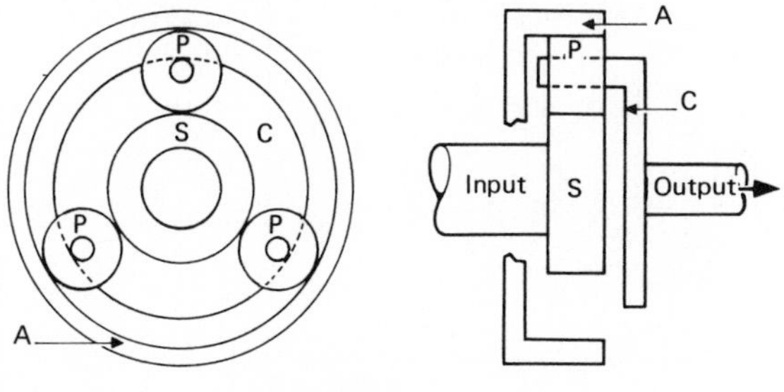

A – Annulus
S – Sun
P – Planet
C – Planet gear carrier

Figure 223  *Planetary auxiliary gearbox layout*

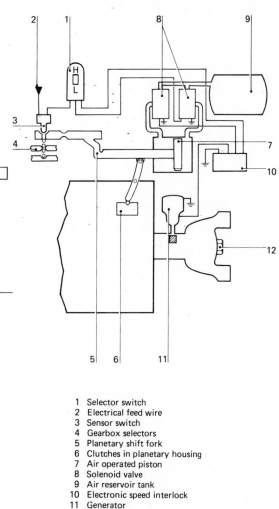

1  Selector switch
2  Electrical feed wire
3  Sensor switch
4  Gearbox selectors
5  Planetary shift fork
6  Clutches in planetary housing
7  Air operated piston
8  Solenoid valve
9  Air reservoir tank
10  Electronic speed interlock
11  Generator
12  Output shaft

Figure 224  *Planetary unit controls*

## Actuation

An air-operated piston (Figure 224) is connected to the shift fork of the planetary unit. The piston is operated by two solenoid valves, one for the high-speed range and the other for the low range. The selector housing of the main gearbox contains a switch which senses the position of the selector shafts. When the gearbox is in neutral, this switch closes the circuit from the electrical input to a switch built into the knob of the gear lever. This switch determines which of the two solenoid valves is to supply compressed air to the operating cylinder of the planetary gear unit. In order to avoid the risk of changing down from the high to low range at high speeds, the circuit between the switch and the solenoid valve for the low range passes through an electronic speed interlock that is also connected to a generator on the output side of the planetary unit. If the speed of the truck is too high to change speed, the generator output will be too high and the speed interlock will not allow the signal to the solenoid valve to pass and therefore prevent the unit to change ratio.

## Power take-off

In order to drive auxiliary equipment, e.g. pumps, winches and mixers, a separate drive controlled by the driver can be fitted to most types of gearbox (Figure 226). The unit is driven by a gear which is usually meshed with a gear on the countershaft.

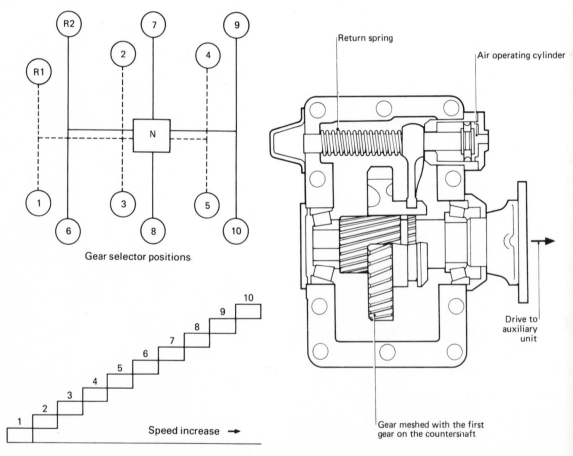

Figure 225   *Speed range in gears*

Figure 226   *Power take-off unit*

This means that the unit can operate when the vehicle is stationary with the gear lever in neutral or when the vehicle is moving. High or low speed ratios can be used to suit the operating conditions, with mechanical or air engaging mechanisms.

In the unit shown in Figure 226, the power take-off is operated by a push button in the cab. Air is supplied through a solenoid-operated air valve which supplies air to the operating cylinder on the power take-off unit – this should only be done when the clutch is 'dipped'. When disengaging the unit, air is released from the operating cylinder and the return spring pushes the gear out of mesh with the countershaft gear.

## Transfer gearboxes

If more than one axle is being driven – front wheel drive or tandem rear bogie – some means of dividing the torque equally to all axles is required. This dividing torque is provided by the transfer box which is usually mounted on the chassis between the main gearbox and the first rear axle.

In its simplest form the transfer box simply provides this means of dividing the torque equally to each axle. It can also provide and house further functions or a combination of any of the following:

1  By using a suitable gear ratio provide an increased torque to each axle.
2  House a third differential.
3  House a third differential and differential lock.
4  Provide means of disconnecting the front or any axle from the drive line.
5  Provide a transfer differential of torque, e.g. 33% to front axle and 67% torque to rear axle.

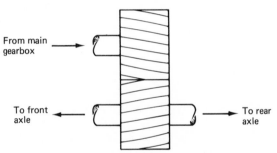

Figure 227  *Simple layout of transfer box with drive equal to front and rear axle with no reduction*

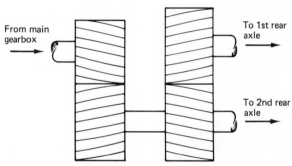

Figure 228  *Transfer box with reduction gear and drive to tandem axle layout*

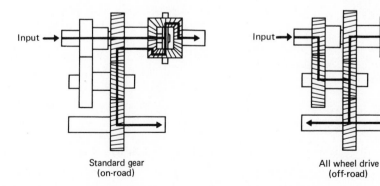

Figure 229  *Transfer box with drive to three axles, also incorporating a third differential*

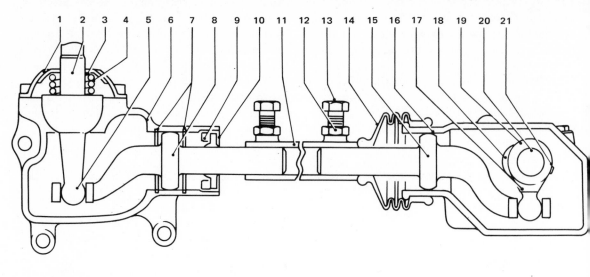

| 1 | Cover | 7 | O-rings | 12 | Lock nut | 17 | Gear shifter |
|---|---|---|---|---|---|---|---|
| 2 | Gear lever | 8 | Shifter rod | 13 | Locking screw | 18 | Bush |
| 3 | Damping plate | 9 | Seal | 14 | Rubber gaiter | 19 | Ball collar |
| 4 | Spring | 10 | Metal ring | 15 | Shifter rod | 20 | Side control shaft |
| 5 | Ball end of gear lever | 11 | Tube for adjustment | 16 | Casing | 21 | Locking screw |
| 6 | Casing | | | | | | |

Figure 230    *Remote control for gearbox*

## Gearbox controls

Gear selection can be by:
1  Direct acting gear level.
2  Remote control gear lever.
3  Pneumatic assistance.

Irrespective of the method used to operate the selector mechanism, the method used to move the dog-clutch or synchromesh hub is basically the same. A selector fork or gear shifter moves the gear and this is fastened to a selector shaft; several shafts are used depending upon the number of gear ratios and these are held in a separate frame or housing.

Also incorporated within the selector housing is a device that holds the dog-clutch or synchromesh hub in the engaged or neutral position (Figure 231a) and a further device which prevents more than one gear from being engaged at any one time – this is usually referred to as the interlock mechanism (Figure 231b).

### Propeller shafts and universal joints

The propeller shaft is usually a hollow shaft, possibly divided into two or more sections, which transmits engine torque from the gearbox to the rear axle. This it must do without vibration and be able to allow for movement of the suspension.

### Hotchkiss drive (Figure 232)

This is the most common layout between the gearbox and rear axle and consists of a rear axle supported by semi-elliptic springs with a swinging shackle at the rear support. At each end of the propeller shaft is a Hooke's coupling or universal joint, and a telescopic or sliding joint at the front. The greater the distance between gearbox and rear axle the more supports are required to prevent vibration and 'whip' in the propeller shaft.

*Sliding joint (Figure 233)*   In order to allow for changes in length of the propeller shaft when the suspension deflects, the front end of the shaft is

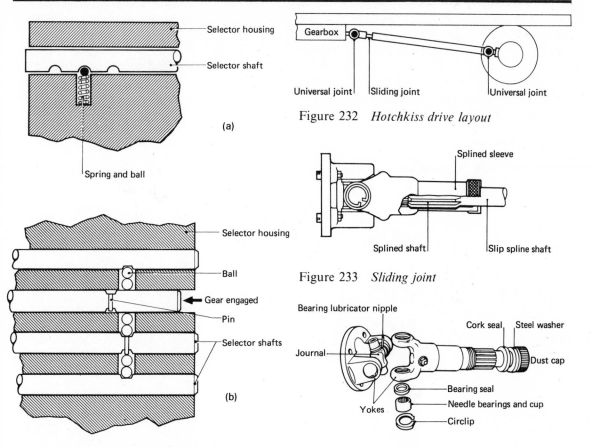

(a)

Figure 232 *Hotchkiss drive layout*

Figure 233 *Sliding joint*

(b)

Figure 231 *Spring-loaded ball holding gear in position (a) and interlock mechanism (b)*

Figure 234 *Universal joint*

splined to the yoke of the universal joint. This is lubricated and usually allows 50–75 mm of movement for the propeller shaft to be lengthened or shortened as the springs are deflected.

*Universal joint (Figure 234)* This is a flexible joint which allows the propeller shaft to transmit torque from the gearbox at an angle which varies according to the position of the rear axle. The joint consists of a spider with cups carrying needle roller bearings which hold the ends of the spider in the yoke on the propeller shaft and in the yoke attached to the flange.

A universal joint is a non-contact velocity joint which means that if the torque is being transmitted through an angle by the universal joint, the speed of the output shaft fluctuates during each revolution even though the input shaft rotates at a constant speed. The greater the angle between the two shafts, the larger the fluctuation of speed of the output shaft. When two universal joints are fitted to a shaft, by correct alignment of the yokes of the universal joints the fluctuation of speed of one joint is balanced by the corresponding phase of the second joint. This means that, if the propeller shaft can be separated at the sliding joint, it is important that it is replaced so that both yokes are in line. Vibration and damage could occur as a result of out-of-phase joints.

A constant velocity joint is a more complicated

type of coupling whereby the velocity of the input shaft and the velocity of the output shaft are always the same throughout each revolution, irrespective of the angle between the two shafts. This type of joint would be used in a front wheel drive vehicle, where a universal joint is required to allow the front driving wheels to turn for steering purposes (Figure 235).

*Centre or support bearings (Figure 236)*   With long wheel-base vehicles, one or more support bearings are required to hold the propeller shaft.

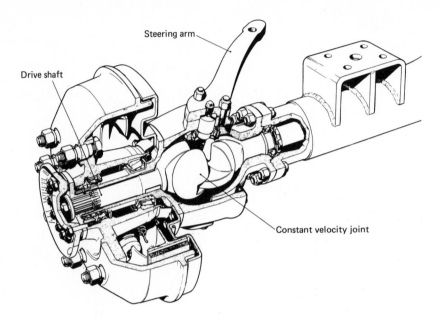

Figure 235   *'Tracta' type constant-velocity universal joint fitted to a front wheel drive axle*

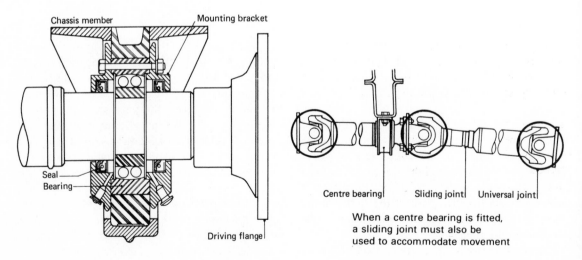

Figure 236   *Sectioned view of centre bearing*

These bearings consist of a ball-type bearing inside a flexible rubber sleeve which is attached to a chassis cross member by a bracket or steel strap.

Figure 237   *Banjo axle construction*

## Rear axle

The rear axle is where the final increase in torque and decrease in engine speed takes place. Because of the large-diameter wheels required to carry the heavy loads, a very high torque is required at the end of the half shaft to turn the wheels and propel the vehicle. The axle casing is usually a banjo-type casting with support bearings for the rear wheels at each end and a detachable casting which houses the differential gears and crown wheel assembly.

On light commercial vehicles, a conventional spiral bevel of hypoid-type rear axle construction is used. As the load-carrying capacity of the vehicle increases, the axle ratio also has to be increased to give the required torque at the rear wheels. When this ratio reaches approximately 8:1 the single bevel gear axle gives way to a worm and wheel arrangement or uses a double reduction arrangement to give the desired ratio with increased strength.

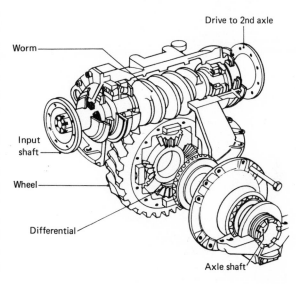

Figure 238   *Worm and wheel axle*

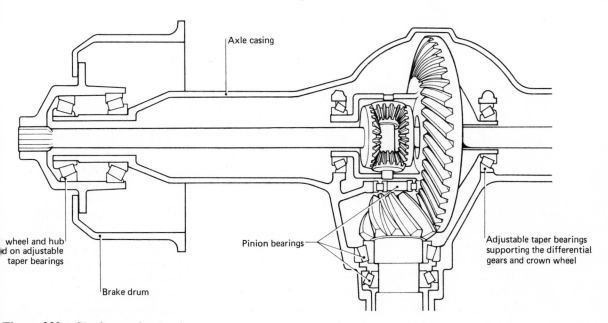

Figure 239   *Single-speed axle*

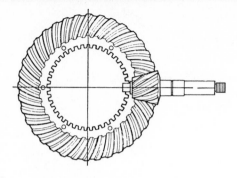

Figure 240(a)    *Spiral bevel axle – pinion on centre line*

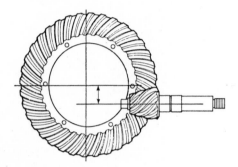

Figure 240(b)    *Hypoid axle – pinion below centre line*

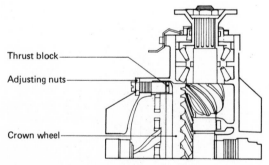

Thrust block
Adjusting nuts
Crown wheel

Figure 241    *Because of the large diameter crown wheel and side thrusts exerted by high torque, a thrust block is often fitted adjacent to the pinion*

### Single-speed axles

The main components of the axle are the reduction gear and the differential assembly. The axle shafts are fully floating with two taper roller bearings on the outside of the axle casing to support the rear wheels. This means that the axle shaft only has to

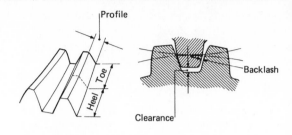

Figure 242(a)    *Backlash adjusted by moving the crown wheel into mesh with the pinion*

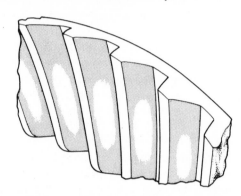

Figure 242(b)    *Correct meshing between the crown wheel and pinion teeth is when the tooth contact is as shown*

take braking and driving torques and in no way supports the vehicle or its load.

### Crown wheel and pinion

These are a matched pair of bevel gears which give the necessary gear reduction and transmit the drive through 90° from the propeller shaft to the rear wheels.

The pinion is supported by two taper roller bearings which are adjusted to the correct pre-load by spacer rings or shims. A pilot roller bearing supports the gear end of the pinion within the axle casing.

The crown wheel is supported by the differential carrier in taper roller bearings, also adjustable to give correct pre-load and correct backlash between crown wheel and pinion. If these adjustments are not accurately set, the axle may 'whine' or wear excessively.

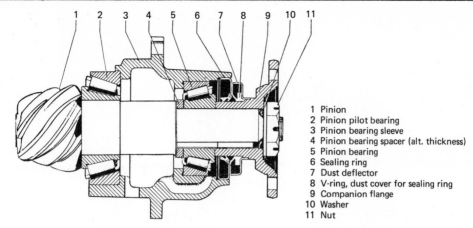

1 Pinion
2 Pinion pilot bearing
3 Pinion bearing sleeve
4 Pinion bearing spacer (alt. thickness)
5 Pinion bearing
6 Sealing ring
7 Dust deflector
8 V-ring, dust cover for sealing ring
9 Companion flange
10 Washer
11 Nut

Figure 243   *The taper roller bearings are pre-loaded by fitting the correct thickness of spacing washer between the two bearings*

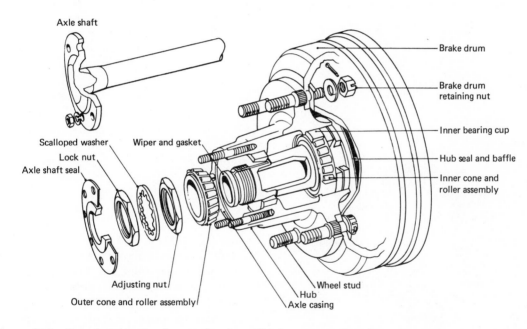

Figure 244   *Rear hub bearing layout showing adjusting nuts and sealing arrangement*

### Double reduction rear axles (Figure 245)

Due to the tremendous torque required to propel a heavy goods vehicle and the large diameter of the rear wheels, the conventional type of rear axle may not be capable of achieving this in a single stage reduction. In order to overcome this, the reduction may be taken in two stages. These extra stages may be taken either immediately before the crown wheel and pinion, immediately after the crown wheel and pinion, or at the rear hubs. When the second reduction is taken at the rear hubs, torsional forces acting on the half shafts are reduced. When taken immediately after the crown wheel and pinion, the loading of crown

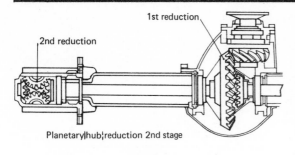

Planetary|hub|reduction 2nd stage

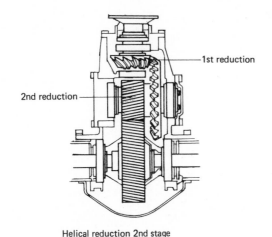

Helical reduction 2nd stage

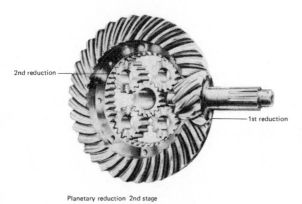

Planetary reduction 2nd stage

Figure 245   *Double reduction gearing*

wheel and pinion gears is reduced. Straight or helical gearing is usually used for the extra stage, but an epicyclic gear train can be used and provides a very compact arrangement particularly when used within the rear hubs.

*Twin driving axles*

In order to comply with legal requirements, the heavier type of goods vehicle may have to have more than one rear axle. This may be a non-driving axle or 'dead' axle which is purely a load-carrying axle or a driven axle which would be able to contribute to propelling the vehicle. This would also mean that maximum use is made of the extra driving wheels when soft ground or slippery conditions are experienced. The arrangement is referred to as a tandem-drive bogie (Figure 246).

*Axle construction*

The axle casing is designed to carry a load via the spring seats and hub bearings and also to house the final drive and differential. The final drive gear arrangement is usually held in a detachable casting which is bolted in front or on top of the main casing. The wheel bearings at each end of the casing support the wheel hub by taper roller bearings fitted to the outside of the casing. The heavy loads carried by these bearings and the side thrusts experienced when the vehicle turns a corner necessitate provision of an adjustment in the form of a nut and lock nut at the end of the axle casing. This allows the elimination of any slackness due to wear, thus increasing the bearing life.

## Differential gears

In order to allow each rear wheel to rotate at different speeds – when cornering, to allow for varying wheel diameters, etc. – but still transmit equal torque to each wheel, a differential gear is incorporated within the reduction gear. This usually consists of a spider with four bevel pinions and two side bevel gears (Figure 247).

*Operation*

When the vehicle is being driven in a straight line, all the bevel gears mounted on the spider (Figure 248a), which is held in the differential housing, are acting as a lever against the side bevel gears. As both the side wheels are splined to each half shaft, they offer the same resistance and the lever action is balanced, so the bevel gears remain stationary.

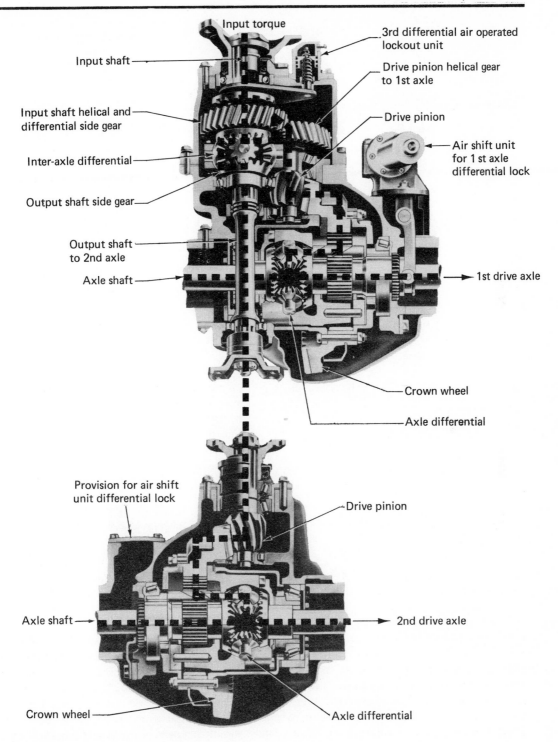

Input torque

3rd differential air operated lockout unit

Input shaft

Drive pinion helical gear to 1st axle

Input shaft helical and differential side gear

Drive pinion

Inter-axle differential

Air shift unit for 1st axle differential lock

Output shaft side gear

Output shaft to 2nd axle

Axle shaft

1st drive axle

Crown wheel

Axle differential

Provision for air shift unit differential lock

Drive pinion

Axle shaft

2nd drive axle

Crown wheel

Axle differential

Figure 246  *Multi-wheel drive arrangements*

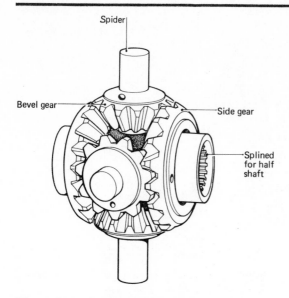

Figure 247    *Differential gears*

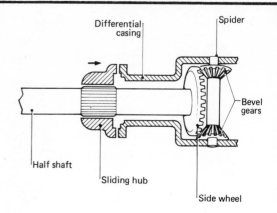

Figure 249    *Differential lock*

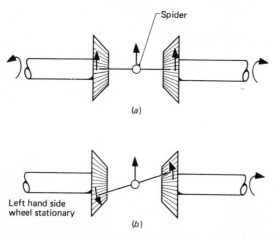

Figure 248    *Equal resistance from both wheels (a) and resistance from one wheel only (b)*

If the vehicle has one of its driving wheels spinning, i.e. because of ice or mud, the lever action on the side wheel is unbalanced (Figure 248b) and the bevel gears begin to rotate against the stationary side wheel, and drive the opposite side wheel as shown. This action does not have any effect on the torque transmitted to the right-hand wheel; it only allows the wheel to turn faster. The left-hand wheel will only turn when there is an increased resistance applied to the right-hand wheel, i.e. if the road wheel can be prevented from spinning, and the balance, as in Figure 248a, is restored. Alternatively, the whole differential can be 'locked'.

*Differential lock*

A vehicle can be provided with a differential lock which would prevent wheel spin when the friction of the road wheels is not equal on both sides. When locked the differential will rotate as a complete unit thus causing both wheels to rotate at the same speed.

When the sliding hub (Figure 249), which is on a splined section of the half shaft, is moved in the direction shown, the half shaft becomes 'locked' to the differential casing. This will prevent the bevel gears rotating independently from the side wheel and prevent any differential action. The operation of the sliding hub can be electrically or pneumatically operated from the driver's cab.

*Third differential*

When more than one axle is being driven, it is usual to fit a differential between these axles to prevent axle wind-up. This is a condition which could exist when a vehicle with two driving axles is being used on hard roads, the transfer box between the two axles divides speed and torque equally between both axles. If one axle had a set of new tyres fitted and the other axle had a set of

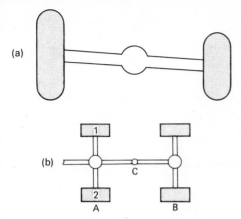

Figure 250    *Third differential operation*

almost smooth tyres, the axle with new tyres would need to be turned at a slower speed than the other axle because of the larger overall diameter of wheels with new tyres.

In the exaggerated example in Figure 250a the right-hand wheel would have to travel faster than the left-hand wheel if it was moving in a straight line. The differential gear would allow this to occur without the differential action 'wind-up' which would put extra stress on the axle and wheels and possibly make a wheel spin in order to catch up, or damage some mechanical component, e.g. half shaft.

In a multi-wheel drive arrangement the same situation would arise. The normal differential gears would allow each wheel to turn at its own speed but a third differential assembly is required to allow each set of wheels, i.e. axle, to turn at their own speed. Without this there would be strain or wind-up between each axle unless the vehicle were travelling on soft ground or across country when each wheel would be able to find its own speed by slipping.

If a vehicle has four driven wheels and each axle is connected via a third differential when only one wheel spins because of ice or soft ground, the vehicle will not move because the differential action divides the torque equally.

Torque required to turn wheel 1 which is spinning is only sufficient to overcome friction, so torque at wheel 2 is the same. Torque required to turn axle A is very small so torque required to turn axle B is also very small because third differential C divides torque equally between the axles. The small amount of torque experienced at the other wheels is insufficient to move the vehicle (Figure 250b).

To overcome this situation, the differentials must be prevented from working or locked. It is possible to fit a lock to all the differentials but this would be expensive, and therefore the third differential is usually fitted with means of locking. In practice, the third differential is usually located in the first drive axle housing.

*Two-speed axles (Figure 251)*

Not to be confused with double-reduction axles which have two fixed-reduction gears, a two-speed axle has a high and low ratio gearing which can be changed by the driver similar to changing a gear in the gearbox. When this unit is fitted, the splitter or auxiliary gearbox fitted to the conventional gearbox is not used but still the gearbox ratios are doubled. This means that the increased torque when in low ratio is not felt by the gearbox or propeller shaft. Because of this change of speed at the rear axle, the speedometer drive ratio has also to be changed otherwise incorrect readings would be obtained. The action of changing the ratio also changes the speedometer drive; an electrically operated or air shift mechanism can be used. Both types of control mechanism are usually fixed to the gear change lever so that axle ratios only can be changed or a 'split' shift can be operated. This means that the axle ratio can be changed at the same time as the gearbox ratio is changed.

The first reduction or high-speed ratio is obtained through the conventional crown wheel and pinion; the second reduction or low-speed ratio is obtained after the crown wheel and usually consists of a planetary gear arrangement within the crown wheel. In high ratio a sliding clutch gear is meshed with the planetary pinions and a locking plate to prevent their rotation, and the drive takes a normal path from the bevel gear crown wheel and pinion to the differential. When low-speed ratio is engaged the sliding gear is moved out of mesh with the locking plate and meshed with a

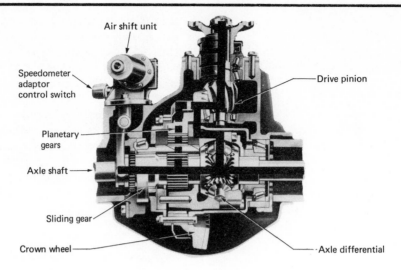

Figure 251    *Two-speed axle*

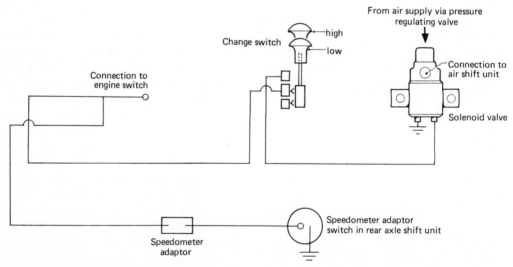

Figure 252    *Layout of circuit for two-speed axle shift*

fixed plate. The pinion gears are then free to rotate around the sliding gear, which now becomes a stationary sun gear. A second reduction now exists between the crown wheel and differential.

*Operation*    In low position, a return spring in the air shift unit moves a sliding gear to lock the planetary unit to the differential and therefore bring a further reduction after the crown wheel

reduction. In high position, an electrical circuit operates the solenoid valve to allow compressed air to flow through the valve and push a piston in the air shaft unit against spring tension. This moves the sliding gear into a position which prevents movement of the planetary pinions and allows normal crown wheel and pinion reduction. In the low position a microswitch energizes the speedometer adaptor to introduce an epicyclic gear reduction and correct the indicated road speed.

*Driving with a two-speed axle*
To shift into low-speed ratio:
1 Keep accelerator pedal down, push button down.
2 To complete shift, disengage and re-engage clutch as quickly as possible, keeping accelerator down.
To shift into high-speed ratio.
1 Keep accelerator pedal down, pull button up.
2 To complete shift, release accelerator and disengage clutch at the same time.

*Split shifting* To shift into next higher gear in the gearbox and at the same time from high to low axle ratio, make the gearbox shift in usual way and, just before engaging the clutch, move the button down. To shift into next lower gear in the gearbox and at the same time from low to high axle ratio, with the accelerator down, move the button up, then complete the gearbox shift in the usual way.

## Lubrication of the transmission

The main components in the transmission system which require lubrication are gears and bearings. In the main it is sufficient if one set of gears dips into the oil as it can then be picked up and thrown about to lubricate all the other gears and bearings. Where this is inadequate, a scoop may be used to pick up oil from a drum wheel which is then fed via troughs or pipes to any bearings that may be inadequately lubricated.

The main function of the lubricant is to prevent wear and to dissipate heat. Because of the very high pressures between the teeth an extreme pressure agent is usually incorporated in transmission oils. This reacts with the metal surfaces to form a protective film which reduces the possibility of metal-to-metal contact. The additive is brought into action by the high temperatures which are developed in these areas. An ordinary type of oil would be squeezed out and result in metal-to-metal contact. Besides a general squeezing action between the teeth, a rolling and

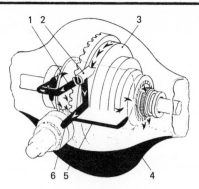

1 Oil channel to differential bearings and planetary gear carrier
2 Oil distributor
3 Oil distributing drum
4 Oil in rear axle casing
5 Oil in planetary gear carrier
6 Oil channel in pinion bearings

Figure 253 *Example of rear axle lubricated by a pick-up tube and distribution troughs*

sliding motion is experienced in hypoid and worm type gears, which further promotes the need for an EP agent.

The viscosity of the transmission oil must be such that it can maintain a film of oil between the wearing surfaces under all operating conditions and temperatures. If an oil is too thick – because of high pressures – it will cause unnecessary power losses and greater generation of heat.

Because of the heat generated within the transmission unit, a breather is usually fitted at the top of the gearbox or rear axle to allow for expansion which may otherwise force oil out through the oil seals.

*Automatic transmission fluids*
The fluid used in an automatic gearbox is a high-quality industrial oil with a viscosity of SAE 5/20. Besides the normal lubricating function, the oil must operate as a hydraulic fluid to control the valve operations, transmit the driving force in the torque convertor and act as a cooling fluid. This means that it has to operate satisfactorily over a wide range of temperatures and operating conditions. No other oil should be used or mixed with automatic transmission fluids.

# 7 Steering and suspension

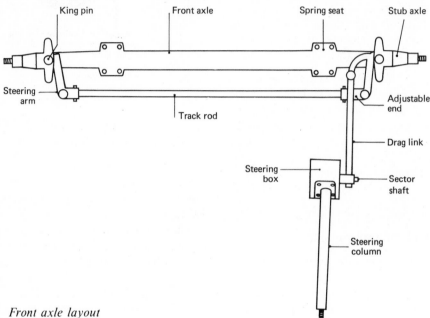

Figure 254  *Front axle layout*

## Steering

Most heavy vehicles employ a solid beam axle for the front axle. This allows a relatively simple steering layout to be used when a single steered axle is used. As the load-carrying capacity of the vehicle is increased, it may be desirable to use twin steered axles. The layout is duplicated for the second steering axle with a linkage to a common steering box.

The main components in a single axle layout are:
1  Front axle assembly.
2  Steering linkages.
3  Steering box.

*Front axle (Figures 254 and 255)*
This is usually an I-section solid beam forging with spring seats for mounting the front springs with an upsweep at each end which is machined to accommodate the swivel pins or stub axles.

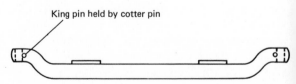

Figure 255  *Reverse Elliot front axle beam*

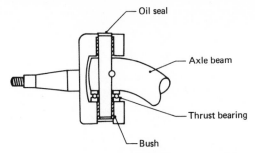

Figure 256 *Stub axle with thrust bearing to support load between axle beam and stub axle*

The most common type used is the reverse Elliot design where the kingpin is held by a tapered cotter pin in the axle end. Because the load acting on the axle beam is transmitted to the road wheel via the stub axle, a tapered roller or similar thrust bearing is fitted between the lower face of the axle and the stub axle.

*Stub axle (Figure 256 and 257)*

Phosphor bronze bushes are fitted between the kingpin and stub axle to give good wearing surfaces. The stub axle provides a mounting for taper roller bearings to support the front hub and road wheel. These are adjustable to accommodate wear. Each stub axle has a fixed arm connected by a track rod which ensures that each wheel is turned through the correct angle. On right-hand drive vehicles, the off-side stub axle also has a steering arm which is connected to the drag link. To allow the wheels to turn, each end of the track rod and drag link is fitted with a ball joint.

All ball joints are screwed into the ends of the steering linkages which means that they can be replaced easily and adjusted to give correct steering alignment. Locking clamps prevent unscrewing. To prevent the wheels from being

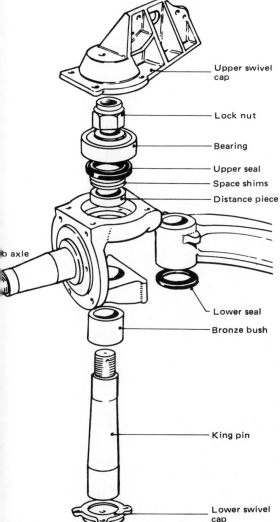

Figure 257 *Exploded view of a stub axle*

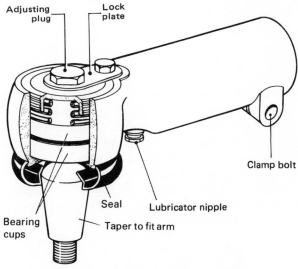

Figure 258 *Adjustable steering connection*

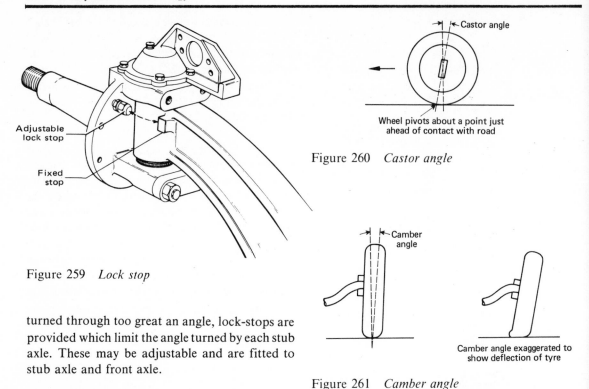

Figure 259    *Lock stop*

Figure 260    *Castor angle*

Figure 261    *Camber angle*

turned through too great an angle, lock-stops are provided which limit the angle turned by each stub axle. These may be adjustable and are fitted to stub axle and front axle.

## Steering geometry

This is the alignment of the road wheels and therefore the stub axles which make sure that the steering is accurate and responsive. Correct alignment will also help to ensure minimum tyre wear. The main angles of steering geometry are concerned with castor, camber, kingpin inclination and Ackerman angle.

*Castor angle (Figure 260)*
This is the inclination of the kingpin towards the rear of the vehicle, which gives the wheel a trailing effect and makes it act very similarly to a castor wheel on a piece of furniture.

In practice the inclination of the kingpin to give castor angle is very small – up to 2° – which means that the wheel pivots about a point just in front of the point of contact between tyre and road surface. The effect of this inclination of the kingpin is to give the steering wheel a self-centring action, which means that if the driver lets go of the steering wheel, the road wheels will return to the straight ahead position. This means that the driver does not have to 'steer' the vehicle when travelling in a straight line. The effect also gives the driver some 'feel' of the position of the road wheels when travelling at speed. It does not affect the manoeuvrability of a vehicle at low speeds as the magnitude of this returning force depends upon the drag force which increases with speed.

*Camber angle (Figure 261)*
This is the inclination of the wheel outwards from the centre of the vehicle. This again is a very small angle – up to 2°. By giving the wheel this inclination, sensitivity through the tyre to the steering wheel is reduced for small movements of the road wheel. Such movements may be experienced when travelling over rough surfaces, e.g. cobbles. Instead of these small movements being transmitted through the steering linkages they are absorbed in the distorted tyre and the vehicle keeps a straight ahead path.

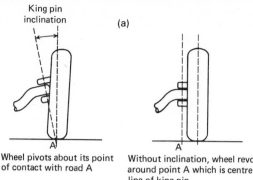

King pin
inclination

(a)

Wheel pivots about its point
of contact with road A

Without inclination, wheel revolves
around point A which is centre
line of king pin

(b)

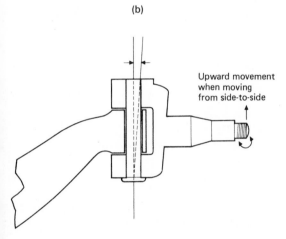

Upward movement
when moving
from side-to-side

Figure 262   *Kingpin inclination*

inclined kingpin the front of the vehicle is slightly raised, and thus the weight of the vehicle tends to help to return the wheels to the straight ahead position (Figure 262b).

*Ackerman angle (Figure 263)*

When a vehicle turns a corner, all the wheels must turn through a common centre in order that they may have a true rolling action and not scrub across the road surface. Although this is impossible to achieve under all conditions, it was found by a man named Ackerman, that by inclining the steering arms towards each other so that a line projected from each kingpin meets at a point on the centre-line of the vehicle just ahead of the rear axle, then almost true rolling action is obtained. The rear wheels are fixed to a solid axle and therefore this centre of rotation must lie on a line projected through the rear axle.

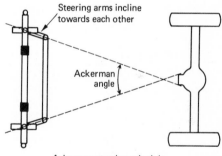

Steering arms incline
towards each other

Ackerman
angle

Ackerman steering principle

*Kingpin inclination (Figure 262)*

This is the inclination of the kingpin towards the centre of the vehicle. A larger angle is usually given – 6–7° for this inclination – in order that the wheel may be 'swivelled' about a point on the road surface. If the kingpin was vertical, the wheel would have to revolve around a point below the centre line of the kingpin. This would lead to very 'heavy' steering, particularly at low speeds, and also a twisting force when the wheels hit a bump or pothole.

This inclination also gives a small amount of self-centring action which is particularly useful at low speeds. When the wheel is turned about the

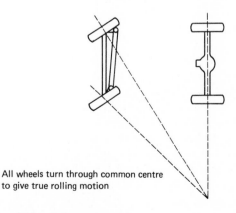

All wheels turn through common centre
to give true rolling motion

Figure 263   *Ackerman angle*

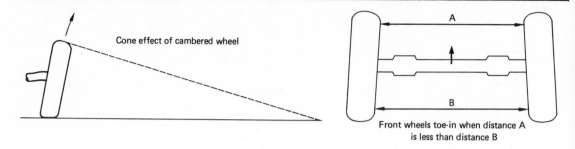

**Figure 264**  *Front wheel alignment*

### Front wheel alignment (Figure 264)

When a vehicle is travelling straight ahead both the front wheels must be parallel otherwise rapid tyre wear will result. Because the wheels are cambered, the cone effect produced by this makes the wheels splay outwards as soon as the vehicle is moved forwards. The track rod prevents this from happening, but any slight play in the track rod ends must be accounted for. This means that the wheels must be set to toe-in when stationary, as soon as they move forward they then assume a straight ahead position.

For twin steered vehicles, when both the front wheels are turned, each axle must have its own Ackerman linkage. This alone does not give true rolling action of all the wheels because the front set of wheels have to turn through different angles from the second set of wheels. In order to achieve this, the connection between the two axles is designed to give a greater degree of turn to the front set of wheels.

When more than one axle is used at the rear of the vehicle, true rolling motion cannot be achieved because these wheels cannot normally be turned. If the centre of rotation was taken along a line through the front of these two axles, the wheels on the rear axle would be subjected to a scrubbing action when the vehicle turned a corner. The further these axles are apart the greater the amount of scrub. In order to even out wear

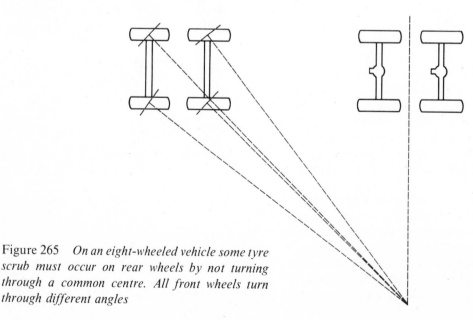

**Figure 265**  *On an eight-wheeled vehicle some tyre scrub must occur on rear wheels by not turning through a common centre. All front wheels turn through different angles*

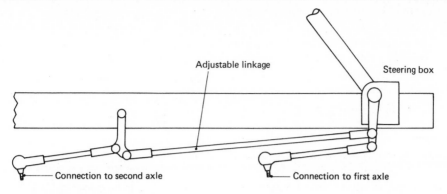

Figure 266   *Linkage between twin steered axles to make all wheels turn through a common centre*

therefore, the axles should be as close together as possible and the centre of rotation taken through a line midway between the axles.

## Steering box

Different types of steering gearbox may be fitted to heavy vehicles but they all perform the same task, and externally look very similar. The reduction which is provided by the steering gear must be suitably chosen to enable the driver to turn the front wheels through approximately 60° with the minimum of effort exerted by the driver at the steering wheel. This means that a ratio of up to 30:1 may be required on heavy goods vehicles which gives a lock to lock turn of six full turns of the steering wheel. Because of the ever-increasing weights carried by heavy vehicles and the greater demands on the driver, many vehicles are adopting some form of power assistance for the steering. This enables the front wheels to be turned with much less effort by the driver and also a reduction in the lock to lock turns of the steering wheel.

By carefully controlling the efficiency of the steering gear a driver is able to experience a degree of 'feel' at the steering wheel without transmitting any road shocks, e.g. when the vehicle hits a bump. A reversible steering assembly allows the steering wheel to be turned by the road wheels when these are lifted off the ground. This means

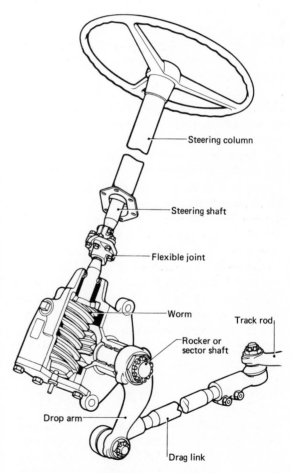

Figure 267   *Steering box assembly*

that all road shocks would be transmitted back to the steering wheel. On the other hand an irreversible steering assembly cannot be turned in this fashion because of the friction and therefore any sense of feel is also lost.

The simplest and earliest form of steering box used on heavy vehicles was the worm and wheel.

### Worm and wheel gear

The worm gear, which is the same principle used as in rear axles, is made from phosphor bronze and is meshed with a steel wheel. As wear occurred, the wheel was able to be turned so that an unworn section could be meshed with the worm, the whole of the wheel not being used at any one time because of the limited movement required to turn the steered wheels.

A natural development from this was to use a worm and sector which only used a section of the wheel and therefore was not as bulky as the original type of box.

This type is not wholly satisfactory mainly because of the high friction forces, but almost all modern steering boxes for heavy vehicles use a worm gear in some form. Meshing with this worm gear however are various devices which keep the frictional forces to a minimum and also provide a certain degree of the reversible characteristics which are not given by the worm and sector type of steering box. The worm, which is mounted at the end of the steering shaft, is usually mounted in taper roller bearings which can be adjusted to the correct pre-load by steel shims. The sector shaft is mounted in phosphor bronze bushes with a taper splined end to hold the steering drop arm. This shaft is also adjustable, to give correct meshing with the gear teeth, by means of shims under the end plate or an adjusting screw and lock nut screwed into the end plate.

### Worm and peg or cam and lever-type steering gear (Figure 270)

Light or medium goods vehicles have a single peg, mounted in roller bearings which engages with the grooved worm gear. This reduces friction to a minimum, as the worm rotates the peg rolls along the groove to move the sector shaft as shown. In

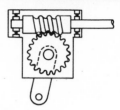

Figure 268    *Worm and wheel steering box*

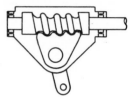

Figure 269    *Worm and sector steering box*

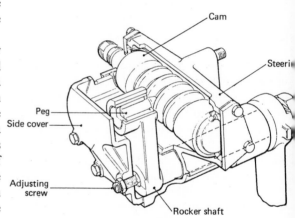

Figure 270    *Cam and lever type steering box*

heavy goods vehicles a double-armed lever is used with two pegs mounted in roller bearings to share out the high loadings experienced, particularly when a twin steer layout is used.

### Worm or cam and roller (Figure 271)

In this type of steering box the worm is shaped like an hour glass to allow the roller to have full engagement throughout its travel. The double or triple roller is mounted on a bush or roller

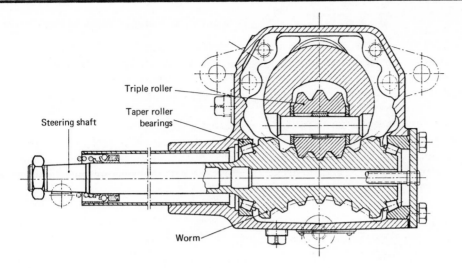

Figure 271   *Cam and roller type steering box*

bearings in the end of the sector shaft. As the worm gear rotates the rollers also rotate, thus keeping frictional resistance to a minimum.

*Recirculating ball steering box (Figure 272)*
A conventional worm gear is again used with a nut travelling from end to end along the 'thread'. The nut is separated from the worm by a series of ball bearings which 'recirculate' as the nut travels along its thread. This also reduces friction and reduces wear between the worm and nut.

## Requirements for power steering

1   Steering must be accurate and free from excess movement.
2   The power assistance must respond immediately the steering wheel is turned.
3   Road feel must be maintained to allow the driver full control of the vehicle.
4   If any fault occurs in the power assistance, the steering must be able to be manually operated.

The effort required to turn the steering wheel on a heavy commercial vehicle may be considerable, particularly when the vehicle is fully laden. Vehicles with twin steered axles have double the number of wheels in contact with the road surface

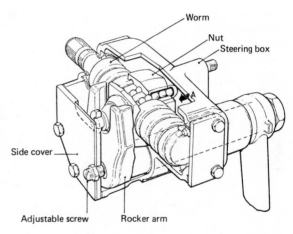

Figure 272   *Recirculating ball type steering gear*

and therefore require an even greater effort. A simple way to overcome this would be to increase the gear ratio of the steering box. This would allow the wheel to be turned more easily but would require more turns of the wheel to move the steered wheels from one full lock to the other. When manoeuvring in confined spaces, when parking or moving slowly in town traffic, this would lead to driver fatigue and may even be dangerous if the vehicle was not capable of rapid steering movements.

In order to make steering wheel movement easy and still retain a low ratio of lock to lock turns, hydraulic or air assistance may be used to boost the effort exerted by the driver. This is usually achieved in one of two ways:

1　By incorporating the booster device inside the steering box (see Figure 273).
2　By using a suitable unit to push against some part of the steering linkage, e.g. drop arm.

## Layout of power steering systems

*Hydraulic assistance*

An engine-driven pump supplies oil under pressure to the assistance unit which gives the desired push against one side of a piston, depending upon the direction turned by the steering wheel.

A very compact arrangement for power-assisted steering is to incorporate the assistance unit integrally with the steering box. In the arrange-

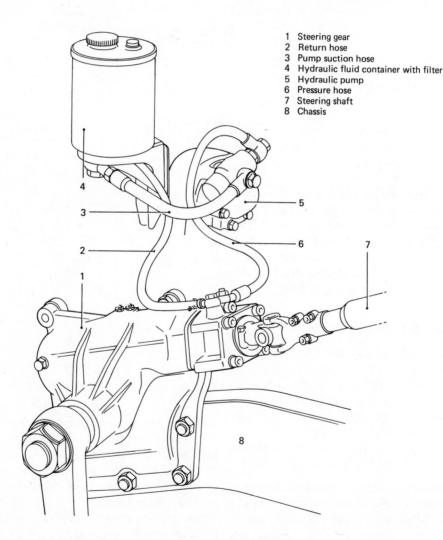

1　Steering gear
2　Return hose
3　Pump suction hose
4　Hydraulic fluid container with filter
5　Hydraulic pump
6　Pressure hose
7　Steering shaft
8　Chassis

Figure 273　*Layout of integral power assisted steering unit*

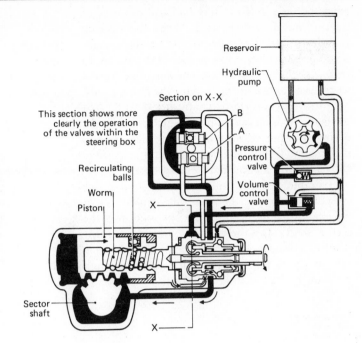

Figure 274 *Operation – left-hand turn – when the steering wheel is turned to the left, valve A is opened and B is closed. This action directs hydraulic fluid to the left-hand side of the cylinder to exert a push against the piston which in turn helps to move the sector shaft and therefore provide assistance. Fluid from the other side of the piston is returned to the reservoir*

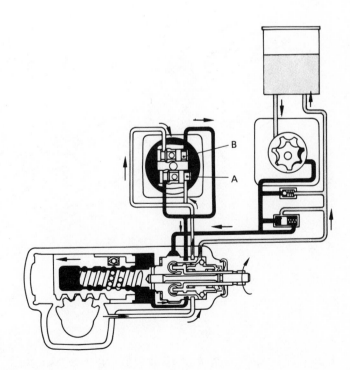

Figure 275 *Operation – right-hand turn – when the steering wheel is turned to the right, valve B is opened and valve A is closed. Hydraulic fluid is then passed to the right-hand side of the cylinder and therefore pushes the piston down the cylinder*

ment shown, a recirculating ball and nut type of steering mechanism is used. When the steering spindle is turned, a valve opens to allow high-pressure fluid to pass to one side of the piston. In this case the piston is the nut surrounding the worm gear and is in mesh with the sector shaft. This hydraulic pressure then pushes the nut up or down the steering gear housing which provides the desired assistance. If this assistance fails, or when the engine is not running, the unit acts as a conventional ball and nut steering box.

Hydraulic steering limiters can be fitted in this type of steering box. These usually consist of two off-loading plungers which are operated from the sector shaft. Just before the working plunger reaches its end position the sector shaft linkage lifts an off-loading plunger which allows the high pressure hydraulic fluid to return to the pump.

A further type of integral power steering unit is shown in Figure 276; this is a column power steering gear. The hydraulic power piston, control mechanism and the mechanical transmission components are fitted to a housing which is also designed as the cylinder for the power piston.

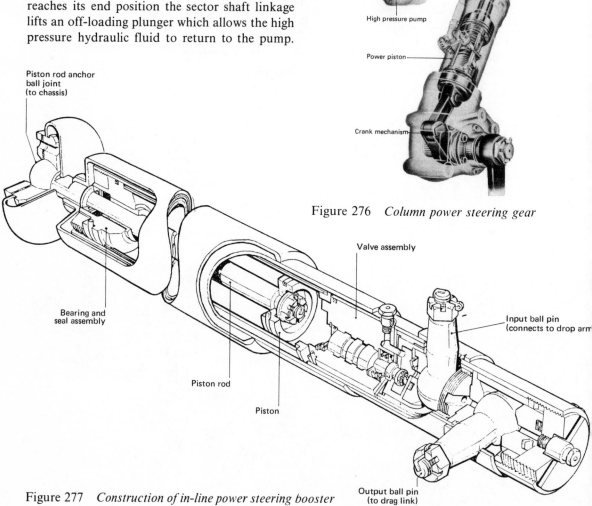

Reservoir

High pressure pump

Power piston

Crank mechanism

Figure 276   *Column power steering gear*

Piston rod anchor ball joint (to chassis)

Bearing and seal assembly

Piston rod

Piston

Valve assembly

Input ball pin (connects to drop arm)

Output ball pin (to drag link)

Figure 277   *Construction of in-line power steering booster*

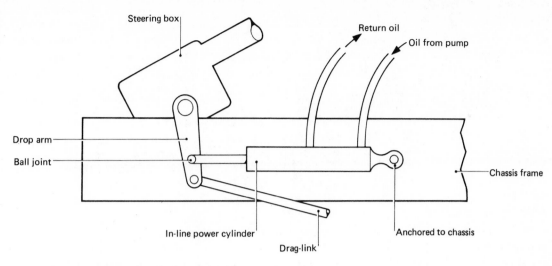

Figure 278(a)   *Connection of in-line booster*

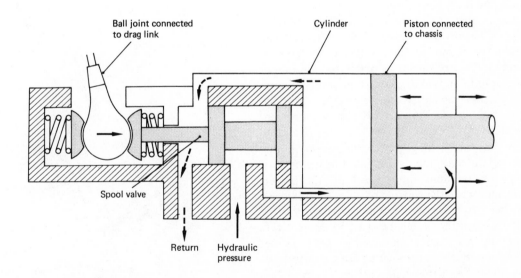

Figure 278(b)   *Principle of operation of in-line booster – when the steering wheel is moved to the right, the ball joint connected to the drop arm moves the spool valve to the right against spring pressure. This allows hydraulic pressure to pass to the rear of the piston, react against the piston and push the cylinder to the right. Fluid from the front of the piston is returned to the reservoir*

*Figure 278(c) – overleaf*

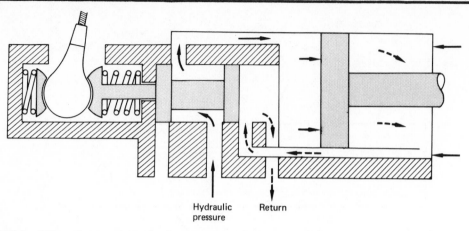

Hydraulic    Return
pressure

Figure 278(c)    *When the steering wheel is turned to the left, the ball joint allows the spring to move the spool valve to the left. This allows hydraulic pressure to pass to the front of the piston, react against it and push the cylinder to the left. Fluid from the rear of the piston returns to the reservoir*

### The engine-driven pump

The pump is usually belt-driven and supplies oil at a maximum pressure up to $10\,000$ kN/m$^2$ (1500 lbf/in$^2$). The pressure is controlled by a relief valve within the pump so that, whilst the engine is running, this pressure is available for use in the booster unit. Should the pump fail, or oil pressure be lost, the vehicle would be steered normally without power assistance. This also occurs when the engine is stopped.

To prevent damage or undue strain in the steering linkages, lock stops fitted to the chassis frame or hydraulic limiters cut off the power assistance when the steering wheel is on full lock.

When an in-line or separate booster device is used, two methods can be used to control the hydraulic assistance. The valve block can be incorporated within the steering box to control the flow of oil from the engine driven pump to the appropriate side of the power cylinder which is connected to the drop arm, or the valve block can be incorporated within the power cylinder. Whichever method is used, movement of the steering wheel moves the valve to open or close corresponding drillings to direct the high-pressure oil to one side of the power cylinder. This force acting against the piston which is fastened to the chassis frame by a ball joint, pushes the cylinder

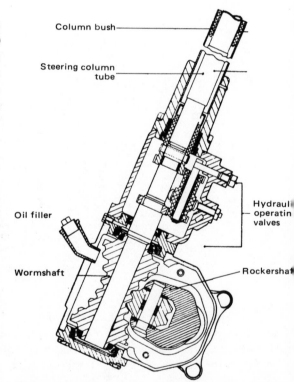

Column bush

Steering column
tube

Oil filler

Wormshaft

Hydraul
operatin
valves

Rockersha

Figure 279    *Cam and roller steering box with hydraulic operating valves which direct oil under pressure to the in-line booster unit which is connected between chassis and drop arm*

against the drop arm to assist the movement of the conventional manual steering box. When the steering wheel is stationary, a compression spring returns the valve to a neutral position and no further oil is passed to the power cylinder.

*Air assistance*

This type uses compressed air which is probably used for power braking in a heavy vehicle. The assistance is provided by a power cylinder connected to the chassis and some part of the steering linkage – usually an arm connected directly to the road wheel. A torque valve is installed in the drag link connection which is a self-centring valve to meter air pressure to the power

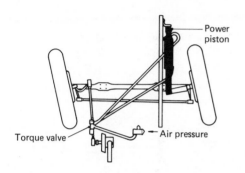

Figure 280   *Layout of air assisted power steering*

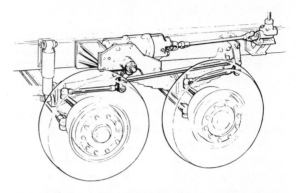

Figure 282   *Steering box mounted between axles gives better turning angles and good steering geometry*

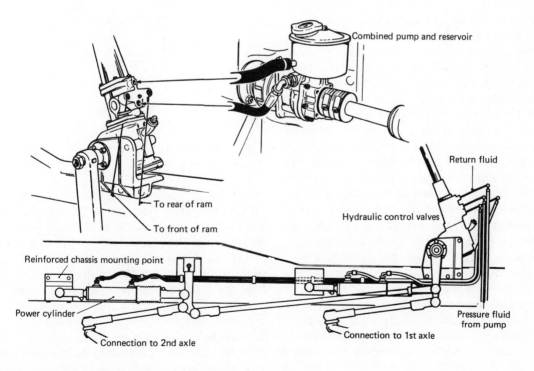

Figure 281   *Layout of power steering for twin steered axles*

cylinder in proportion to the effort applied to the steering wheel. A safety valve is also incorporated which permits manual control to override the air system automatically when air pressure drops below 490 kN/m$^2$ (70 lbf/in$^2$).

## Suspension system

The suspension system separates the axles from the vehicle chassis, so that any road irregularities are not transmitted directly to the driver and the load on the vehicle. This not only allows a more comfortable 'ride', and protection of the load from possible damage, but it also helps to prevent distortion and damage to the chassis frame.

On most heavy vehicles, suspension is by means of laminated leaf springs, but on some special applications rubber or air may be used as the suspension medium. Passenger vehicles often use some form of air suspension to give extra passenger comfort, but this is offset by an increase in cost.

*Laminated leaf spring (Figures 283 and 284)*
This is built up from several layers or leaves commencing from the main leaf and gradually reducing in size. The length, width and number of leaves are decided by the load carried – very heavy springs with a large number of thick leaves are used for carrying very heavy loads, reducing in number as the load-carrying capacity decreases.

The main leaf is rolled into an eye at each end which is then fitted with bushes to accommodate the shackle pin. This is used to connect the spring to the chassis. The second leaf also follows a similar contour to the main leaf to give it extra support. At intervals, as the spring leaves become shorter, clips are fitted to hold the leaves together. The main purpose served by these clips is to support the main leaf when the wheel drops into a 'pot' hole or when the chassis frame carries on rising when the wheel has gone over a bump, i.e. the spring is on rebound. Without these clips the main leaf would be supporting all the weight of the axle assembly and a very high bending load would be applied to the leaf at the 'U' bolt end. A secondary purpose of these clips is to keep the

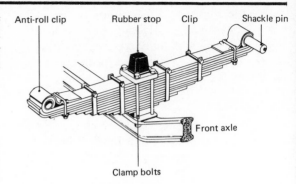

Figure 283   *Laminated leaf springs*

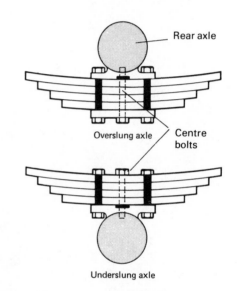

Figure 284   *Rear axle connection to springs*

spring leaves aligned and prevent 'splaying'. A centre bolt passes through all the leaves at the centre of the spring, and its head is used to locate the spring in the axle casing – without this the leaves may slide over each other which would lead to the vehicle 'crabbing'. 'U' bolts or clamp bolts hold the spring on to the axle casing on many vehicles with an overslung axle, but when the axle is fitted beneath the springs – underslung, to lower the loading height or the centre of gravity – the 'U' bolts also carry the load acting on the axle. This means that very high tensile steel must be used and the nuts must be very tightly secured and locked.

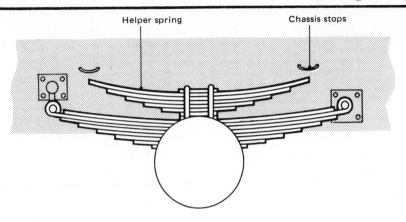

Figure 285   *Helper spring fitted to rear spring*

## Helper spring (Figure 285)

An ideal suspension system would not affect the 'ride' of a vehicle irrespective of whether it is fully laden or unladen. Unfortunately, because of the heavy loads carried by most heavy vehicles, an ideal suspension system is impossible. Large stiff springs are required to support the load and this gives a very harsh 'ride' when the vehicle is unladen. Conversely if the spring were too soft it would deflect too much or break when carrying a full load. The spring 'rate' is the amount of deflection of the spring for a given load. If the spring could have a variable rate it would be possible to stiffen the spring when more load was added and still give an acceptable ride when unladen. On vehicles fitted with laminated leaf springs, this stiffening effect is achieved by fitting a helper spring above the main spring. When lightly loaded the main spring carries the weight but as the load is increased the helper spring contacts spring seats on the chassis and the suspension is stiffened as both the helper and main springs now support the load.

## Single leaf spring (Figure 286)

On many light commercial vehicles, a single leaf spring is often fitted. Modern materials give what is essentially a main leaf, the same strength as a conventional spring which will bend but not break. This has the advantage therefore of reducing the unsprung weight of the vehicle.

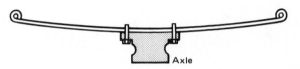

Figure 286   *Single leaf spring*

## Taper leaf spring

This is a single leaf spring which, because of its strength, is able to support up to 16 tonnes. It usually has slipper seatings because it would be difficult to form the ends into an eye. The spring is more suitable for trailer applications where its main purpose is load bearing and it does not have to take braking and driving torque reactions.

## Connections to the chassis (Figures 287 and 288)

Most leaf springs are fixed at the front end of the spring by a shackle pin to a spring hanger bracket which is bolted or riveted to the chassis frame. The rear connections can also be held by shackle pins but are connected to the chassis frame by a swinging linkage which allows the spring to lengthen as the load increases to deflect the spring. All shackle connections use a steel pin with a phosphor bronze bush to act as a bearing surface. An alternative connection which may be used on the rear connection to the chassis frame is a slipper seat. The end of the spring is not formed into an eye but is left

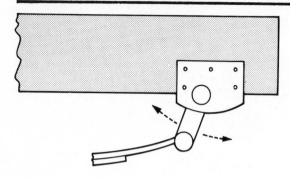

Figure 287 *Swinging shackle connection to chassis*

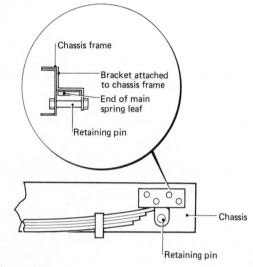

Chassis frame

Bracket attached
to chassis frame

End of main
spring leaf

Retaining pin

Chassis

Retaining pin

Figure 288

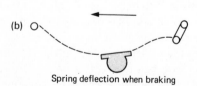

(a)

Spring deflection when accelerating

(b)

Spring deflection when braking

Figure 289 *Spring deflectors when braking and accelerating*

flat which bears on a flat slipper bracket fastened to the chassis frame. This is a much simpler arrangement which also eliminates the need for lubrication but can only be used on the rear connection as the front half of the spring has also to take braking and driving forces.

When accelerating, torque reaction due to the pinion wanting to 'climb around' the crown wheel makes the springs deflect as shown in Figure 289a. It is this same reaction which tends to lift the front end of a vehicle when accelerating very hard. When braking, an opposite torque reaction again deflects the springs in the opposite way (Figure 289b). The front half of the spring also 'pushes' the vehicle forward when the vehicle is being driven in a forward direction and helps to hold it back when braking. This is why the swinging shackle is fitted to the rear of the spring – if fitted to the front it would not give a positive driving and braking connection to the chassis.

*Suspension systems for tandem rear axles*
On heavier goods vehicles, which use two axles at the rear because of the weight regulations, the axles must be mounted as close together as possible in order to eliminate tyre scrub when cornering. The wheels must try to follow a common turning point, but this is impossible when two axles are used. Apart from this, both axles must be interconnected to eliminate overloading of one axle when this goes over a 'bump' (Figure 290).

Various forms of interconnecting linkage are used and some are more effective than others in equalizing the loading under all conditions.

The simplest form of interconnection in a

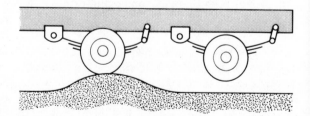

Figure 290 *Exaggerated view showing what would happen if rear axles are not interconnected*

double drive layout is a simple balance beam (walking beam) (see Figure 291) which connects the rear swinging shackle of the forward spring to a swinging shackle on the front of the rear spring. When the front axle negotiates a bump the balance beam pivots at the centre and allows load equalization on each axle to the limit of travel of the beam.

When accelerating, as mentioned previously, the spring is subjected to twisting. In this particular layout, under these conditions, the forward spring will tend to move down at the rear and the rear spring will tend to move up at the front owing to the torque reactions. Both of these reactions will tend, through the balance beam, to have some load transference under these accelerating conditions to the front of the two axles. This means that the forward axle is temporarily

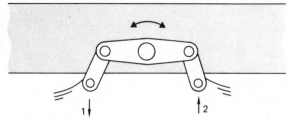

Figure 291 *Balance beam method of connecting rear suspension*

subjected to more load than the rear axle which could lead to possible wheel spin on the rear axle wheels under this condition. When braking, the torque reaction acts in the opposite way with similar effects. This type of suspension is referred to as a *reactive suspension* (Figure 291).

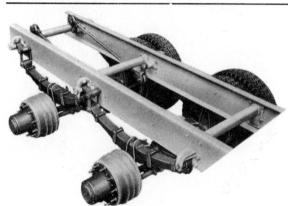

*(a)   Non-reactive rear suspension*

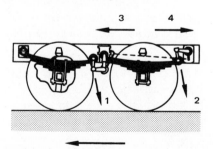

*(b)   Torque reaction when accelerating – (1 and 2) rear of springs tend to move in direction shown but are prevented by a linkage inside the chassis frame (3 and 4) where both forces are balanced out*

Figure 292

*(c)   When the front or the rear axles goes over a bump the linkags move in the direction shown, and any tendency to overload the axle is transferred to the rear axle*

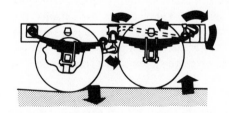

*(d)   When the rear axle is higher than the leading axle, the connecting linkage balances out the loading as shown*

More complicated linkages are required to equalize axle loading under conditions of abnormal loading, braking and driving torque reactions. This type of suspension is referred to as a *non-reactive suspension*.

Figure 292a shows a typical non-reactive suspension system. When the forward axle moves over a bump, the linkages equalize the loading with the rear axle. When accelerating, the torque reaction in the forward spring tends to move the linkages as shown. At the same time the torque reaction in the rear spring moves to oppose the movement by the forward spring, therefore any transfer of load under this condition is balanced against each axle and no movement takes place. Even if one axle were negotiating a bump at the same time, the axle loading would be balanced out. Torque reaction due to braking is balanced out in the opposite direction to driving torque reaction under all conditions.

When a degree of movement between the axles in a tandem bogie layout is desirable – vehicles used on site work or vehicles which spend more of their driving time in off-road situations – a further type of suspension layout can be used. This can be either a single spring or a twin spring layout with the springs mounted on trunion bearings (Figure 293a). When using this layout, the springs can be laminated leaf, taper leaf or single leaf with slipper type mountings at both ends of the springs. This means that the driving thrust, driving and braking torque reactions cannot be taken by the springs. Both axles are then held by torque bars and Panhard rods which locate the axle to the chassis frame and take all other torques usually taken by the springs. This layout also means that the springs can be designed for suspension only and allows a greater difference in levels between the two axles. Both systems are of course non-reactive layouts.

When a conventional suspension system is too harsh for the type of load carried or the type of body or especially a bulk tanker with special linings fitted, a rubber suspension may be used. This uses rubber 'springs' in torsion – as each axle moves the bonded rubber units are subjected to more torsion.

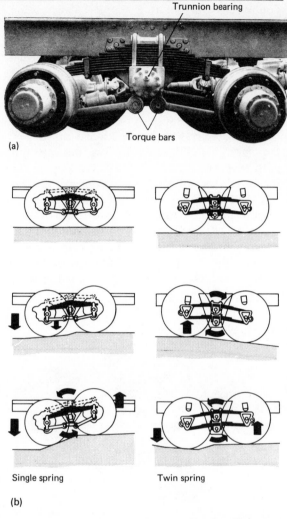

(a)

(b)

Single spring          Twin spring

Figure 293   *Springs mounted on trunnion bearings which allow greater degree of movement. Loads are balanced between both axles under all conditions*

When the second axle is a non-driving type of axle, the second axle, which is purely for load carrying, must still be interconnected with the front axle in order to share out the load (Figure 296).

A second axle may also be fitted which has the capability of being lifted off the road when the vehicle is lightly laden or unladen. This type of axle can be fitted to the rear of the vehicle but is often used as a second steering axle. The axle uses

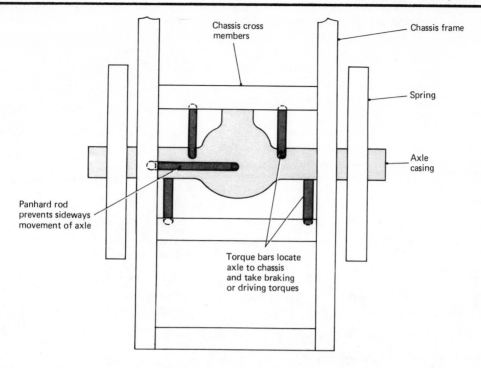

Figure 294   *Location of axle when taper leaf, rubber, or air suspension is used*

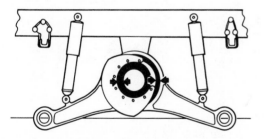

Figure 295   *When rubber is used in place of conventional springs, each axle is supported on arms which are separated by rubber subjected to torsional stresses as each axle moves*

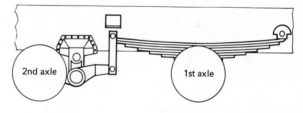

Figure 296   *Rear axle layout with the second axle non-driving*

a conventional leaf spring layout but a driver-operated control pressurizes an air bag fitted between the spring and the axle to push the wheels on to the road when they are required for load carrying. When the air is released, the spring 'lifts' the axle just clear of the road surface which therefore reduces tyre wear (Figure 297).

## Dampers

When a vehicle goes over a bump, energy is stored in the springs as in a ball that is bounced. When this energy is released, the springs will tend to continue oscillating just as the ball carries on bouncing. On a heavy vehicle, because the springs are very stiff for load-carrying purposes, control of the springs is more difficult and many heavy vehicles only fit dampers to the front axle.

Two types of damper are used, a lever type and a telescopic type. Both use hydraulic pressure to change mechanical energy into heat energy by forcing oil through small holes or valves as the axle moves in relation to the chassis. The heat generated is then dissipated to the atmosphere. When the spring is being compressed, very little damping effort is required but when it is releasing its energy, maximum restraint or damping effect is required. The damper fitted to a conventional suspension system is, therefore, single acting.

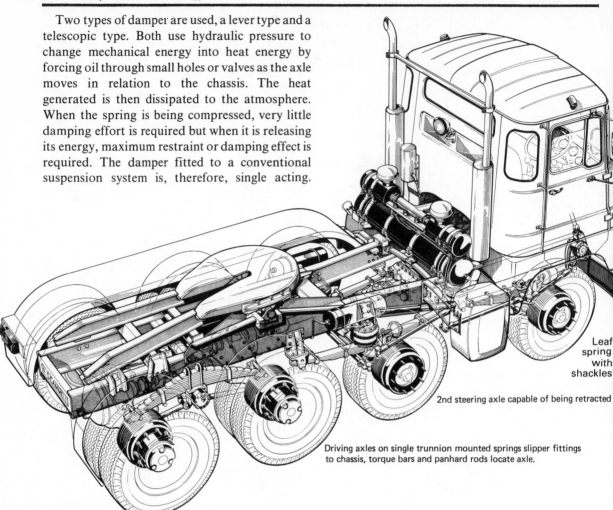

Leaf spring with shackles

2nd steering axle capable of being retracted

Driving axles on single trunnion mounted springs slipper fittings to chassis, torque bars and panhard rods locate axle.

Figure 297    *Combination of suspension systems used on a four-axle vehicle*

This means that little effort is required to operate one way and maximum effort required on the return stroke.

### Lever-type dampers (Figure 298)

This unit is bolted to the chassis with an operating lever and link providing the connection to the chassis. As the axle moves up and down a double piston arrangement forces the oil through a valve block from one chamber to the other which provides the desired resistance. This pressure can be varied according to the type of vehicle the unit is fitted to. Due to the leverage provided by the operating linkage and the corresponding small movement of the pistons, the operating pressures in this type of damper are very high. Oil sealing and manufacturing tolerances need to be very precise, in order to give reliability, and this also tends to increase the cost of this type of unit.

### Telescopic dampers (Figure 299)

This is a direct-acting unit which is mounted between the chassis and the axle. Many different types of construction are used but the principle of

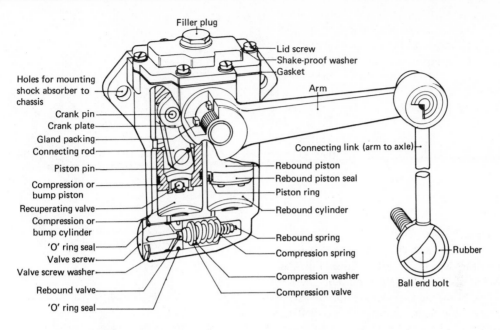

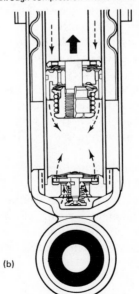

Figure 298  *Lever type shock absorber*

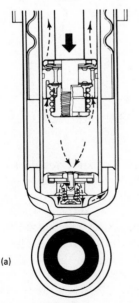

Descending piston forces oil through compression valve and metering spacer, and also upwards through piston intake valve.

Limited oilflow through rebound valve in ascending piston. Piston intake valve closed. Oil is drawn from reserve tube through compression intake valve.

(a)  (b)

Figure 299  *Telescopic dampers*

operation is still the same. A single piston is usually used which can be used either to move the oil in a circuit around the damper through valves or to pass the oil from one side of the piston to the other, through valves in the piston. The whole unit is filled with oil and is usually sealed for life. This direct-acting damper has a long stroke with a correspondingly lower working pressure, which means that the unit does not need to be manufactured to the high precision of the lever-type damper.

## Wheels

### Road wheels (Figure 300)

Together with the tyres, the road wheels must support the weight of the vehicle and also be capable of withstanding the torsional forces when driving and braking and various side-thrusts when cornering. This means that the wheel construction must withstand these forces without damage or distortion. Two types of construction are used, but both are basically the same shape. The wheel centre or nave and the rim may be pressed steel and welded or riveted together to form a relatively light but very strong structure. Alternatively the whole wheel may be a single casting to give a rather heavier but strong structure.

The wheel centre is dished which allows the wheel hub and brake drum to be accommodated within the space, this would otherwise increase the track of the vehicle unnecessarily. The off-setting (Figure 300b) also allows two wheels to be mounted back to back when twin wheels are needed and still come within the legal limit of spacing.

Without weakening the wheel centre, ventilation holes (Figure 300c) are usually left to allow more air-flow around the brake drums and therefore help to maintain braking efficiency. Without this feature the brake drums would be almost totally enclosed which would lead to serious overheating.

### Rim construction

In order to carry heavy loads the side walls of the tyres must be very stiff and therefore very strong.

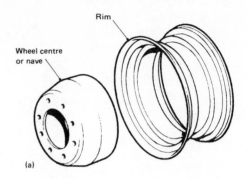

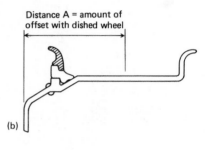

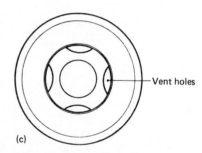

Figure 300   *Wheel construction*

This means that it would be difficult to remove the tyre by levering the bead over the flange. To overcome this, various types of rim construction are used.

Wheel sizes are dependent upon the carrying capacity of the vehicle. The size is measured as a diameter across the wheel from rim to rim, the most common being 50 cm (20 in) for heavy vehicles. The whole unit is held on to the wheel hub by conically faced studs which locate the wheel centrally with a mating seat in the wheel

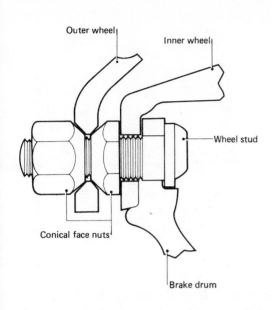

Figure 301    *Wheel studs*

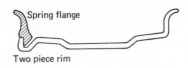

Figure 302    *A two-piece rim can be used on light commercial vehicles*

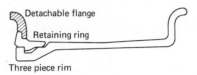

Figure 303    *Three-piece rim construction*

Figure 304    *The 'O' ring is used to seal the retaining ring when a tubeless tyre is used. The tyre seals normally against the detachable flange*

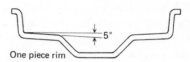

Figure 305    *Wheel sizes – one-piece rim*

centre (Figure 301). All near-side wheels have 'left-hand' threaded studs to reduce the risk of unwinding. This would lead to eventual wear of the conical seating and therefore the self-locking capacity of this type of fitting eliminates this risk.

A one-piece rim is generally used only on the smaller commercial vehicle but when tubeless tyres are fitted, one-piece rims with a deep centre well are used on heavy goods and passenger vehicles.

In the two-piece rim (Figure 302), the detachable flange is made from spring steel and is split so that it can be sprung over the edge of its retaining groove. When this is removed the tyre can then slide off the rim. On vehicles carrying heavier loads, a three-piece rim is usually used where a solid flange is held in position by a split locking ring which sits in a groove in the rim. When tubeless tyres are used a special ring with an extended tail accommodates a rubber O-ring (Figure 304) to provide a seal at the detachable end.

When inflating wheels with detachable rims, a steel cage should be used which will prevent any damage in the event of a rim being incorrectly assembled and the flange or ring being forced off due to the high inflation pressures.

## Tyres

Because of the nature of the work undertaken by heavy vehicles, many different tyre designs are used. The load-carrying capacity of any vehicle is determined by the tyres, therefore many different sizes and ply ratings are also required in order to match the tyres to the vehicle. Besides the function of load carrying, the tyre is also subjected to many

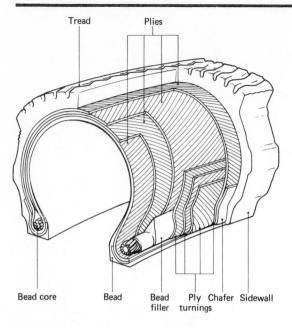

Figure 306   *Tyre construction*

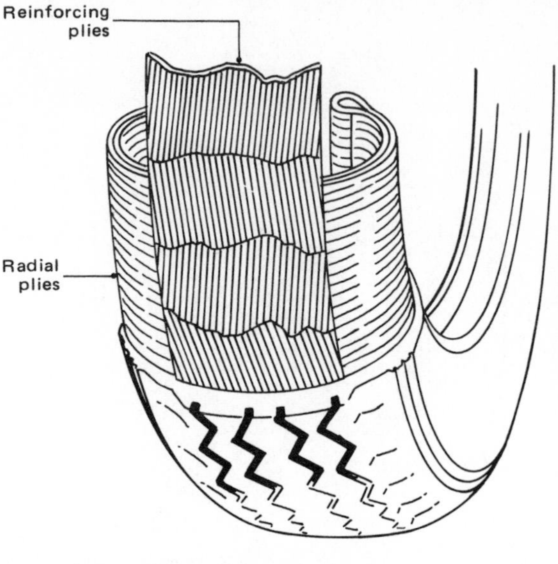

Figure 308   *In a radial-ply tyre the body plies run at right angles to the crown of the tyre. Breaker strips or reinforcing plies give support to the tread*

other forces whilst driving, braking, steering and cornering. In order to perform all of these functions correctly it must also provide a good grip between itself and the road surface in all conditions and in all directions. During this time it must also be appreciated that the area in contact with the road surface is very small – approximately equal to the area covered by a large sized boot.

All tyres come under two main types of construction and both of these may be tubeless or

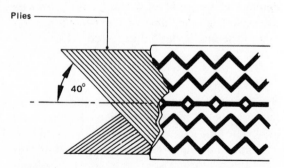

Figure 307   *In a cross-ply tyre the plies cross from bead to bead*

fitted with an inner tube. Both types consist mainly of a casing, beads, plies and tread and may look very similar in appearance but their internal structure is different. This difference in construction gives very different performance on the road.

### Cross-ply tyres (Figure 307)

The plies are built up from several layers of rubber-impregnated rayon, polyester or nylon fabric which cross from bead to bead at approximately 40° to the circumference of the tyre. Subsequent layers are laid in opposite directions and are built up until the required strength is obtained. The bead is heavily reinforced by steel wire hoops which give support and strength to the side wall and ensure a tight grip between the tyre and wheel rim when inflated. This prevents the wheel from spinning inside the tyre.

### Radial ply tyres (Figure 308)

In this type of tyre the plies pass from bead to bead at right angles to the circumference, i.e. radially. Fewer layers of plies are used in this construction but these are strongly reinforced by several layers

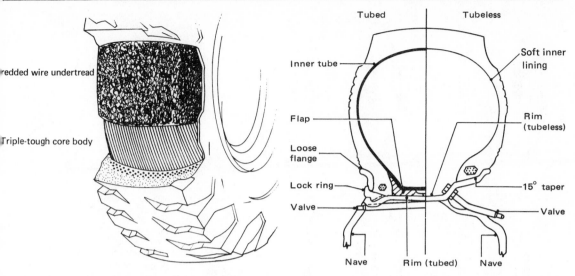

Figure 309   *A more heavily reinforced undertread helps to resist damage to the tyre, particularly when used 'off the road'. The tyre is basically cross-ply construction*

Figure 310   *A tubeless tyre*

of breaker strips or reinforcing plies which run around the circumference of the tyre directly beneath the tread rubber. Steel wire is often used in place of fabric in the construction of radial ply tyres, which provides a flexible but very strong tyre casing.

*Ply rating*
The load carrying capacity of a tyre depends upon its strength. This is directly related to the number of plies used in its construction, but early tyres used cotton fabric as ply material. In these early tyres therefore a 16-ply tyre had 16 layers of material in its side wall. With the use of modern man-made fibres however the ply material is much stronger and a side-wall may only have 10 ply layers but still have the strength of an original 16-ply tyre. Ply rating is now used as an indication of tyre strength but does not relate to the actual number of plies in the tyre. A PR is usually found on radial tyres.

*Tubeless tyres (Figure 310)*
This type of tyre relies upon the making of a good

seal between the tyre bead and the wheel rim when inflated to the correct pressure. This is achieved by using a layer of soft rubber which extends from the outer surface of the bead and around the inner casing of the tyre. The soft lining also provides a self-sealing characteristic should a foreign object penetrate the tyre casing.

*Tread pattern (Figure 311)*
The tread pattern of a tyre is decided by its use. A vehicle which is mainly used for relatively high-speed motorway-type running would greatly benefit from different tyres to those used by a vehicle used mainly off the road and *vice versa*. Under ideal conditions, i.e. smooth roads and no water, a perfectly smooth tyre would be serviceable. These conditions rarely exist, and therefore the main purpose of the tread pattern is to provide the grip necessary to propel the vehicle. A tyre for normal road work generally consists of several zig-zag ribs running circumferentially round the tyre. These ribs give lateral stability when cornering and directional stability when running in a straight line. If the tyre is mainly used in off-the-road or

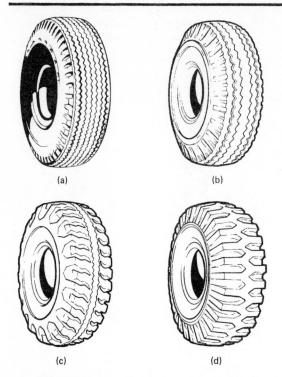

(a)    (b)

(c)    (d)

Figure 311

(a)   *Rib pattern – a general-purpose, high-speed tyre. Ribs in a zigzag pattern*

(b)   *Reinforced side walls with a scuff band are used for tyres on local delivery work. A simple zigzag pattern is used*

(c)   *A multi-purpose tyre for on and off the road application uses a combination of ribs and cross bars. The cross bars give increased traction and the ribs give lateral stability*

(d)   *An off the road tyre usually uses staggered cross bars for grip and slightly inclined to give a self-cleaning action*

cross-country type of work, the tread consists of inclined cross bars which are designed to give grip and a self-cleaning action.

### Inflation pressures

The load carried by a vehicle is suspended finally on the air in the tyres. To obtain maximum tyre life and vehicle performance it is important that this air is maintained at the correct pressure. If a tyre is

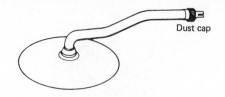

Dust cap

Figure 312   *Offset tyre valve*

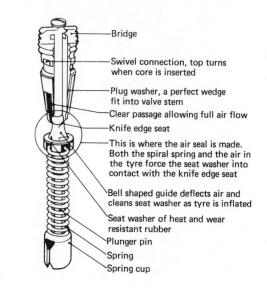

Bridge

Swivel connection, top turns when core is inserted

Plug washer, a perfect wedge fit into valve stem

Clear passage allowing full air flow

Knife edge seat

This is where the air seal is made. Both the spiral spring and the air in the tyre force the seat washer into contact with the knife edge seat

Bell shaped guide deflects air and cleans seat washer as tyre is inflated

Seat washer of heat and wear resistant rubber

Plunger pin

Spring

Spring cup

Figure 313   *Valve core*

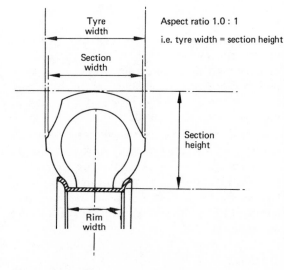

Tyre width

Section width

Aspect ratio 1.0 : 1

i.e. tyre width = section height

Section height

Rim width

Figure 314   *Tyre size and aspect ratio*

under-inflated, the tyre wall flexes too much which creates excessive heat and increases its wear rate. If a tyre is over-inflated, its casing will be under too much tension and not allow the tread to contact the road properly. In both conditions excessive wear will occur and the road holding and steering characteristics will be upset. When inflated to the correct pressure – which varies according to the weight carried – the tyre assumes the correct shape to give optimum performance.

The valve fitted to heavy vehicle tubes or wheels if a tubeless tyre is fitted is usually on an extended stem which compensates for the large offset in the wheel and allows easier access when tyres are twinned. The valve core, which is threaded into the end of the stem, provides a one-way path which allows the tyre to be inflated to its correct pressure. A dust cap fitted to the end of the stem acts as an extra air seal and prevents entry of dirt and water which may impair the sealing quality of the valve.

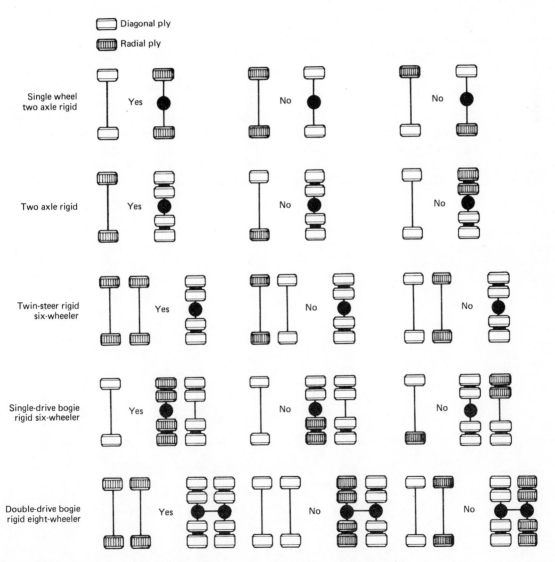

Figure 315  *Cross-ply and radial-ply tyre combinations – legal and illegal*

*Tyre selection*

When a tyre is used for a job it is not designed for, very high rates of wear occur. If a tyre is overloaded by only 10%, then up to one-fifth of its expected mileage may be lost. Because the main purpose of a heavy vehicle tyre is to support a load it is important that a tyre of the correct size, tread pattern and ply rating is used. Most manufacturers supply tables of maximum load limitations for each tyre and other facts about design that might affect its performance for a particular application.

When tyres are fitted to twin wheels it is advisable that both are the same make which means that they are exactly the same size and therefore wear at the same rate. When radial and cross-ply tyres are in use, it is important that these are not mixed on any one axle.

*Tyre size*

The sizes marked on a tyre refer to the width of the tyre and diameter of the rim to which it is fitted, e.g. a 9.00–20 tyre is approximately 9 in wide and is fitted to a 20 in diameter wheel rim. The aspect

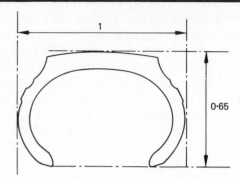

Figure 316   *Aspect ratio of a super single tyre*

ratio, i.e. the ratio of width to height of tyre, is approximately 1:1 with this type of conventional tyre. Most manufacturers now make an extra wide tyre – Super Singles – which can replace twin tyres. These have an aspect ratio of 0.65:1 with a typical size 15–19.5. This tyre can give better performance because of the larger surface area in contact with the ground and it is also lighter than the twin wheels it replaces.

# 8 Braking system

As the road speeds and weight of heavy vehicles have increased over the years, it has been necessary to match these changes with a more powerful system of braking. Vehicle brakes make a direct contribution to road safety and it is most important that they should be sufficiently powerful to control the speed of the vehicle to which they are fitted.

The function of vehicle brakes is to control the speed of the vehicle when travelling downhill, to reduce the speed of the vehicle when required, and to stop the vehicle and hold it stationary. The layout and equipment of a braking system varies with each type and make of vehicle and systems are generally more sophisticated on larger vehicles than on the smaller ones, but the principle of vehicle braking applies in every case. The basic principle is that when the brakes are applied to a vehicle in motion, the kinetic energy stored in the vehicle is converted, through the force of friction between the brake lining and the drum, into heat energy which is then dissipated into the atmosphere.

## Leading and trailing shoe brake (Figures 317 and 318)

This is one of the simplest brake assemblies and is often adopted by heavy vehicle manufacturers. The brake shoes pivot about the same point and are actuated by a cam or a single expander unit. This assembly requires much larger pedal forces than are required with the two-leading-shoe arrangement but it has the advantage of giving the same stopping power in both directions of wheel rotation which makes it suitable for the rear wheel brakes on many vehicles.

The leading shoe in this assembly can be identified by observing the position of the cam or expander and the direction of rotation (DOR) of the drum. Where the expander forces a shoe outwards in the same direction as the rotation of the drum, the friction caused by the mating surfaces forces the shoe harder into the rotating drum, this being known as self-servo action. The leading shoe provides approximately three-quarters of the total retarding force.

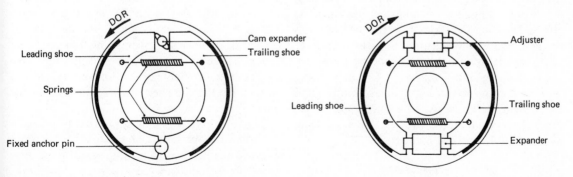

Figure 317  *Leading and trailing shoe brake – cam operated*

Figure 318  *Leading and trailing brake – expander operated*

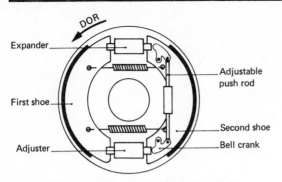

Figure 319   *Girling two-leading-shoe brake*

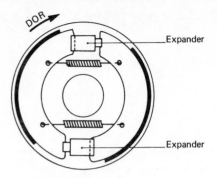

Figure 320   *Lockheed two-leading-shoe brake*

The trailing shoe is the shoe which the cam or expander forces outwards in the opposite direction of rotation of the drum and the resulting friction tends to force the shoe off the drum. This shoe provides approximately one quarter of the total retarding force of this assembly.

## Two-leading-shoe brake

Each brake shoe in this arrangement is forced outwards in the same direction as the normal rotation of the drum. The servo-action is less than that of the leading shoe used with a trailing shoe but the two-leading-shoe arrangement provides a more powerful and stable brake.

### Girling front brake (Figure 319)
When the brakes are applied, the expander tappet moves the upper bell crank which actuates the lower bell crank by the push rod. The lower bell crank presses against the adjuster which has the effect of forcing the shoe outwards with an even lining pressure on the drum. The secured adjuster and expander housings act as shoe anchors.

Two-leading-shoe action is usually only necessary in the forward direction of motion and for this reason the second shoe only is fitted with the bell cranks and push rod, the first shoe being actuated in the normal manner.

### Lockheed front brake (Figure 320)
The two wheel cylinders are secured to the brake back plate diametrically opposite each other and

the pistons force out each shoe tip. The two cylinders are connected by a rigid pipe, and the farthest one from the master cylinder is fitted with a bleed nipple.

### Weight transfer
When the brakes are applied, the normal weight distribution of the vehicle is altered and, considering a four-wheeled rigid vehicle, about 60% of the total vehicle weight is transferred to the front axle. The additional load or weight on the front axle increases the grip between the tyre and the road surface which makes the two-leading-shoe brake popular for front axle brakes as greater deceleration on the front wheels can be obtained without the danger of the wheels locking and skidding.

## Cam-operated brake (Figures 321 and 322)

This type of brake shoe expander is often used in heavy vehicle and trailer braking systems. When the brakes are applied, the camshaft is turned in its bushed housing which expands the brake shoes until they contact the drum. When the brakes are released the brake shoe pull-off springs retract the shoes and keep them in contact with the cam.

The camshaft is usually supported in nylon or phosphor bronze bushes, or needle roller bearings. and is often used in the leading-and-trailing shoe assembly with the cam action pivoting both brake shoes about the fixed anchor pin. With this arrangement pedal travel remains fairly constant

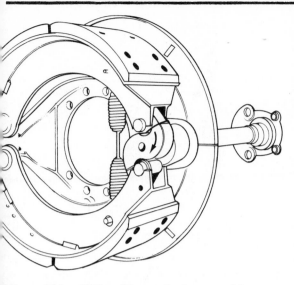

under severe usage, but a high pedal effort is required to produce the necessary cam force for brake operation. The reason for this high pedal effort is the lack of servo-action of the trailing shoe, and this is aggravated by the greater wear and greater shoe–drum clearance of the leading shoe causing the greater amount of cam force to be exerted on the trailing shoe.

## Wedge expander unit

When the brake is applied, the draw link pulls the taper wedge which operates through the rollers and forces the tappets outwards causing the brake shoes to contact the drum. When the brake is released, the brake shoe pull-off springs retract the brake shoes and the tappets are forced inwards to the position where the circlips contact the body.

Figure 321    *Girling 'S' cam brake assembly*

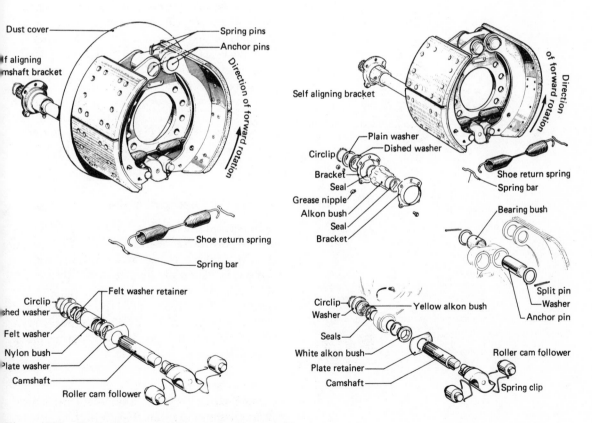

Figure 322    *Exploded view of 'S' cam brake assembly*

The wedge action magnifies the force in the draw link providing a greater force on the tappets.

## Adjusters

Brake shoe adjusters are fitted to limit the travel of the expander which will normally increase to its maximum as the linings wear thinner with use. A correctly adjusted lining will have a very small shoe clearance which normally limits the travel of the expander. Two types of adjuster are the wedge type and the clicker wheel type.

*Wedge type (Figures 323 and 324)*   This type consists of a screwed conical wedge which can be turned from the rear of the back plate by the squared end of its shaft. Flats on the wedge contact the tappets, acting as a locking device and providing a means of 'feel' for shoe adjustment.

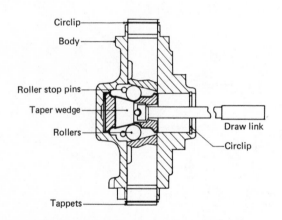

Figure 323   *Wedge expander unit*

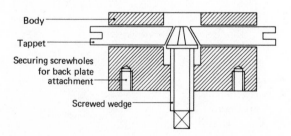

Figure 324   *Wedge-type brake adjuster*

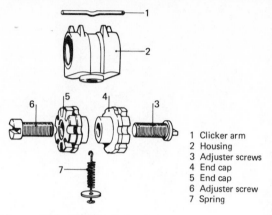

1  Clicker arm
2  Housing
3  Adjuster screws
4  End cap
5  End cap
6  Adjuster screw
7  Spring

Figure 325   *Clicker wheel type*

*Clicker wheel type (Figure 325)*   This type consists of a body containing two opposed end wheels which have right-hand and left-hand threads, respectively, to accommodate the adjuster screws. The clicker arm locates in the teeth on the periphery of the wheels and rests between lugs on the housing. It is spring-loaded by the spring which passes through the body.

During adjustment, each end wheel is turned by means of a lever through a slot in the back plate which moves the adjuster screws inwards or outwards depending upon the direction of rotation of the end wheels. This movement will adjust shoe–drum clearance.

## Mechanically operated brakes

Rod-operated brakes are still used on some heavy vehicles. Figure 326 shows the layout of a cam-operated braking system where rods are entirely used for the handbrake linkage and partly used for the footbrake system in conjunction with air operation. The rods are linked to cross shafts, and accurate adjustment of the linkage is necessary or the vehicle will pull to one side during brake applications.

### Compensation
A compensating system is used in mechanical braking systems to ensure that the braking effort is evenly divided between each wheel brake as

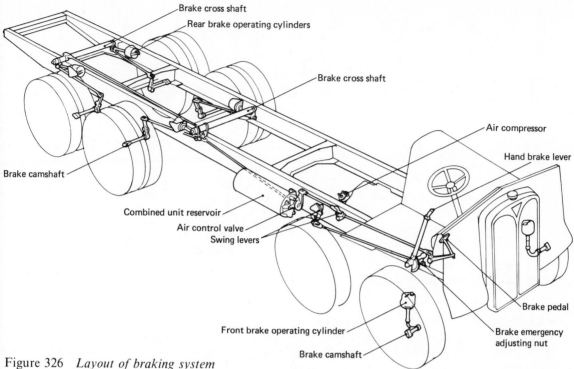

Figure 326 *Layout of braking system*

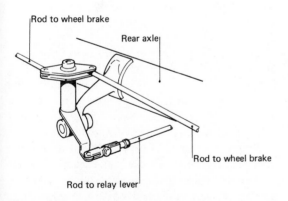

Figure 327 *Compensating linkage*

intended. Where a mechanical linkage (see Figure 327) is used to apply the rear brakes only on a four-wheeled rigid vehicle, a single compensator is used, this being positioned on the rear axle casing. A full mechanical braking system requires a greater number of compensators.

This compensator functions as a beam. When the brake is applied and the brake shoes make contact with one of the drums, the end of the beam operating the brake will become the fulcrum or pivot about which the beam will tilt until free movement in the other brake is taken up.

### Hand-operated brake

Some heavy vehicle braking systems have a multi-pull hand lever to operate the parking brake. Figure 328 shows the type used on an eight-wheeled goods vehicle and consists of a hand lever, toothed quadrant, brake-operating lever, two pawls and a trigger rod.

The brake is of the progressive ratchet type and operates the brakes on the four rear wheels only, by means of levers and rods connected to a cross shaft. On brake application, when the hand lever has been pulled up as far as it will go, it may be pushed forward and given another pull up, or if

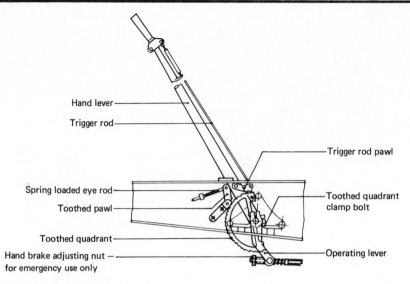

Figure 328   *Arrangement of handbrake lever assembly*

easier for the driver the brake may be applied by a number of small pulls. When applied, the brake will stay on until it is released by giving the hard lever handle a sharp push forward. This will knock the spring-loaded toothed pawl out of mesh with the quadrant, allowing the quadrant and the brake-operating lever to return to their original positions, and in doing so releasing the brakes on the wheels.

This type of brake has been superseded by a more easily operated parking brake on modern vehicles.

## Brake linings

One of the most important properties of a brake lining material is its coefficient of friction. When the material is in contact with cast iron the combination produces a coefficient of friction of 0.3 to 0.4 over a wide range of operating conditions. Other important properties of the material are that it must have high resistance to wear and it must not be affected by the variations in operating temperature to which it is frequently subjected, particularly in the operation of buses on local services. The stress resistance of a lining material must be high enough to withstand severe braking conditions on loaded vehicles operating under arduous conditions. The lining material must be flexible enough to conform to the curvature of the shoe when being fitted, and the cost of the finished lining is important to the operator for reasons of economy.

### Brake fade
Heating of the brake drums caused by prolonged or hard braking during fast driving or descending long steep hills results in drum expansion leading to excessive pedal travel and loss of retardation known as brake fade. Brake linings for heavy vehicles are usually made with high fade resistance to ensure that there is little fade during normal operating conditions. Some brake drums have ribs or fins on their outer surface which assist in dissipating heat from the drum to the atmosphere. An adequate air flow over the drums is essential for cooling purposes.

The ingress of water in a brake drum will cause fade. This is due to the water acting as a lubricant on the friction surfaces and dramatically lowering the coefficient of friction. Heavy vehicle drivers should be aware of the effects of water on brake friction surfaces and make allowances for drying out and recovery of braking efficiency.

## Types of lining

Two types of friction lining are usually used for vehicle brakes. These are known as the solid woven-asbestos type and the moulded type.

The solid woven type consists of asbestos and resin impregnated with zinc wire. The zinc content slightly reduces the coefficient of friction of the lining material but assists in conducting some of the heat away from its friction surface. Zinc also produces better anti-fade characteristics and increases the wear and resistance of linings.

Some heavy vehicle brake linings are manufactured by a moulding process. The material 'mix' includes asbestos fibres, resin powders and fillers, which are finely mixed and processed under high pressure and heat. Moulded linings have good wear characteristics and the coefficient of friction is fairly constant throughout the working range of temperatures. Care must be taken when fitting moulded linings to brake shoes as they are more brittle than the woven type. Moulded linings are less prone to brake fade than the woven type, this being due to the greater density of the moulded material. Response to water is better than the woven type which have a more porous composition.

## Fitting of linings

A large number of heavy vehicles have brake linings secured to their shoes by rivets, although the alternative method of bonding the lining to the shoe is occasionally used.

The riveted lining is fitted to the shoe by using brass, copper or aluminium rivets. A disadvantage of this type of fitting is the risk of lining distortion often caused by the rivet holes in the lining and shoe not being coincident. Other disadvantages of the riveted lining are the reduction in surface area and the accumulation of dirt in the rivet holes which causes scoring of the drum. The limit of wear is controlled by the rivet head and a considerable amount of time is required for refitting linings to shoes.

Bonded linings are firmer than riveted types and give a longer life owing to the absence of rivets which control lining life. A special process is used to fit the lining to the shoe which involves high pressures and temperatures followed by a buffing process which is necessary to obtain the correct curvature of lining.

## Disc brakes

This system of braking is seldom used on heavy vehicles. The principle of operation of the disc brake is the application of pressure on friction pads acting against a disc which is driven by the road wheel. The pads are supported by a caliper (see Figure 329) which straddles the disc and is mounted on a torque arm secured to the suspension. The pad is about one quarter of the area of a drum brake lining and operates with higher temperatures and pressures which can cause overheating problems with seals and fluids. The volume of lining available for wear is considerably less than the shoe lining which would be a disadvantage on passenger vehicles where linings wear rapidly due to the arduous operating conditions on local services. A further disadvantage of the disc brake is the smallness of components which, when coupled to air-operating systems, would lead to design problems.

Future vehicles may, however, be fitted with disc brakes if these disadvantages can be overcome.

Some advantages of disc brakes when compared with drum brakes are better heat dissipation caused by the larger proportion of the brake

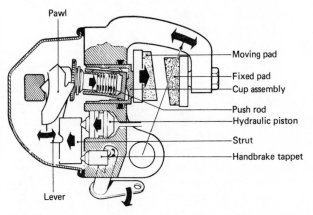

Figure 329 *Single-sided swinging caliper disc brake*

assembly being exposed to the air stream which reduces the risk of brake fade, and the pedal travel remains fairly constant. The disc brake assembly is lighter in weight than the drum brake assembly, the construction is simpler and the pads can be easily observed for wear and replaced within a few minutes if necessary. The disc is usually made from cast iron and is more substantial than a brake drum thus eliminating the risk of drum distortion caused by excessive heating during arduous braking conditions.

## Hydraulically operated brakes

Hydraulic brakes (Figure 330) are often used with footbrake operation for vans and light commercial vehicles. They are preferred to mechanically operated systems because they have the following advantages:

1   The hydraulic system provides equal pressure throughout the enclosed system and is fully compensating.
2   The force exerted on each brake shoe depends upon the area of its wheel cylinder piston. This is determined by the manufacturer during the design and development stage.
3   The system is, to a large extent, self-lubricating which reduces the risk of seizure, a common defect in mechanical systems where the linkage is exposed.

4   There is no loss of motion and reduction of the applied force caused by worn mechanical linkages and ineffective angularity of levers.
5   The system of rigid and flexible pipes lends itself to complex vehicle layouts, particularly vehicles with independent wheel suspension.

Vehicles fitted with hydraulically operated brakes have, in addition, an independent braking system which is used to operate the brakes of at least two wheels for parking and emergency purposes. This is a legal requirement and is satisfied by including a mechanically operated handbrake system on the rear wheels.

*Layout of system*
The system consists of a supply tank, a master cylinder, a system of rigid and flexible pipes, pipe junctions and unions, and wheel cylinder assemblies. The supply tank is either an integral part of the master cylinder unit or a separate unit mounted in a convenient position for accessibility and connected to the master cylinder by a pipe.

*Brake pipes (rigid and flexible)*
The fluid supply tank, master cylinder and wheel cylinders are connected by a system of pipes. Rigid pipes are used for most of the system and flexible pipes are used where there is movement of components.

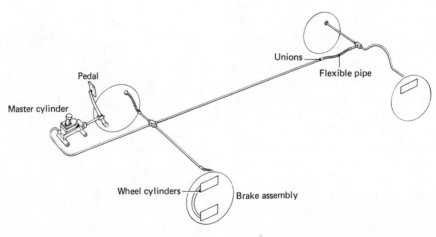

Figure 330   *Layout of hydraulic braking system*

The rigid pipes are manufactured from steel and are shaped to follow the contours of the vehicle chassis to which they are attached by securing clips, straps or brackets which should be periodically examined for security. Union nuts and connecting nipples are usually used to connect the pipes to components or other pipes. A material which will withstand mechanical vibration and corrosion by road salts and other substances is used for pipe manufacture.

Flexible brake pipes should be periodically examined for leaks and wear which are usually caused by ageing of the material, excessive movement and stretching, or chafed by rubbing contact with another component.

## Master cylinders

The purpose of the master cylinder is to transmit fluid pressure from itself to the wheel cylinders during brake applications which will actuate the wheel cylinder pistons and brake shoes. Some master cylinders operate by increasing an existing residual line pressure, others permit the free passage of fluid to and from the lines when in the 'off' position.

### Lockheed type (Figure 331)

The unit consists of a cylinder and piston assembly combined with the supply tank all housed in the body which is secured to the vehicle by fixing bolts.

The principal parts are the piston, the main and secondary seals, the spring and the double-acting check valve. The main seal is located in front of the piston and they are separated by a thin flexible metal disc which prevents the seal being drawn into the small holes in the piston head. The rear of the piston is sealed in the bore by the secondary seal and the brake pedal operates the push rod which is located in the hollow part of the piston. The spring returns the piston when the brake is released and loads the check valve when in the 'off' position.

*Brakes applied*   When the pedal is depressed the push rod forces the piston along the cylinder,

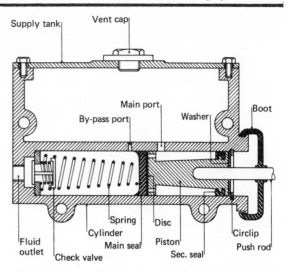

Figure 331   *Lockheed master cylinder – the disc (dished water) should be fitted with the convex side against the head of the piston*

cutting off the by-pass port and building up the pressure in the cylinder. When fluid pressure exceeds the residual line pressure 55–83 kN/m$^2$ (8–12 lbf/in$^2$), the pressure difference will open the check valve and fluid will pass into the lines and operate the brakes.

*Brakes released*   When the brake pedal is released quickly the spring returns the piston more quickly to the 'off' position, then fluid is returned from the pipe lines. The sudden piston movement causes a depression in the forward part of the cylinder and the pressure difference forces fluid through the small holes in the piston head and over the main seal to make up the temporary fluid deficiency. This action also reduces back pressure on the piston and assists in releasing the brakes quickly. The portion of the cylinder around the waist of the piston is immediately refilled with fluid from the supply tank via the main port. The fluid in the wheel cylinders and pipe lines is now at a higher pressure than the fluid in the master cylinder and the brake shoe pull-off springs are retracing the wheel cylinder pistons. The returning fluid lifts the check valve off its seat, compressing the spring, and displaces the fluid in the forward part of the cylinder by forcing it through the bypass port to the supply tank. The return of the fluid from the pipe lines continues until the fluid pressure in the lines is equal to the spring loading of the check valve. The check valve closes at this instance and the lines are sealed off from the master cylinder at residual line pressure.

*Girling centre valve (CV) type (Figure 332)*

This type of master cylinder is made in two styles. One has a separate fluid supply tank which is connected to the cylinder inlet port by a length of pipe, and the other has an integral supply tank. The operating principle is the same for both.

The cylinder is an alloy casting, with an accurately machined bore. A port connects the end of the cylinder bore with the fluid supply and fluid can pass through the outlet port to the brake pipes and wheel cylinders. The inner assembly consists of a push rod, dished washer, circlip, plunger, main seal and, on some models, end seals, spring thimble, plunger return spring, valve stem and centre valve assembly.

*Brakes applied*   When the brake is depressed, the push rod takes up its small clearance and moves the plunger into the cylinder. The first 0.78 mm (1/32 in) of plunger has the effect of closing off the fluid supply port by moving the centre valve on to its seat. Further plunger movement increases the fluid pressure throughout the system which forces the wheel cylinder pistons outwards to apply the brake shoes to the drums.

*Brakes released*   When the brake pedal is released the plunger-return spring returns the plunger assisted by the brake shoe pull-off springs which retract the shoes and wheel cylinder pistons and return fluid from the lines to the cylinder. As the plunger reaches the end of its stroke, the centre valve is lifted off its seat, and fluid can pass freely between the cylinder and supply tank. The centre valve, sometimes referred to as a compensating valve, automatically functions to allow for fluid expansion or contraction with temperature variations and compensates for fluid losses in the system.

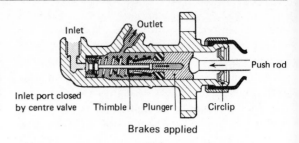

Inlet   Outlet

Push rod

Inlet port closed
by centre valve   Thimble   Plunger   Circlip

**Brakes applied**

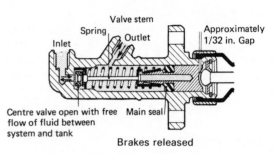

Valve stem
Spring   Approximately
Inlet   Outlet   1/32 in. Gap

Centre valve open with free   Main seal
flow of fluid between
system and tank

**Brakes released**

Figure 332   *Girling CV master cylinder*

*Girling compression barrel (CB) type (Figure 333)*

This type of master cylinder has a separate supply tank and is designed to be bolted to the chassis by side-fixing lugs or by flange mounting. There are a range of sizes from 15.9 mm (5/8 in) diameter bore to 25.4 mm (1 in) diameter bore for light vehicles including vans, and from 38.1 mm (1½ in) diameter bore up to 50.8 mm (2 in) diameter bore for heavy vehicles.

The master cylinder plunger is operated by a push rod connected via the brake linkage to the foot pedal or connected to a vacuum servo unit or air cylinder. The main (recuperating) seal is stationary in the body of the cylinder and the plunger moves through the seal when the brakes are operated. The smaller types of cylinder have four small holes in the plunger which bypass the main seal and allow free movement of fluid through the system and supply tank, when the brake is off. The larger types of cylinder have a check valve fitted in the end cap which provides a residual line fluid pressure of 55–83 kN/m$^2$ (8–12 lbf/in$^2$).

*Brakes applied*   When the brake pedal is depressed, the push rod moves the plunger

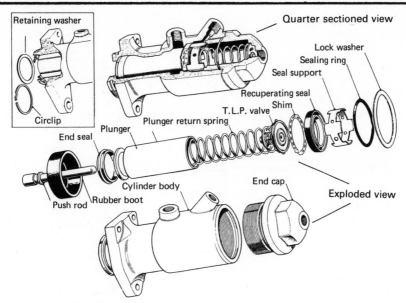

Figure 333    *Girling compression barrel (CB) type*

inwards and applies pressure to the fluid which expands the wheel cylinder pistons causing the brake shoes to contact the drum.

*Brakes released*    When the pedal is released the plunger is forced outwards by its spring, assisted by the returning fluid caused by the action of the brake shoe pull-off springs.

## Tandem master cylinder

To increase road safety and comply with legislation, the tandem master cylinder may be used in a hydraulic braking system. These master cylinders are usually larger and more expensive than the single types and function as two single cylinders in series although they are often more complicated in design. One part of the master cylinder supplies the front axle brakes and the other part supplies the rear axle brakes. Some later systems are designed to operate diagonally. Each part has its own supply tank and in the unlikely event of one part of the braking system failing the other part will provide an effective brake even though pedal travel may be slightly increased.

Figure 334 illustrates the basic principle of the

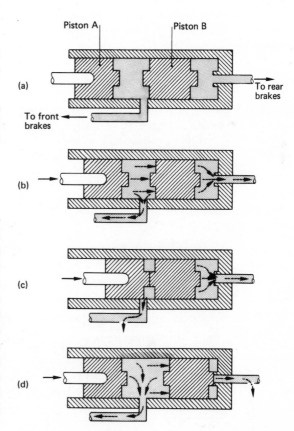

Figure 334    *Principle of tandem master cylinder*

tandem master cylinder without inlet ports and fluid supply tanks. (a) shows the brakes in the 'off' position. When the brake pedal is depressed as shown in (b), the push rod forces piston A into the cylinder which increases the fluid pressure between the pistons and transmits hydraulic pressure to the front brakes. At the same time, fluid pressure acts on piston B which also moves inwards and transmits hydraulic pressure to the rear brakes. When the system is functioning normally the hydraulic pressure in both the front and rear braking systems is equal and fully compensated.

In the event of a failure in the front brake system as shown in (c), contact would take place between pistons A and B during brake application which would transmit fluid to the rear brake system. Alternatively, if failure occurred in the rear brake system as shown in (d), piston A would cause piston B to travel inwards to its stop during initial application followed by further pedal movement which would transmit fluid to the front brakes.

### Lockheed type (Figure 335)
Both parts of the cylinder are supplied with fluid from the partitioned supply tank. The primary piston is operated by the push rod and has a projecting stop on its pressure face. The secondary piston has stops on each end and a hollow piston stop is situated at the outlet end of the cylinder.

Check valves are situated at the outlet ports and the screwed-in piston stop limits the outward position of the secondary piston.

### Girling type (Figure 336)
When the brake pedal is depressed the push rod moves the primary plunger along the cylinder and allows the spring-loaded tipping valve to return to its central position. The primary supply port is closed as a result of the movement of the tipping valve and further movement of the primary plunger causes hydraulic pressure to be transmitted, via the trapped-line-pressure valve, to the wheel cylinders operating the rear brakes. At the same time the pressure created acts together with the increasing force of the primary spring to overcome the resistance of the stronger secondary spring and so moves the secondary plunger along the cylinder.

Initial movement of the secondary plunger closes the centre valve supply port and hydraulic pressure is transmitted via another trapped-line-pressure valve to the wheel cylinders operating the front brakes.

If either of the cylinder chambers or circuits fail, physical contact of the plungers takes place within the cylinder and the remaining chamber and circuit build up to normal pressure and operate the brake line – front, rear or diagonal – in the usual way.

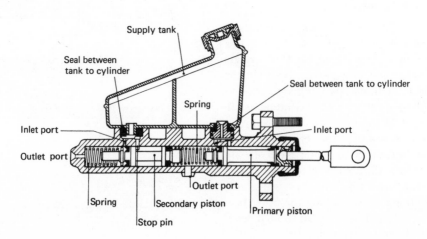

Figure 335   *Lockheed tandem master cylinder*

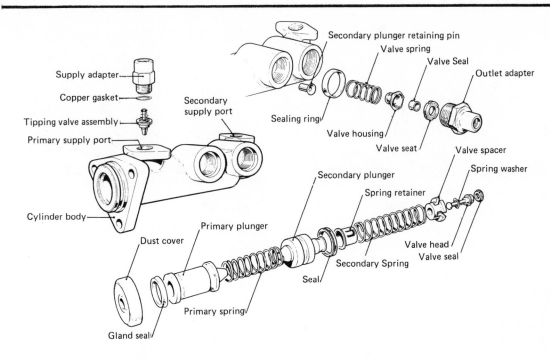

Figure 336   *Girling tandem master cylinder*

## Check valve (Figures 337 and 338)

Some master cylinders incorporate a check valve or trapped-line-pressure valve. Other types do not have such a valve and therefore allow the free passage of fluid between the pipe lines and master cylinder. The reasons for fitting a check valve in some systems are:

1   To maintain a residual or line pressure of about 55 kN/m$^2$ (8 lbf/in$^2$) when the brake is 'off' which will cause fluid to flow out rather than air to enter the fluid system in the event of a slight leak.

2   To prevent the return of fluid pumped into the lines during bleeding operations. This ensures that a fresh charge of fluid at each stroke of the brake pedal enters the system and helps to expel air from the system.

3   The wheel cylinder seals are maintained under slight pressure which prevents a tendency for them to collapse and allow air to enter the fluid system through the wheel cylinders.

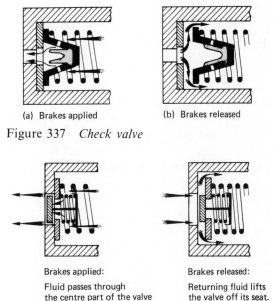

(a) Brakes applied          (b) Brakes released

Figure 337   *Check valve*

Brakes applied:
Fluid passes through the centre part of the valve

Brakes released:
Returning fluid lifts the valve off its seat.

Figure 338   *Check valve (alternative type)*

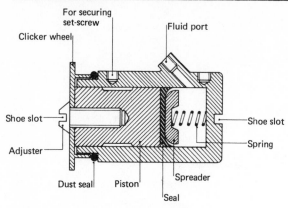

Figure 339   *Lockheed wheel cylinder – single piston type*

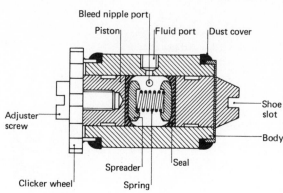

Figure 340   *Lockheed front wheel cylinder – double piston type*

## Wheel cylinders

*Single piston type (Lockheed) (Figure 339)*
Each cylinder is accurately machined and has a polished bore. This type contains a piston, a rubber seal, a spreader, a spring and an adjuster.

Fluid enters the cylinder through the port and when braking pressure is applied to the piston it moves outwards and expands the brake shoe against the action of the brake shoe pull-off springs. When braking pressure is released the shoe pull-off springs retract the shoes and return the piston assembly to its original position. The light spring holds the seal against the piston under operating conditions. The outer seal is used to exclude dirt and moisture from the cylinder. The end cap has a series of notches on its outer surface and a clicker spring locates in the notches as the cap is rotated during brake adjustment.

*Double piston type (Lockheed) (Figure 340)*
The cylinder body is bolted to the backplate and differs from the single acting type by having two pistons. The ends of the pistons are slotted to locate the ends of the brake shoes.

When braking pressure is applied both pistons are forced outwards causing the brake shoes to contact the drum. Release of braking pressure causes the brake shoe pull-off springs to retract the brake shoes and return the pistons to their original positions.

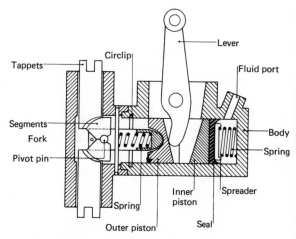

Figure 341   *Lockheed transverse wheel cylinder and bisector unit*

## Lockheed transverse wheel cylinder and bisector expander

This type of unit (see Figure 341) is often used on heavy vehicle braking systems. It has the advantage of being located on the rear brake backplate with part of the unit on the outside and exposed to the air stream which keeps it cool during operation. The unit is used on braking systems where the brake shoes are actuated by a wedge action controlled by fluid pressure during footbrake application and mechanical operation during handbrake application.

The unit consists of two main assemblies: (1) the expander which consists of a body housing two opposed tappets, a bisector fork carrying two segments which rotate on the pivot pin and a return spring; (2) the wheel cylinder consisting of an accurately machined bore containing two pistons whose adjacent faces are slotted to admit the heel of the handbrake-operated lever which pivots upon its pin, the seal, the spreader and the spring.

*Operation* When the brake pedal is depressed, fluid pressure forces both pistons along the cylinder applying force to the bisector fork causing the segments to expand the tappets and apply the brake shoes to the drums. When the brake pedal is released, the brake shoe pull-off springs retract the shoes, the tappets contract and return the bisector fork and pistons to their 'off' position. The clearance between the heel of the lever and the inner piston prevents movement of the handbrake linkage during footbrake operation.

When the handbrake is applied, the lever pivots on its pin and forces the outer piston and bisector fork outwards, expanding the tappets and applying the brake shoes to the drum. When the handbrake is released the brake shoe pull-off springs retract the shoes and contract the tappets returning the bisector fork and outer piston to the 'off' position. The position of the inner piston is not affected by operation of the handbrake.

## Girling transverse wheel cylinder

There are basically two types of wheel cylinder, the pusher type and the puller type. The pusher type is usually used on the front brakes where no separate mechanical linkage is required for handbrake operation. The puller type is used for rear brake operation and is designed to operate by both the hydraulic system controlled by the foot-brake and the mechanical linkage controlled by the handbrake. Both types are secured to the back plate and they can be removed and fitted as a complete unit from the outside of the drum. The fluid is maintained at a low temperature by the

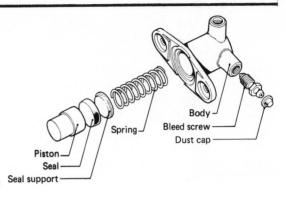

Figure 342   *Girling pusher-type wheel cylinder*

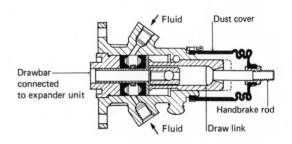

Figure 343   *Girling puller-type wheel cylinder*

unit being located on the outside of the drum exposed to the cool air which is advantageous in heavy vehicle braking systems.

### Operation of pusher type (Figure 342)
Application of the brake pedal causes an increase in fluid pressure which forces the piston outwards applying force to the expanding unit and brake shoes. When the pedal is released, the brake shoe pull-off springs retract the brake shoes and the expander, returning the piston to its original position.

### Operation of puller type (Figure 343)
Application of the brake pedal causes an increase in fluid pressure which forces the piston outwards pulling the draw link away from the backplate and applying the shoes to the drum. The handbrake linkage is not affected by this action as the draw link will pass over the end of the handbrake rod.

Return of the brake pedal will cause the draw link to return to its original position.

Application of the handbrake causes the handbrake rod to pull the draw link outwards and apply the brake shoes to the drum without affecting the hydraulic piston chamber volume or piston position. Release of the handbrake causes the draw link to return and the brake shoes are released from the drum. The footbrake and handbrake therefore function independently of each other in this unit.

## Seals

The rubber seals (Figure 344) used in a hydraulic braking system usually give long service and little trouble, although a periodic examination of all seals in a system is usually recommended for safety and reliability.

A contaminated fluid can cause the seals to perish and wear. Perished seals usually expand and cease to work correctly. A seal affected by a contaminated fluid can often be identified by comparing it with a new seal (but do not let them touch). If the used one has a larger diameter – 1.59 mm (1/16 in) or more on a 1-m diameter seal – fluid contamination has caused the seal to deteriorate.

Seals usually wear on their outer edges often in the form of a fine scored groove caused by particles of grit or rust existing in the system. Seals should be examined for wear together with the cylinder in which they operate and both renewed if necessary. Worn seals can cause air to enter the system without any sign of leaking fluid.

It is common practice to replace a hydraulic cylinder as a complete unit. This method reduces the time to do the job and eliminates the skill and knowledge necessary to strip, examine and rebuild the original unit. Some manufacturers recommend changing wheel cylinders, master cylinders and hydraulic hoses every 80 000 km (50 000 miles) or every two years whichever is reached first.

Scrupulous cleanliness should be exercised at all times when dealing with the internal parts of a hydraulic system, particularly the seals which should never be handled with greasy hands.

New seal                    Affected seal

Figure 344   *Rubber seals used in hydraulic braking systems*

## Brake fluid

It is extremely important that the correct fluid is used in a hydraulic braking system. There are various fluids used which have a vegetable oil base compounded with suitable dilutents.

Brake fluid should have a low freezing point, high boiling point, a low viscosity throughout its working temperature and should not perish rubber or corrode any metal components with which it comes into contact. Fluid does not quickly deteriorate in quality but if it is contaminated with oil, fuel, water or other similar liquids it is likely to cause corrosion or have a perishable effect on the seals which may lead to a dangerous condition of the braking system. The fluid level in the supply tank should be regularly checked and topped up if necessary to prevent air entering the system.

Cleaning of hydraulic brake components should be carried out with industrial methylated spirit or the recommended cleaning fluid and the components reassembled with a smear of the specially prepared rubber grease or fluid used for the system. Flushing with methylated spirit at periodic intervals is often recommended for a system and may have to be carried out at additional times if the fluid is contaminated which can often be identified by its dirty and thick appearance. On no account should a vehicle be driven if the brake fluid is contaminated; it is in a dangerous condition and should be given immediate attention.

## Hygroscopic properties of fluids

Brake fluids have a tendency to absorb moisture from the atmosphere so giving them a hygroscopic property. Absorption occurs during the operating life of a vehicle and can enter the hydraulic system through the flexible hoses which are slightly permeable.

The temperature at which brake fluid vaporizes decreases in proportion to the increase in moisture content within the fluid. Under conditions of prolonged or heavy braking, a vapour-lock point may be reached which could seriously affect braking performance. One of the first signs of vapour-lock can be detected by a 'spongy' brake pedal. An alert driver is likely to observe this effect which will cause deterioration in performance. If this condition occurs the vehicle should be stopped, time should be allowed for the fluid to cool, and the fluid should then be tested.

Improvements in the quality of fluid are constantly being made and instruments are available to test the fluid for moisture. It is recommended that samples for testing should be taken from a low point within a system, as fluid at a lower level is more prone to 'locking'. Regular testing of fluid is recommended by suppliers to reduce the risk of 'locking'.

## Bleeding the hydraulic system

If air enters the hydraulic system, part of the master cylinder piston or plunger movement will be used in compressing the air. This gives a 'spongy' feel to the brake pedal movement and reduces braking efficiency. Bleeding is necessary to expel the air from the system.

The vehicle should be prepared by placing wheel chocks in position and releasing the handbrake. It is vitally important that absolute cleanliness is maintained throughout the bleeding operation. Rag of linty texture should not enter the system via the supply tank. One method of bleeding is carried out by attaching a flexible tube on each bleed nipple in turn and entering the free end of the tube into a jar containing a small quantity of brake fluid.

The nipple is unscrewed half to three-quarters of a turn while the brake pedal is depressed and the nipple re-tightened as the pedal reaches the end of its stroke. The pedal should then be allowed to return slowly to its 'off' position followed by a pause of three to four seconds before the procedure is repeated. The operation is continued until no air bubbles are visible in the jar of fluid during pedal movements. It is important to ensure that at no time during bleeding operations should the fluid level in the supply tank be allowed to fall to a level where air is admitted. Frequent checking and topping up will be necessary.

There are important differences in manufacturer's recommendations for the method and order of bleeding a hydraulic system which should be strictly adhered to. It is also important that all air should be expelled from a hydraulic system as any trapped air may have the effect of becoming compressed instead of producing an increase in fluid pressure during brake pedal operation. This action may result in insufficient fluid pressure being built up to actuate the brakes.

Fluid which has been bled from a hydraulic system should not be used for topping up the supply tank as it may be aerated or contaminated. A supply of the manufacturer's recommended brake fluid should always be available for bleeding operations.

The conventional method of bleeding requires the attendance of at least two people. A servicing unit can be used for the bleeding operation which permits the operation to be performed with one person and reduces the time to do the job.

Some heavy vehicles use an air hydraulic system. The pedal 'feel' with this system does not give any indication of air in the system. A more technical examination of the system is necessary for these vehicles if the braking efficiency is low and air is suspected to exist in the system. The correct way of checking a Girling system is to charge the air reservoir fully and, with the brake shoes fully locked in the drums, apply the brake pedal and check the indicator (Figure 345) on the air cylinder actuating the master cylinder. If the indicator rod protrudes more than approximately 2 cm (¾ in), air is probably present in the system.

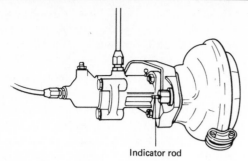

Indicator rod

Figure 345    *Girling indicator for air-hydraulic system*

## Air-operated braking systems

Air-operated braking systems are used on heavy goods vehicles – rigids, tractive units and trailers and passenger vehicles. Compressed air, operating on large-diameter diaphragms, provides very large operating forces at the brake shoe assembly which is necessary on this type of vehicle to give good braking efficiency.

The system can be split up into three main units:

1  Compressor and storage equipment.
2  Control equipment consisting of various valves required to operate the brake chambers.
3  Actuation equipment consisting of brake chambers which convert compressed air into mechanical energy to apply the brakes.

There are many variations and combinations of these units which make up a complete vehicle system. This is generally decided by size and weight of vehicle together with cost. Two basic layouts are generally used:

1  A dual system for rigid vehicles with two separate air supplies which operate front and rear brakes independently.
2  A three-line system used on articulated vehicles which provides service, emergency and secondary systems of operating the brakes.

Actuating equipment may use single, dual or triple diaphragm brake chambers, spring brake actuators or lock actuators or combinations of each to provide the effort which applies the brakes.

## Compressor and storage equipment

*The compressor*

This is usually driven at half engine speed from the timing gears at the front of the engine. The single or twin cylinder piston-operated pump is normally lubricated from the main engine's lubrication system and can be either air or water cooled.

The output of the compressor is controlled by unloader and governor valves which maintain a pre-determined pressure in the reservoirs and allow the compressor to run 'light' once this pressure has been reached.

One type of unloader valve is incorporated in the cylinder head of the compressor and is connected to the reservoir through the governor valve. When the correct pressure has been reached in the reservoir, the governor valve opens and passes air back to the unloader valve which in turn holds the inlet valve open. When the compressor is on compression stroke, air is forced back through the open valve and prevents any further compression. As pressure in the reservoir falls, the unloader valve returns the inlet valve to its normal position and air is again delivered to the reservoir. An alternative method is to mount the unloader and governor valves in a single unit which isolates the reservoir from the compressor once working pressure has been reached and the compressor is opened to atmosphere to prevent further increase in pressure. Both methods mean that the temperature of the pump and wear of its moving parts are considerably reduced.

Figure 346 shows the normal operation of the compressor – air is drawn through the inlet valve and forced out through the spring-loaded delivery valve to the reservoir. The safety valve is also fitted above the delivery valve which blows off at 1060 kN/m$^2$ (150 lbf/in$^2$) should the governor/unloader mechanism fail.

Figure 347 shows the compressor running light – pressure in the reservoir lifts the governor valve off its seat, passes to the unloader plunger which holds the inlet valve off its seat. As the pressure in the reservoir falls, the valves are reseated and the compressor operates normally.

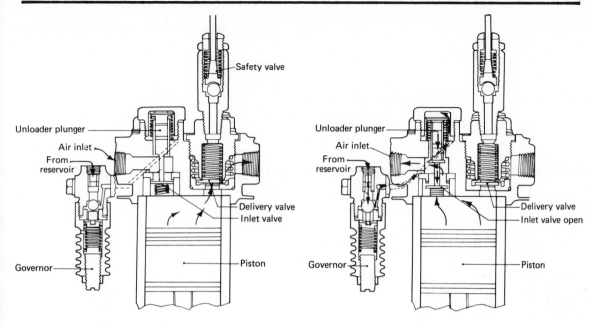

Figure 346   *Compression of air*

Figure 347   *Unloading*

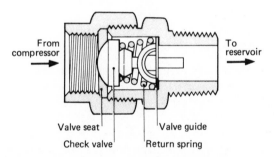

Figure 348   *One-way valve fitted to the reservoir which prevents back-flow should the feed pipe fail*

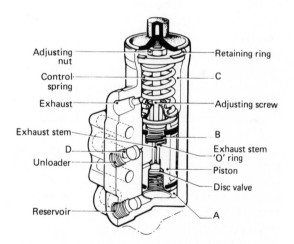

Figure 349   *Governor fitted between reservoir and compressor*

*Governor valve*
This controls air output from the compressor to the reservoir by causing the compressor to 'cut-out' when a pre-determined pressure is reached in the reservoirs. Similarly, when pressure falls in the reservoir, the governor 'cuts-in' to allow the compressor to build up lost pressure. The difference in pressure between cut-in and cut-out is usually 103 kN/m² (15 lbf/in²); cut-out pressure can be adjusted by the adjusting screw.

*Operation*   Under normal working conditions, chamber A (Figure 349) is at reservoir pressure and chambers B and C are exhausted. Figure 349 shows the valve at rest. As pressure rises in the reservoir, the same pressure is felt in chamber A

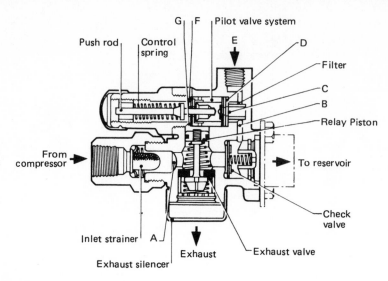

Figure 350    *Unloader valve*

and begins to push the piston up and bring the disc valve into contact with the spring-loaded exhaust stem. This will then be pushed off its seat and allow air to pass, through a drilling in the piston, to chamber D and along to the unloading mechanism in the compresser, at the pre-determined cut-out pressure. The unloader plunger then holds the inlet valve off its seat and therefore prevents any compression of air.

When the reservoir pressure falls, the unloader piston is pushed down by the control spring. This allows the disc valve to reseat on the piston, and isolate the unloader connection from reservoir pressure. Further movement opens the exhaust valve – top of disc valve/bottom of exhaust stem – and allows air to escape from the unloader passages, and exhaust through the hollow exhaust stem holes, in the lower spring seat, to atmosphere through the exhaust port. The compressor begins to recharge the reservoirs and the whole process is repeated until normal operating pressure is reached [827 kN/m$^2$ (110 lbf/in$^2$)].

*Unloader valve*
The unloader valve does a similar job as the governor valve, but whereas the governor can be fitted near to the compressor and the reservoir, the unloader valve is fitted in the air line between the two components. Pressure in the reservoir is controlled by diverting compressed air, at cut-out point, to atmosphere. Cut-out pressure is approximately 827 kN/m$^2$ (110 lbf/in$^2$).

*Operation*    Air from the compressor passes to the reservoir (Figure 350) via chamber A and the spring-loaded check valve. Air at reservoir pressure has access to the face of the pilot valve piston and port E via passage B. Port E is provided for the use of a safety valve, low-pressure indicator or pressure gauge.

When the reservoir pressure acting on the face of the pilot valve piston at C reaches the cut-out setting, controlled by the force of the control spring, the pilot valve moves towards seat F. As soon as the seal between the pilot valve piston and the seat D is broken – by contacting the push rod – a larger area of pilot valve is exposed to the reservoir pressure, which snaps the valve piston over to seat F. At the same time reservoir pressure will pass from passage B to chamber G via the annular clearance between the valve piston and bush. This pressure on top of the relay piston, together with compressor pressure in chamber A, opens the exhaust valve and holds it open by pressure via chamber G. The compressor now pumps to atmosphere and the pressure in the reservoir, plus spring action, holds the check valve on its seat to seal off the air in the reservoir. As pressure in the reservoir is reduced to below the cut-out setting, the control spring overcomes the reduced air pressure on the face of the pilot valve piston at C and it moves towards its seat at D. As soon as the piston moves away from its seal at F, pressure from chamber G leaks to atmosphere through the control spring housing. This allows the return springs of the relay piston and exhaust valve to return them to their original position and the compressor will be able to charge the reservoir again.

*Reservoirs*

These are usually heavy-gauge cylindrical steel tanks containing air at a pressure of approximately 827 kN/m² (110 lbf/in²). All inlet unions from the compressor are fitted with single check valves which prevent loss of air should the compressor valves or pipe lines fail. Because air which is delivered to these tanks may contain a certain percentage of oil and water vapour which may foul valves in the system, some means of extracting these contaminants is necessary. All reservoirs are fitted with drain cocks at their lowest parts and manual operation of these will extract the water and oil. A more satisfactory system is to fit a 'wet tank' before the main reservoirs where the vapours are condensed and collected. An automatic drain valve is fitted to the lowest point in this tank, which opens when the governor or unloader valve operates and releases any condensate which has collected.

An alcohol evaporator is often fitted to the inlet side of the compressor to prevent freezing of the water vapour which may form ice, preventing operation of the valves in extremely cold operating conditions. A check valve prevents loss of alcohol when the compressor is running 'light'.

*Operation* When the compressor is charging, a partial vacuum is present above the alcohol in its bottle. Air drawn through a filter bubbles up through the alcohol and, carrying alcohol in

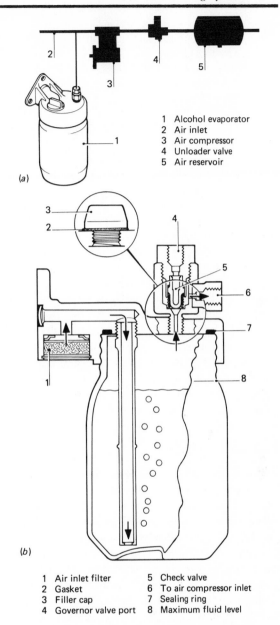

1 Alcohol evaporator
2 Air inlet
3 Air compressor
4 Unloader valve
5 Air reservoir

(a)

1 Air inlet filter
2 Gasket
3 Filler cap
4 Governor valve port
5 Check valve
6 To air compressor inlet
7 Sealing ring
8 Maximum fluid level

(b)

Figure 351 *Alcohol evaporator and check valve*

vapour form, passes into the air inlet pipe to the compressor.

To prevent the loss of alcohol when the compressor is running 'light', a check valve is fitted (Figure 351b). Normally, this is held off its seat by the return spring, but when the governor valve stops the compressor charging, compressed air passes to the check valve which closes the vapour passage to the compressor.

*Automatic drain valve operation* When the system is being charged, the edge of the diaphragm is moved away from the inlet seat by the compressed air. This allows any water or oil to collect in the cover (Figure 352). When the governor or unloader valve cuts out, the diaphragm-type spring, under the diaphragm, pushes it to seal against the inlet seat. If there is any loss of air due to a control valve being operated [0.14 kg/cm$^2$ (2 lbf/in$^2$)], the pressure in the cover, acting on the lower face of the valve A which is higher than the pressure acting above, lifts the valve away from the exhaust seat. Compressed air, oil and water can now escape from the cover, until the higher pressure above the valve closes the exhaust seat. The procedure begins again with air pressure moving the edge of the diaphragm away from the inlet seat and building up until there is a further drop in pressure. Manual draining can be carried out by depressing the wire protruding from the drain port.

## Indication equipment

Pressure gauges and low-pressure audible or visual warning devices are fitted in the driver's cab and connected to the air storage reservoirs. When pressure is low – below 400 kN/m$^2$ (60 lbf/in$^2$) – on initial starting of vehicle or when air is lost from a reservoir, these gauges, buzzers or warning lights are used to inform the driver that it is dangerous to use the vehicle. Low-pressure indicators consist of a spring-loaded diaphragm acting against an electrical contact which completes an electric circuit when pressure is low. This in turn operates the buzzer or light until sufficient pressure is built up to separate the contacts and break the circuit.

*Low-pressure indicator*

*Operation* When the reservoir air pressure rises above the setting pressure of the indicator (usually

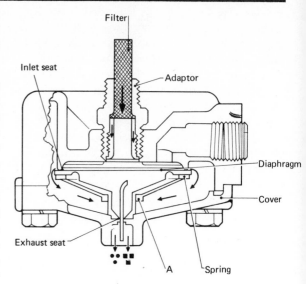

Figure 352　*Automatic drain valve*

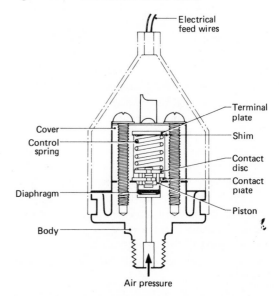

Figure 353　*Low-pressure indicator switch*

4.1 bar, 60 p.s.i.) pressure behind the diaphragm raises the piston and the contact disc against the pressure of the control spring, thereby breaking the electrical contact.

Should the pressure fall below the setting pressure (Figure 353), the reverse operation takes place and electrical contact is made to operate a

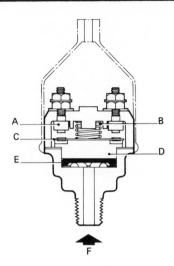

Figure 354    *Stop light switch*

buzzer or warning light in the driving compartment.

### Stop lights

These are fitted into all brake circuits, e.g. in a dual-line circuit there will be two stop light switches, one in the front circuit and one in the rear. The type of switch used in a pressure circuit, i.e. service line, will be shown, as in Figure 354, where the contacts are closed by air pressure. In a secondary circuit, however, when spring brake chambers are used, the spring brake is applied by spring tension when the air is released. In this case, the stop light switch is a low-pressure indicator, as used in Figure 353, whose contacts close when pressure falls below 60 p.s.i. and the stop lights then come on.

*Operation*  Whenever air pressure is applied to the brake chambers (Figure 354), this same pressure is fed to the port F. This acts on the combined diaphragm and seal E which moves the nylon piston D upwards, compressing the spring B thus causing the contact strip C to bridge the contact points in the bases of the two terminal screws A. As these terminals are connected in series with the stop light circuit, the circuit is completed and the stop lights are switched on.

When the brakes are released, the applied pressure will drop at F until overcome by the return spring B, which will push away the contact strip and break the electrical circuit, switching off the stop lights. The switch has been arranged to make contact at approximately 5 p.s.i., thereby ensuring that the stop lights come on immediately a brake application begins.

## Control equipment

### Foot control valves

These units provide the normal means of operating the service brakes on a vehicle. The action of this valve ensures that the pressure in the brake chambers is proportional to the pedal effort.

A single foot control valve regulates the air pressure being delivered to or released from all brake operating cylinders. In a dual-brake valve, one valve normally controls the operation of the rear brakes and a second valve controls the operation of the front brakes.

Normally, line pressure to both valves is balanced during application and release, but as both are supplied from separate air reservoirs failure of one does not affect the other, and 50% of the braking system is still available should any failure occur.

*Operation*  The sectional view in Figure 355 shows the pedal in its released position. As the

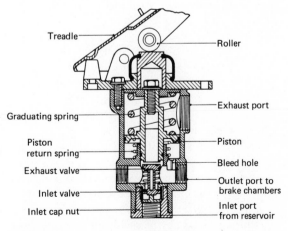

Figure 355    *Sectional view – released position*

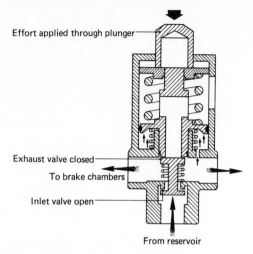

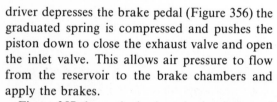

Figure 356    *Applying position*

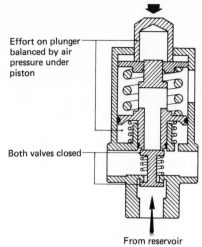

Figure 357    *Balanced position*

driver depresses the brake pedal (Figure 356) the graduated spring is compressed and pushes the piston down to close the exhaust valve and open the inlet valve. This allows air pressure to flow from the reservoir to the brake chambers and apply the brakes.

Figure 357 shows the brake valve in a balanced position – brakes held in applied position according to pressure exerted by driver. In this condition, air pressure, equal to the pressure applying the brakes, builds up below the piston to raise it sufficiently to close the inlet valve but still to hold the exhaust valve closed. When the driver releases the foot pedal (Figure 358), air pressure lifts the piston to open the exhaust valve and all air pressure in the brake chambers is exhausted. When the foot pedal is fully depressed, full air pressure from the reservoir passes to the brake chambers to give full braking effort.

*Quick release valve (Figure 359)*

Instead of air having to travel back to the foot control valve when the brakes are released, a quick release valve is often fitted to front and rear axles. This allows the brakes to be released as quickly as possible and give a more efficient operation.

When air pressure enters through the inlet port, the diaphragm moves down and closes the exhaust

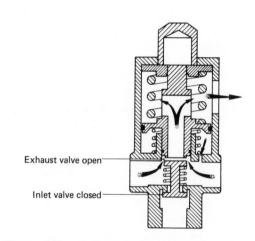

Figure 358    *Releasing position*

port. Air then deflects the outer edges of the flexible diaphragm and flows to the brake chambers. When this pressure is released, brake chamber pressure flexes the diaphragm the other way to open the exhaust port and so release the brakes.

*Pressure protection valve*

These are fitted in the pipe line to check the flow of air to other parts of the system until sufficient pressure has been built up in the system

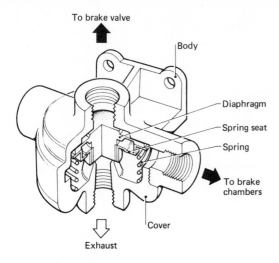

Figure 359    *Quick release valve*

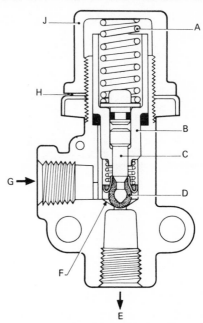

Figure 360    *Operation of pressure protection valve*

immediately preceding the valve. It can be used also to safeguard a system against loss of air, e.g. if the trailer coupling is disconnected from a tractive unit this valve prevents loss of air from the main tractor system. Another use is to fit a pressure protection valve between reservoirs to ensure that the first reservoir is sufficiently charged before allowing air into the second reservoir.

The valve consists of a spring-loaded diaphragm which is balanced against air pressure which, when approximately 400 kN/m$^2$ (60 lbf/in$^2$) is reached, lifts the diaphragm to allow free flow of air through the unit.

*Operation*    When air is applied to the supply port G (Figure 360), pressure will build up under the piston B until it overcomes the force of the control spring A. The piston then rises, lifting the valve stem C, and opening the inlet valve D at F. This allows the applied air to flow through the valve and out of the delivery port E. When the air pressure beneath the piston is reduced to a force lower than that exerted by the control spring, the piston is pushed down to close the inlet valve, preventing any further flow to the delivery port. The force of the spring, and therefore the amount of air pressure required to open the valve, is controlled by the setting of the cap J. Turning this

cap clockwise raises the pressure setting, and turning it anti-clockwise lowers the pressure setting.

*Pressure-reducing valves and limiting valves*
These are used to reduce pressure in a part of the circuit and maintain a predetermined value below normal line pressure. Their main use is in auxiliary circuits, e.g. air-operated windscreen wiper motors and air horns.

*Relay valve*
This valve is used to increase the speed of application of the brakes. On a long wheelbase vehicle or on a unit and trailer, the rear brakes will be applied later than the front brakes if air had to travel from the reservoir, through the foot valve, to the brake chambers. The valve can be fitted in a convenient position where a 'signal' pressure from the controlling valve can be used to 'open' the relay valve and allow air, straight from the reservoir, to pass straight to the brake-operating chambers.

*Operation*    When a signal pressure is applied to port D (Figure 361) air flows into chamber C

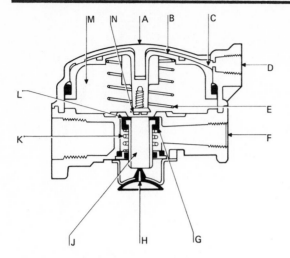

Figure 361    *Relay valve*

between the cover A and the top of the piston B. A relatively small applied pressure reacts quickly over the large area of piston B, which is forced down against the spring E. This movement of the piston closes the exhaust passage as the valve seat N seals against the inlet/exhaust valve G, which is also moved down against the return spring K and opens the inlet at L. Air now flows from the reservoir port F past the open valve chamber M, and from there it passes out of one of the delivery ports. This flow continues until the combined forces of the piston and valve return springs and the air pressure beneath the piston balance the force of the applied air pressure above the piston. The piston now lifts sufficiently to allow the valve to rise and close the inlet at L. The valve is now in the 'lapped' condition with both the inlet and the exhaust closed.

If the signal pressure is reduced at D, the forces below the piston are now the greater, and the piston rises until the valve seat N is lifted clear of the valve, allowing air to exhaust through the hollow in the piston at J, and out to atmosphere past the rubber flap at H.

The exhaustion continues until the force below the piston is reduced to balance that above the piston, and the exhaust closes again, lapping the valve.

These procedures are repeated instantly the applied pressure at port D is varied, either up or down, the valve being self-lapping under all conditions.

*Relay emergency valve*
This is used on a trailer as an ordinary relay valve which applies the brakes; also incorporated with this assembly is an emergency valve. This valve

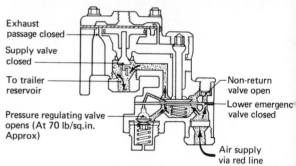

(a)    *Charging trailer reservoir*

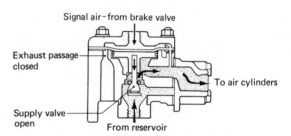

(b)    *Normal relay valve operation*

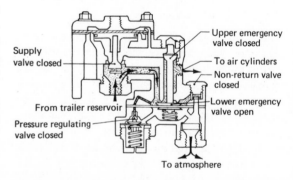

(c)    *Emergency application – when supply line is exhausted*

Figure 362    *Principle of operation of relay emergency valve*

automatically applies the brakes to the trailer and prevents loss of air when tractive unit and trailer are disconnected.

### Principle of operation

The emergency line connection from the tractive unit supplies air pressure to the trailer reservoir. This pressure lifts the diaphragm against its spring (Figure 362) to allow air to flow to the reservoir. The movement of the diaphragm also unseats another valve which allows air to pass to the brake chambers when required, and at the same time isolates them from either reservoir. When the trailer line is disconnected, pressure falls beneath the diaphragm, allows the diaphragm and valve to seat, and prevents loss of air. At the same time air from the trailer reservoir passes to the brake chambers to apply the brake. Before the brakes can be released, a pressure has to be re-applied via the emergency line, or the trailer reservoir supply has to be exhausted.

### Differential protection valve

This is a valve fitted to a system using spring brake actuators, where both the service air pressure and the secondary system spring pressure may be applied at the same time. If this were to happen, the spring brake actuator push rod, slack adjuster and the back plate would be overloaded leading to possible damage.

*Operation* When all the brakes are off, the service line is exhausted (Figure 363), and air pressure in the secondary line – holding the springs off – passes through the secondary port D to A and C, and the spring chambers. If the spring brakes are applied whilst the service brake is 'on', air exhausts normally through the hand control and relay valve. As the air pressure in the service line quickly becomes greater than that in the secondary line, it is able to push the inner piston across and seal off the secondary port D. The outer piston can then be pushed open and allow service air to pass through ports A and C to hold the springs off. When the pressure in the service line is reduced, first the outer piston, then the inner piston move back, by spring pressure, to

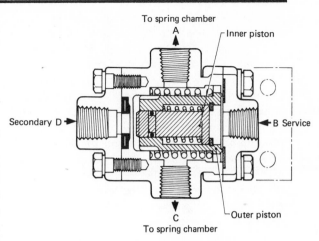

Figure 363    *Differential protection valve*

open port D and allow the spring chambers to exhaust and apply the secondary brake.

If the service brake is applied whilst the spring brake is 'on', because the secondary port D and all the spring chambers are exhausted, air pressure from the service line can push the inner piston, to close port D, and then push the outer piston off its seat. This will allow service air into the spring chambers and hold the springs off. When the service brake is released, air pressure to the valve is released and allows the springs to reapply the brake.

### Variable-load valve

This is fitted to the vehicle or trailer chassis with a link to the axle (Figure 364). Its purpose is to

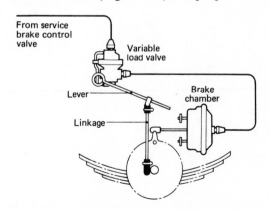

Figure 364    *Connection of variable-load valve*

regulate air pressure and therefore braking force, usually to tractive unit rear axles and trailer axles. When a particular axle is unladen it may require less braking force than when laden to prevent the brakes 'locking' and therefore skidding and possibly allowing a unit and trailer to 'jack-knife'. When the axle is unladen, the springs are only slightly compressed and the lever is in its lowest position and delivers a lower air pressure to the brake chambers on that axle. As the load on the axle is increased, the distance between the axle and the chassis decreases and the lever moves up to allow more air pressure to pass to the brake chambers.

### Hand-operated brake control valves

This type of hand valve (Figure 365) is used in the air brake system of a rigid vehicle. Control valves within the unit direct air as required to the spring brake chambers.

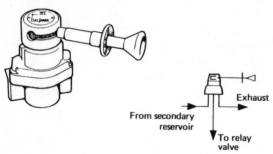

Figure 365　*Spring brake control valve – rigid*

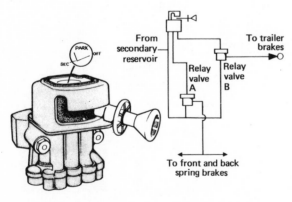

Figure 366　*Spring brake control valve – tractive unit*

In the 'off' position, air from the secondary reservoir is directed through the valve to send signal pressure to a relay valve which opens up and allows air pressure to pass to the brake chambers to compress the springs and therefore hold the brakes 'off'.

As the handle is moved towards secondary position, the air in the signal line is exhausted which closes down the relay valve and exhausts air in the line to the quick release valve which in turn releases air from the spring brake chambers to apply the brakes. Speed of movement of the lever controls the speed of application and release of the brakes. Full application of the control handle automatically locks it in park position. To release, the driver has to withdraw the spring-loaded outer sleeve before it can be moved.

The valve shown in Figure 366 is designed for use where the tractive unit has spring brakes and the trailer has diaphragm brake chambers.

When the brakes are 'off', air is supplied to the spring brake chambers to hold the springs off and no air is supplied to the trailer brakes. To make a secondary brake application, the handle is moved to the secondary position and in the process, valves inside the unit:

1　Exhaust air pressure to relay valve A to allow application of the spring brakes.
2　Send air pressure to relay valve B which opens up and allows air pressure from the secondary reservoir to pass through and apply the diaphragm brakes on the trailer.

When the handle is moved into 'park' position, air is released from all brake chambers. If the tractive unit is to be separated from its semi-trailer, the driver must first apply the mechanical ratchet brake to hold the trailer brakes on.

### Actuation equipment

Brake operating chambers are usually mounted on the axle or direct to the backplate. Operation is either through a mechanical linkage which rotates a cam to operate the brake shoes or directly to a wedge which forces the shoes apart.

Single-diaphragm chambers consist of two steel pressings with a rubber diaphragm clamped between them (Figure 367). A push rod and plate assembly, against which the diaphragm operates, is held in the released position by a return spring. When compressed air is introduced into the sealed chamber, the diaphragm, acting against the push plate, forces the push rod assembly outwards. The force of this application depends upon the area of the diaphragm and the pressure of air which is allowed into the chamber. When this pressure is released, the return spring returns the push plate and diaphragm back to its original position.

Double-diaphragm brake chambers (Figure 368) contain two separate sealed chambers with separate diaphragms. Each is able to operate the brake push rod and provides an independently operated source of braking. The service diaphragm is fed from a side port and the secondary or parking diaphragm is fed from a central rear port. If any diaphragm should fail the remaining one will still operate the brake shoes.

### Lock actuators (Figure 369)

A lock actuator is a diaphragm-operated brake chamber with rollers that can be used to lock the brake push rod in position after application of the brake. This provides a mechanically operated parking brake which is still operative when all air has left the brake chamber. The parking function is operated by releasing air pressure in the lock port which acts against a small piston. This allows the spring to push the rollers against the collar and so wedge the push rod in position.

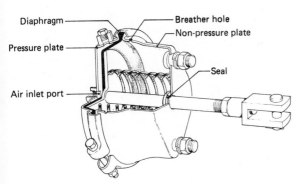

Figure 367 *Cut-away single-diaphragm brake chamber*

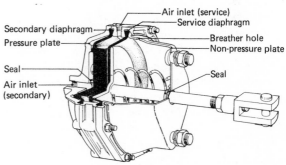

Figure 368 *Cut-away double-diaphragm brake chamber*

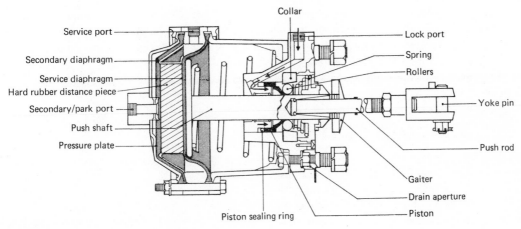

Figure 369 *Lock actuator chamber*

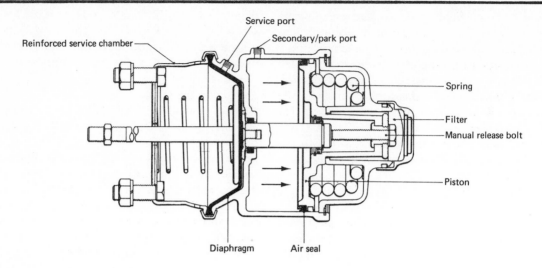

Figure 370   *Spring brake actuator*

### Spring brake actuators (Figure 370)

The front portion of a spring brake chamber is similar to a conventional brake chamber. The rear portion contains a piston and powerful coil spring. Under normal operating conditions this spring is held compressed by an air supply acting against the piston. When the service brake is applied, the front chamber is filled with air and the diaphragm applies the brake. When the secondary brake is applied, air from the rear cylinder is expelled and the spring applies the brake. Parking brake function also releases air from the rear cylinder and the spring force holds the brakes applied until air pressure is reintroduced. The manual release on the rear of the actuator allows the brakes to be released when air pressure is not available – when the bolt is screwed out, it shortens the effective length of the push rod to prevent it operating the foundation brake. It also allows service diaphragms or brake linings to be changed without removing the actuator from the vehicle.

### Slack adjusters

These serve as a lever during normal braking operations and provide a quick and easy method of adjusting the brake shoes. When the adjusting screw is rotated (Figure 372), the worm gear rotates the camshaft which in turn spreads the brake shoes to give the correct brake lining clearance. Automatic slack adjusters are also used, which eliminate the need for manual adjustment by continuously and automatically compensating for wear of the brake linings.

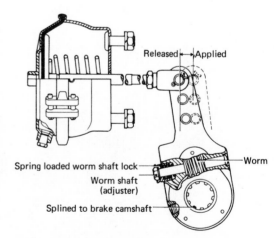

Figure 372   *Slack adjuster*

Figure 371   *Operation of a spring brake actuator*

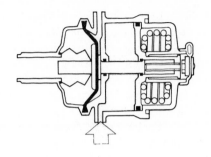

(a)   *Normal driving   In its 'off' position the hand control valve in the driver's cab maintains a constant air pressure on the spring brake piston. The resulting compression of the powerful brake spring releases the vehicle brake and allows the vehicle to move. This system ensures that the vehicle cannot be moved until sufficient air pressure is available to hold off the brake spring*

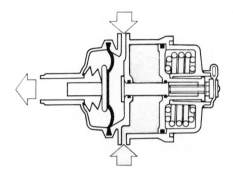

(b)   *Service brake   The service brake chamber is of the conventional diaphragm type. The vehicle service braking effort is controlled by a foot operated brake valve in the driver's cab. The valve supplies a gradual air pressure to the service brake chamber while the spring brake continues to be held off by the air pressure from the hand control valve*

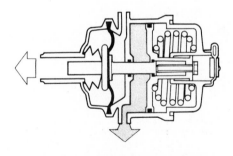

(c)   *Secondary and parking brake   Moving the hand control valve handle from 'off' towards 'secondary park' gradually releases air pressure from the spring brake chamber and allows the brake spring to extend. Progressive secondary braking is provided by the increasing spring pressure on the service brake push rod. At 'park' the air pressure has been exhausted and the vehicle brake is held on by the force of the brake spring alone. Any loss of air pressure from the braking system will also result in an automatic application of the spring brake*

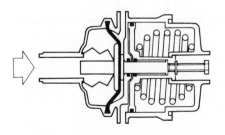

(d)   *Manual release   The readily accessible brake spring release bolt allows the vehicle to be moved in the absence of air pressure and permits the safe and speedy servicing of the actuator and foundation brake. Note that the spring brake is still applied, but the foundation brakes are released*

## Braking system layouts

### Dual system

This is a system used on rigid vehicles. Figure 373 shows a typical layout using single- and double-diaphragm brake chambers. The main system is divided up into two separate circuits. A dual foot valve is supplied with air from a divided reservoir – one half operates the front brake chambers and the other half the rear. Air pressure from a third reservoir supplies air for the parking brake. When the handbrake lever is operated, an air valve supplies air pressure to the secondary diaphragms on the rear axle. At the same time the mechanical linkage is applied and holds the brakes in the locked position.

### Three-line system (Figure 374)

This system is used on articulated tractive units which are also required to supply air to a trailer braking system. Double-diaphragm actuator units are fitted to all wheels and the tractive unit service brakes are operated by a single or dual foot valve.

This supplies air to one of these diaphragms and to the relay valve which sends an air pressure signal only to the trailer braking system. The large air reservoir supplies air for service operation of tractive unit brakes and supplies air to the trailer reservoir through the emergency line. The pressure protection valve and the relay valve prevent loss of air in the tractive unit system if there is failure in trailer brake or couplings. The second air reservoir supplies air for power operation of the handbrake, as in the dual system, and also for the secondary brake system. This is operated by a graduated hand valve which, when operated, supplies air to the front chambers of the tractive unit brakes and also through the secondary brake coupling to all trailer brakes. This reduces the risk of jack-knifing when the secondary brake is applied in an emergency.

### Trailer braking (Figure 375)

A separate reservoir is fitted to a trailer or semi-trailer which receives its supply from the main tractive unit reservoir. When the service brake is

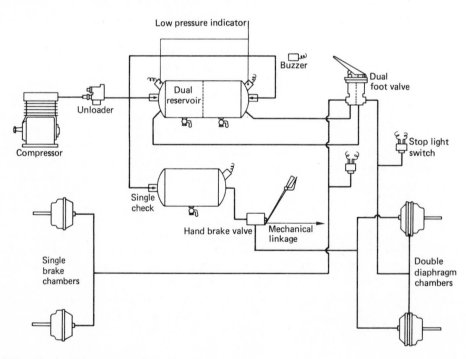

Figure 373  *Dual air brake system*

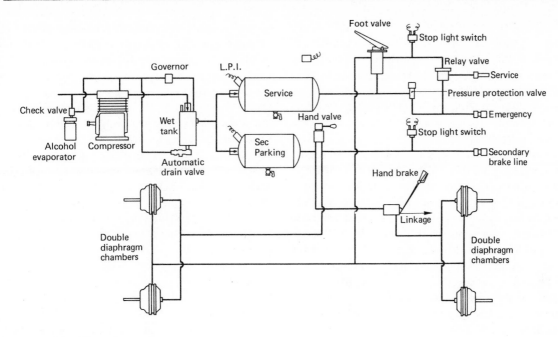

Figure 374   *Three-line system*

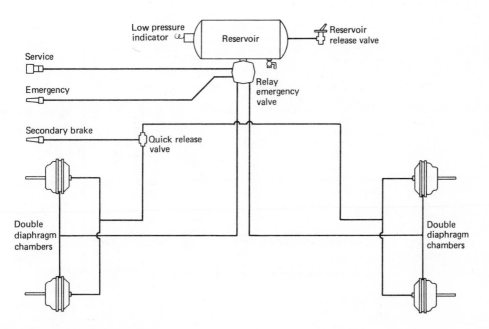

Figure 375   *Three-line trailer system*

applied, the signal received from the relay valve operates the relay emergency valve fitted to the trailer, which in turn allows an equal pressure to operate the trailer service brakes from its own reservoir. This system speeds up the application and release of the trailer brakes which may be some distance from the driver's foot control and may also reduce the drain on the tractive unit's main reservoir.

Secondary brake application is controlled by the driver's hand-operated lever which operates the outer diaphragm of the double-diaphragm brake actuators. If any drop in pressure occurs in the emergency line – below a pre-determined pressure – the emergency relay valve will automatically apply the trailer service brakes from the reservoir on the trailer. The reservoir release valve is fitted to allow the trailer air system to be exhausted when the emergency valve has operated, when the trailer is disconnected, for example.

*Spring brake circuit (Figure 376)*
A single foot valve operates the diaphragms in the spring brake chambers to provide service braking. The hand valve controls secondary and

parking brake operations. Vehicles fitted with this system cannot be moved until sufficient air pressure has been built up in the reservoirs to compress the springs in the brake chambers. As the hand valve is moved from the park position, the relay valve allows air to pass to the brake chambers and compress the springs which release the brakes. When the lever is moved to the park/secondary position, air pressure is exhausted from the hand control valve, relay valve and quick release valves and allows the springs to apply the brakes. Service and secondary lines are connected by a differential protection valve which prevents both systems applying the brakes at the same time which may seriously overload the mechanical components.

*Lock actuator system (Figure 377)*
This is very similar to a dual system with the addition of a control line to operate the locking device. The service reservoirs are fitted with a biased non-return valve which maintains the reservoir air pressure $100–135$ kN/m$^2$ ($15–20$ lbf/in$^2$) below the secondary reservoir pressure. This ensures that, even if the service brake valve is fully applied when the lock mechanism is engaged,

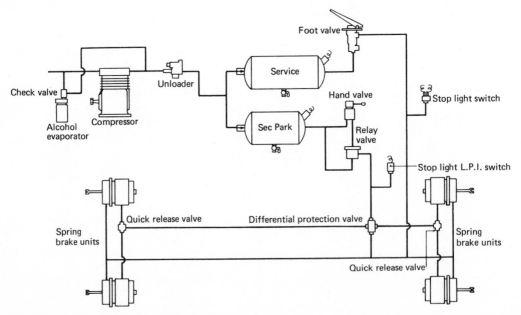

Figure 376   *Rigid vehicle with spring brake chambers*

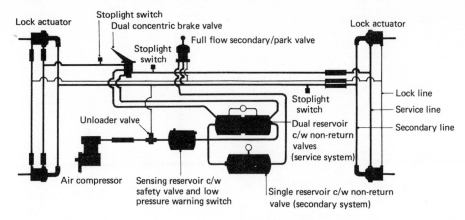

Figure 377  *Typical air pressure braking system with lock actuators*

the locks can still be released by correctly moving the secondary/park valve lever across the gate. To ensure that sufficient pressure is available to free the locks under abnormal conditions, the governor or unloader valve is prevented from cutting out when the control lever is moved to the 'unlock' gate.

Operations to release the parking lock and brake:

1 Air enters to operate the secondary diaphragm.
2 Air enters lock port and acts against the piston.
3 Normal secondary reservoir pressure is applied to the secondary diaphragm giving it a further slight movement which allows the piston to push the rollers against spring

pressure and so release the push shaft. If this pressure is insufficient to release the rollers, the lever can be held in the unlock position which overrides the governor and therefore gives additional effort to the secondary diaphragm.

4 Air pressure exhausts to atmosphere through the hand valve and the brake is released.

When applying the parking brake, auxiliary and unlock positions are not used:

1 Air pressure acting against secondary diaphragm applies the brake.
2 Air pressure holding rollers is released.
3 Air pressure is released and the spring-loaded rollers are wedged between the collar and push shaft to lock the brake in the applied position.

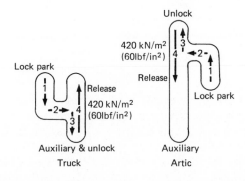

Figure 378  *Releasing the parking lock and brake*

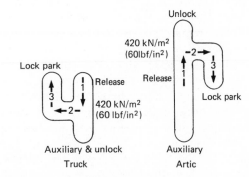

Figure 379  *Applying the parking brake*

### Exhaust brakes (Figure 380)

The function of an exhaust brake is to increase an engine's natural braking effect. This is achieved by blocking off the exhaust system and turning the engine into a low-pressure single-stage compressor.

There are many ways of bringing the system into operation but basically a butterfly valve, or sliding vane valve – electrically or air-operated – closes the exhaust pipe between the engine manifold and silencer. When this valve is closed the fuel supply to the combustion chambers is also cut off.

Pressure builds up as air is pushed into the closed-off manifold. When the air has built up sufficient pressure, it is strong enough to overcome the exhaust valve springs and force its way back into the cylinder. Maximum working pressure is the pressure required to overcome the exhaust valve springs sufficiently to allow this flow back of air. The piston is therefore working against this air pressure on every compression and exhaust stroke. When at working pressure sufficient new air is drawn in through the inlet valve to replenish any air lost through leakage.

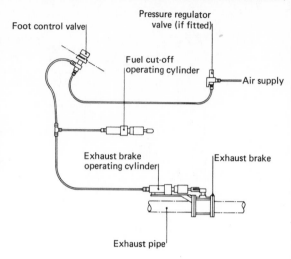

Figure 380   *Typical exhaust brake air pressure system*

### Electric retarders (Figure 381)

This type of retarder is installed somewhere in the transmission line – propeller shaft, directly on the gearbox or directly on the rear axle. Its action is electromagnetic with progressive application by a hand control situated in the driver's cab.

The retarder consists of two main components:
1  A stator fixed to the chassis frame.
2  A rotor running on taper roller bearings inside the stator.

When the hand lever is operated by the driver, groups of four electromagnetic pole pieces in the stator are energized according to the position of the lever. These poles are energized by battery current through a relay box, and the resulting magnetic field creates eddy currents in the rotor discs as they revolve. These eddy currents in turn set up a magnetic drag force tending to stop the rotor. The electrical circuits for each group of

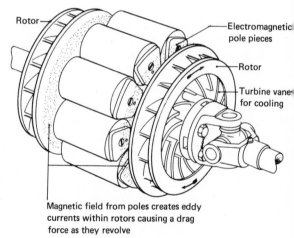

Figure 381   *Electric retarder*

poles are independent, so that failure in any group of pole pieces still leaves the remainder fully operative. A special feature of this type of retarder is its ability to maintain a braking force for long continuous periods owing to the ease with which heat can be dissipated from the rotors which are revolving in the open air.

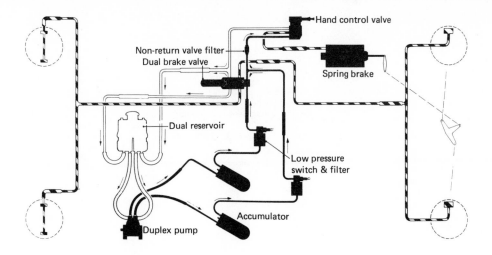

Figure 382  *Full power hydraulic brake system*

## Power-assisted systems

A full-power hydraulic braking system (Figure 382) uses an engine-driven pump to supply hydraulic pressure to operate brake cylinders at each wheel. The pump is fed from a dual-compartment reservoir and supplies fluid at a delivery pressure between 12 500 and 14 500 kN/m² (1800 and 2100 lbf/in²) through two separate pipe lines, to a dual foot valve. Accumulators in the circuits hold a reserve volume of pressure which is available to operate the brakes when pressure is not sufficient, e.g. when several brake operations are required with engine idling, braking is also available in case of engine failure.

The dual foot valve is sensitive to effort exerted by the driver which varies the pressure available to operate the brake shoes. One half of this valve supplies pressure to operate the front brakes, the other half supplies pressure to the rear brakes.

A spring brake, operating through a mechanical linkage is used as a parking brake. During normal running, the spring is held compressed and inoperative by hydraulic pressure acting against the piston. When the hand control valve is operated by the driver, this controls the pressure opposing the spring and allows a gradual application of the parking brake by spring pressure through the independent mechanical linkage.

### Air/hydraulic servo-assisted brakes

An Airpak system combines compressed air and hydraulic fluid for power braking. Figure 383 shows a typical layout. Power for its operation is supplied from an engine-driven compressor which is fed to the integral reservoir. The compressor is controlled by a governor valve and also incorporates a safety valve. The Airpak unit is controlled from hydraulic pressure exerted on the brake pedal by the driver; in the event of loss of air pressure, the brakes will still operate but require much greater pedal pressure.

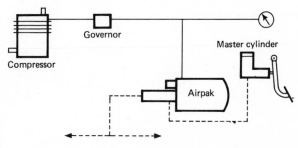

Figure 383  *Air/hydraulic servo assisted brake system*

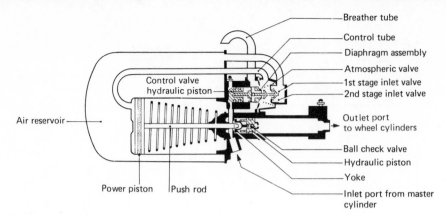

Figure 384   *Airpak in released position*

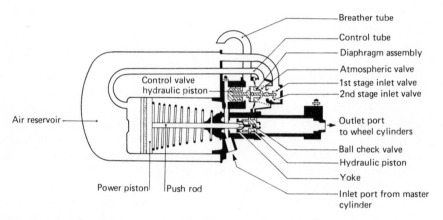

Figure 385   *Applying position*

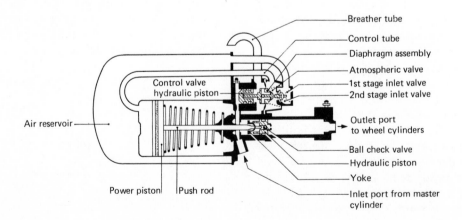

Figure 386   *Applied – valves in 'lap' position*

*Principle of operation* Figure 384 shows a cross-sectional view of an Airpak unit. This consists of an air reservoir, a power piston and cylinder, a hydraulic slave cylinder and a hydraulically actuated control valve. Working in conjunction with a conventional master cylinder, hydraulic pressure applied through the driver's foot pedal actuates the Airpak unit which acts against its own hydraulic cylinder to apply the brakes.

As the brake pedal is depressed (Figure 385), initial fluid pressure from the master cylinder passes through the centre of the hydraulic piston, past the ball check valve and along to the wheel cylinders. This initial pressure is also applied to the control valve hydraulic piston which begins to move to the right against the diaphragm and spring. This initial movement closes the atmospheric valve and further movement opens the first stage inlet valve and allows air to pass from the reservoir, along the control tube to the power cylinder. The yoke remains stationary during initial movement of the power piston which closes the ball check valve; further movement forces hydraulic fluid to the wheel cylinders.

A pressure difference across the control valve diaphragm assembly is equal to the pressure difference across the power piston. The reaction force transmitted back to the driver's foot is therefore proportional to the power piston force and gives 'pedal feel'. When the brake pedal is held stationary, both air inlet and atmospheric valves are seated to assume a lap or holding position. When the brake pedal is fully applied, the control valve hydraulic piston is moved completely to the right which pushes the second stage inlet valve off its seat. This is a larger-diameter valve than the first-stage valve and so a greater volume of air is admitted to the power cylinder which rapidly applies the brakes.

*Dual air/hydraulic braking system*
In this layout (Figure 387) an engine-driven compressor supplies air to a dual reservoir; it is then fed via a dual foot valve to the dual actuator. The actuator contains two power pistons which operate a single push rod in the tandem master cylinder. Each power piston is connected to one of the reservoirs through the brake foot valve. In the

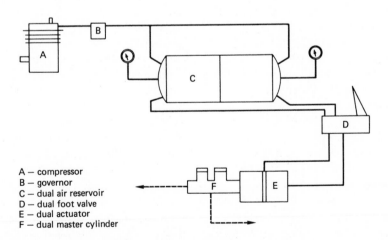

A — compressor
B — governor
C — dual air reservoir
D — dual foot valve
E — dual actuator
F — dual master cylinder

Figure 387 *Dual air/hydraulic braking system*
*In this layout an engine-driven compressor supplies air to a dual reservoir, it is then fed via a dual actuator. The actuator contains two power pistons which operate a single push rod in the tandem master cylinder. Each power station is connected to one of the reservoirs through the brake foot valve. In the event of air pressure loss or failure in one of the air systems, the remaining system would continue to operate the master cylinder but at a reduced pressure*

event of air pressure loss or failure in one of the air systems, the remaining system would continue to operate the master cylinder but at a reduced pressure.

## Air brake systems to meet EEC (European Economic Community) Directives

When the United Kingdom joined the Common Market, we also agreed to abide by a common set of rules and standards. Some of these standards apply to the braking systems of commercial vehicles. In 1964, Plating Regulations in this country were introduced for a three-line system of braking for vehicles drawing a trailer. EEC requirements now recommend that new vehicles and trailers should have a two-line system as a basis for type approval. Other regulations, mainly related to safety, fail-safe and speed of operation and release, mean that new valves and layouts are required to comply fully.

Air dryers are also becoming a popular fitment in place of the alcohol evaporator. The dryer is fully automatic and is designed to remove water, oil, carbon and dirt from compressed air before it enters the storage reservoirs. Air enters the dryer when it is first cooled by contact with the outside wall of the unit. It is then filtered before passing through a dessicant chamber where water vapour is removed – the dessicant is a crystal-type material which can adsorb water in its pores. The dry, cool air then enters a purge chamber before passing to the reservoirs. Everytime the governor valve unloads the compressor, air from the un-loader line opens a purge valve – similar to the way it operates the automatic drain valve. When the purge valve opens:

1  All the condensate collected in the bottom of the dryer is expelled.
2  The dry air collected in the top of the dryer is forced back down through the dessicant, taking the water collected in the crystals with it and out through the open purge valve to atmosphere.

(The crystals a*d*sorb water, i.e. take in droplets of water into their micropore structure without changing their structure or composition. This means that a small quantity of dry air will blow the water out of the pores ready for re-use.)

The crystals are now ready to absorb more water vapour. A heating element in the bottom of the dryer prevents any condensate from freezing in cold weather.

The dry air in the reservoirs increases the life and efficiency of the air braking system. Dry air also prevents the lubricant in the valves and actuators from being washed away by moisture carried along in the air stream.

*Rigid or truck layout (Figure 388)*

This layout is similar to the system already in use with the exception of:

1  Two separate service tanks, one each for front and rear brake chambers, to meet the EEC Directive: 'If there is a failure in a part of the main brake, a sufficient number of wheels must still be braked by the action of the main brake, so the residual efficiency of the main braking equipment is equal to 30% of the efficiency of the vehicle (loaded).'

2  Single-circuit protection valves which replace check valves in the reservoirs. These valves are necessary to comply with the requirement that, should one portion of the complete system fail, the feed to the part not affected by the failure must continue to be ensured as necessary to enable the vehicle to be stopped with the efficiency above. Unlike a check valve, which allows air to flow one-way all the time, a protection valve isolates an affected circuit from the supply and allows the other circuits, operated by air from separate reservoirs, to be charged up normally.

*Tractive unit layout*

In this two-line system, it is permissible under EEC rules to couple a semi-trailer with the braking system of the combination as a dual system split tractor/trailer. The dual foot valve then controls from one side the unit brakes and from the other side, via a multi-relay valve, the trailer brakes. The secondary system and park are combined and work from the hand-operated L gate valve. When the valve is in the 'off' position, the spring

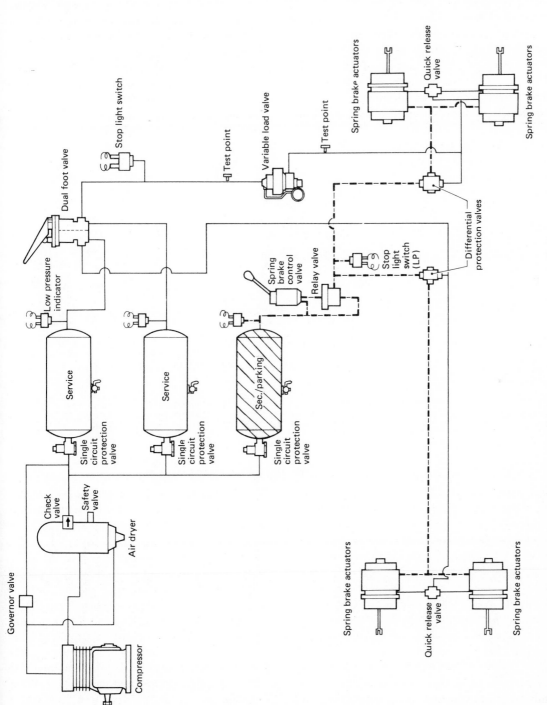

Figure 388 *Rigid vehicle with spring actuators*

actuators are fed with air from the secondary/ park reservoir, via the valve and the differential protection valve to compress the springs and release the brakes. (This means that when the vehicle has been parked overnight, the driver has to wait until sufficient pressure has been built up in the reservoir before the spring brakes can be released.) When a secondary brake application is made, movement of the hand lever:

1    Exhausts air pressure up to the quick-release valves via the exhaust port – release of pressure at the quick-release valves allows air in the spring brake chambers to escape and apply the brakes (application depends upon movement of the handle, i.e. move handle halfway and brakes are applied by half).

2    A pressure signal is sent to the multi-relay valve, which in turn signals the trailer relay valve, via the service line, to apply the trailer– diaphragm brakes.

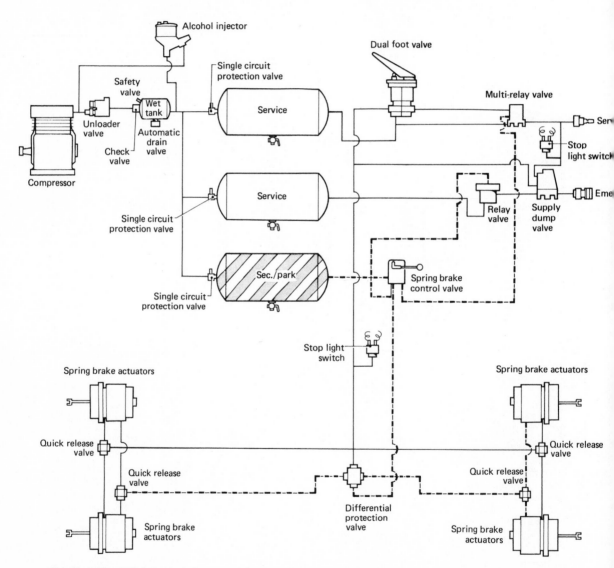

Figure 389    *Tractive unit layout with a two line trailer coupling*

3 When the hand lever is moved to 'park' position, the spring brakes remain on and the trailer brakes are exhausted.

The supply dump valve is used to meet the EEC Directive that should the trailer service line fail, the next full brake application will, within two seconds, automatically reduce the trailer emergency line pressure, which in turn will signal the trailer emergency valve to apply the trailer brakes from air stored in the trailer reservoirs.

*Principle of operation of the supply dump valve*
The valve acts to compare the pressures in the tractive unit service brake system and the trailer service line when a two-line system is used. If the pressure in the unit service brake system is sufficiently in excess of that in the trailer service line, the valve will exhaust the trailer emergency line to apply the trailer brakes.

As can be seen from Figure 391, the multi-relay valve can receive pressure signals from various

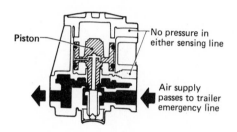

(a) *Normal running When there is no pressure in either sensing line, the valve will allow air to pass from the trailer control or service reservoir on the tractive unit to the emergency (red) coupling line to the trailer*

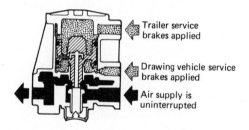

(b) *When a normal brake application is made, i.e. the two sensing lines receive equal air pressure, the piston remains in the same position as in (a)*

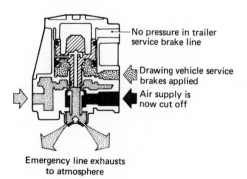

(c) *If the trailer service line is not coupled or has failed, the next service brake application will lift the piston away from the exhaust port and cut off the air supply. Further movement will allow the emergency line to exhaust to atmosphere. This pressure drop will signal the trailer relay emergency valve to make a full trailer brake application from the trailer reservoir*

Figure 390   *Operation of supply dump valve*

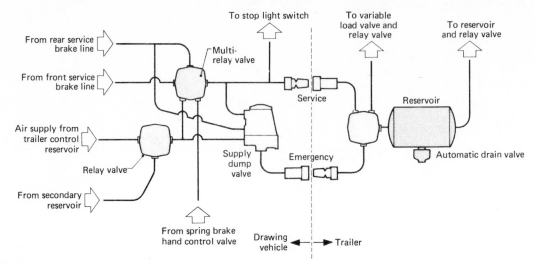

Figure 391    *Alternative connections to the multi-relay valve and dump valve*

sources. The operation is basically the same as a single relay valve which, when signalled, opens up a supply line to quicken the application of the brakes. In this example, the multi-relay valve, attached to the drawing unit, is used to signal the relay emergency valve on the trailer via the service coupling (yellow) and apply the brakes.

### Two-line trailer layout

When a brake application is made, tractor service pressure is passed along the service (or control) line to signal the relay portion of the relay emergency valve, which in turn signals the relay valve via the variable load valve. This relay valve delivers a braking pressure to the diaphragm chambers. Should the pressure in the emergency line fall below a predetermined level, the 'emergency' feature of the relay emergency valve will automatically apply the trailer brakes.

A reservoir is fitted at the front of the trailer, fed from the tractor main reservoir through the emergency (or supply) line and a relay emergency valve. Additionally, a second reservoir with a relay valve is fitted towards the rear of the trailer. The use of relay valves speeds up the application and release of brakes remote from the driver's brake valve. A variable load valve is fitted into the circuit

between the relay emergency valve and the relay valve. This means that air pressure to the diaphragm chambers is varied in accordance with the load carried on the axle or axles.

The reservoirs are fitted with automatic drain valves and the trailer has its own pressure signal to operate a warning device in the tractor cab via an electrical circuit. A brake release valve is fitted so that the trailer air system can be exhausted when the trailer is detached from the tractor to release the brake application which occurs when the emergency line is exhausted.

### Two-line tractive unit with tube-mounted brake chambers

This layout is basically similar to that shown in Figure 389 with the exception that the foundation brakes are of the twin-wedge type operated by tube-mounted brake chambers. The service line operated diaphragm chambers. A, one single (Figure 394) and one in the spring actuator B. The secondary/park system is provided by the spring brake actuators.

### Twin-wedge foundation brake

This type of brake can either use two diaphragm chambers – for front wheel brakes, a diaphragm

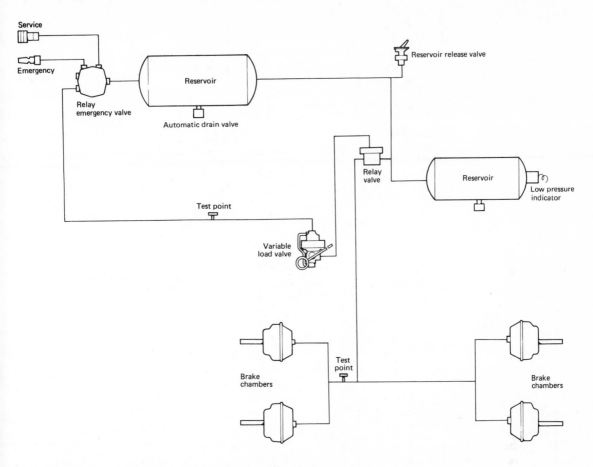

Figure 392 *Two-line trailer layout with two-line coupling*

chamber and a spring brake chamber – to give a two-leading-shoe normal operation and leading/trailing shoe for parking, or two spring brake chambers for a two-leading-shoe operation in all conditions. The two-leading-shoe facility means that a far better braking efficiency can be achieved which is particularly useful for the ever increasing demands to improve safety standards.

The brake chambers are screwed directly into the double-acting expander units. When the brakes are applied, the brake operating chamber pushes a wedge between two tappet faces which in turn push the brake shoes against the drum. An automatic adjuster can be incorporated within the

expander unit or alternatively a manual adjuster, with a hexagon-headed adjuster behind the brake back plate, can be used.

The spring brake chambers used in this system have the usual facility of applying the brake automatically should any loss of air occur, and the spring action may be released by unscrewing the manual release bolt.

## Braking efficiency

Braking efficiency is generally known as the ability of a vehicle's brakes to perform their mechanical

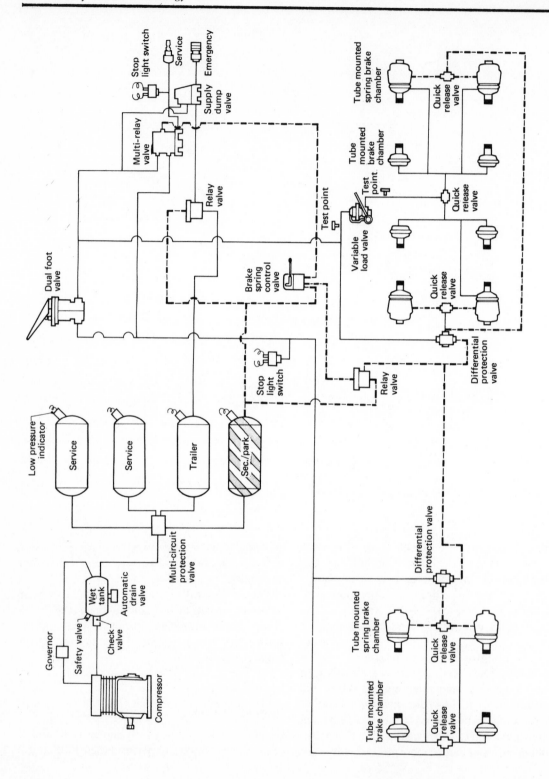

Figure 393   *Two-line tractive unit with tube-mounted brake chambers*

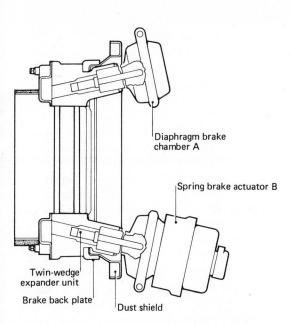

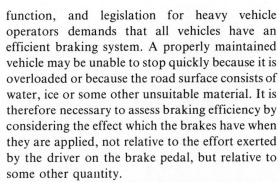

Figure 394   *Tube-mounted brake chambers*

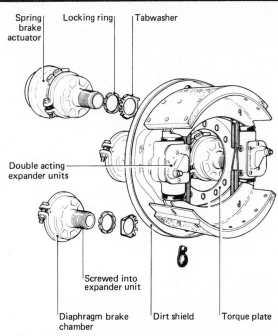

Figure 395   *Two-leading-shoe brake layout*

function, and legislation for heavy vehicle operators demands that all vehicles have an efficient braking system. A properly maintained vehicle may be unable to stop quickly because it is overloaded or because the road surface consists of water, ice or some other unsuitable material. It is therefore necessary to assess braking efficiency by considering the effect which the brakes have when they are applied, not relative to the effort exerted by the driver on the brake pedal, but relative to some other quantity.

When a vehicle is travelling along a level road and the effects of rolling resistance and wind resistance are ignored, the deceleration produced by the braking force depends only on the gross vehicle weight. The expression used for this method of calculating braking efficiency is

Braking efficiency

$$= \frac{\text{Braking force}}{\text{Gross vehicle weight}} \times 100$$

which expresses the braking efficiency as a percentage.

An alternative expression often used for braking efficiency is by comparison with the acceleration due to gravity (*g*). The braking force acting on the gross vehicle weight produces a deceleration which is used in the expression

Braking efficiency

$$= \frac{\text{Deceleration}}{32.2 \text{ or } g} \times 100$$

which expresses the braking efficiency as a percentage.

As the braking force and deceleration are directly related, both expressions give the same answer.

### Determination of braking efficiency

Braking efficiency may be determined in practice by one of the following methods:
1   Measuring the stopping distance or stopping time for a given test speed.
2   Using a brake testing machine.
3   Using a decelerometer.

### Measuring stopping distance

This method consists of driving the vehicle at a constant speed on a level road and measuring the distance covered between the instant when the brake is applied and stopping the vehicle. The test should be carried out at least twice in opposite directions at the same speed to reduce possible inaccuracies resulting from wind resistance and variations in road gradients. The value of the stopping distance is used to determine the value of the braking efficiency from a chart supplied by brake manufacturers and trade associations.

### Measuring stopping time

This method is rarely used as it gives an indication only of vehicle deceleration.

### Brake testing machine

The brake testing machine is used by the Department of Transport for statutory vehicle tests. It is important that vehicle operators check the braking efficiency of their vehicles at regular intervals in the interests of road safety. Many operators include periodic checks in their inspection and service schedules.

The brake testing machine is used in the workshop location and in this respect differs from the decelerometer which is used on a vehicle during road tests. A common brake testing machine is the roller type which tests each axle in turn, either on both wheels at the same time or separately. The vehicle wheels stand on the steel rollers of the testing machine, the rollers have a diamond tread pattern which provides a good grip for the tyre tread.

The testing machine rollers are driven by low-speed electric motors which are worked harder when the vehicle brakes are applied. A load cell is built into the mountings of the machine and measures the braking force as the vehicle brakes are applied. The force is indicated on a dial panel usually remote from the rollers, but visible to the person who is testing the brakes. The braking efficiency is calculated by dividing the total braking force by the gross vehicle weight.

This type of testing machine is expensive to purchase and install, but it is often necessary as a test instrument for use in the interest of braking efficiency legislation. Little skill is required to use this type of machine and it is also useful for diagnosing faults on individual wheel brakes.

### The decelerometer

Deceleration, a reduction in speed, is a direct effect produced by the braking force and can be measured within the vehicle by using a decelerometer. The principal part of a decelerometer is either a pendulum, a spring-mounted mass or a volume of fluid enclosed in a 'U'-shaped tube. When the vehicle and instrument are travelling at constant speed, the movable part assumes a constant neutral position and a zero reading can be observed on a visible scale.

When the decelerometer is to be used in a vehicle to be tested for braking efficiency it must be positioned so that it faces towards the observer and is adjusted for level on its adjustable scale. During brake application the instrument records the effect of deceleration by the movable part which swings from the vertical position. The greater the deceleration the greater will be the swing of the part against its restraint and *vice versa.* A mechanism for damping the action of the movable part is incorporated in the instrument so that vibrations and shocks in the vehicle will not have any effect on its action.

One type of decelerometer carries a stylus at the lower end of the pendulum which swings during brake applications causing the stylus to mark a curved card which is secured below it. The card is printed with a braking efficiency scale and the stylus mark is read against the scale giving the braking efficiency. Another type of instrument incorporates a steel ball fitted inside a curved tube. The tube tilts during brake application and causes shutters of different colours to become visible through small windows from which the braking efficiency is indicated.

Most decelerometers are designed so that their indicating mechanism remains stationary after brake application and has to be cancelled manually. This relieves the driver from making observations of the instrument readings during driving activities. Some instruments are suitable for windscreen mounting, others are recommended to be secured to the vehicle and positioned as close as possible to its centre of gravity.

A decelerometer can be used at any road speed, and provided the brakes are applied for long enough to enable the instrument to give its reading, it is not necessary to keep the brakes applied until the vehicle stops. The instrument is suitable for routine testing of heavy vehicle brakes to ensure that the required minimum braking efficiency is being obtained, although individual brake faults cannot be as easily identified with the decelerometer as with the brake testing machine.

## Factors affecting brake testing and efficiency

### Adhesion
The frictional grip between the tyre and road surface depends upon the nature and condition of the two mating surfaces. The value of this grip is often expressed as the coefficient of adhesion, and when this value is multiplied by the load on the wheel it is known as the adhesive force. If the braking force at any wheel exceeds the adhesive force on that wheel it will lock. A braked wheel exerts maximum deceleration just before its rotation is stopped or locked and exerts a greatly reduced decelerating force when locked which also causes skidding and loss of control.

In order to achieve maximum braking on any type of road surface the braking force on each wheel must be in proportion to the load carried on the wheel concerned. The braking ratio between the different axles of a vehicle needs to be variable if maximum possible braking is to be achieved, and valves are fitted into braking systems to control the braking force on selected axles.

### Severe braking
The effects on the goods or passengers carried on a vehicle during braking, whatever the value of the braking efficiency, is that they are pressed forward relative to the vehicle by a force equal to the same percentage of the weight of goods or passengers. A driver in a goods vehicle who weighs 76 kg (168 lb) who brakes his vehicle with 70% deceleration has to resist a force of 53.3 kg (117.6 lb) which could produce disastrous results if he is not prepared for this effect, or he is not using a seat belt. A similar effect occurs to standing passengers on a bus or coach or to loads carried on goods vehicles. When the vehicle comes to a halt after a sudden deceleration the driver and passengers are subjected to a jerk as the inertia force which their muscles have been resisting suddenly ceases to exist. The maximum braking efficiency of a passenger vehicle is limited for this reason.

### Reaction time
Reaction time is the period that elapses between the instant when the driver perceives a hazard ahead or receives an order to stop and the instant when the brakes first function by his efforts.

When braking efficiency is determined by measuring braking force or deceleration, reaction time is not included but it may be included when the stopping distance or stopping time is measured. Reaction time varies between individuals depending upon their state of alertness or tiredness but a minimum value can be as low as 0.5 s. If a similar value is included in a calculation together with the actual stopping time it will considerably influence the value of the braking efficiency being calculated.

### Braking on gradients
It is more usual to conduct brake tests on a level surface but tests may be carried out on an incline with equally accurate results provided that simple allowances are made for the angle of the gradient.

### Weight transfer
Weight transfer during braking varies the loading on axles and wheels and so affects the adhesion available at the contact point between tyre and road surface. If a decelerometer is used with a vehicle having a suspension system which dips forward during braking a slight error in the reading will occur. However this affects the reading of braking efficiency to the value of about 0.5 and may be ignored.

### Brake fade
Excessive and prolonged braking will increase the

operating temperature of brake linings and reduce the braking efficiency of the vehicle.

## Legal requirements for braking efficiencies

25%  Minimum secondary brake requirement for goods vehicles registered on or after 1 January 1968.

50%  Minimum requirement for main brakes of goods vehicles registered on or after 1 January 1968.

60%  Satisfactory for main brakes of goods vehicles. Maximum desirable for passenger safety in PSVs.

70%  Normal maximum for goods vehicles under favourable conditions.

100%  Seldom achieved except under ideal conditions.

*Note:*  Parking brakes for goods vehicles registered after 1 January 1968 are required to hold on a 1 in 6.25 gradient. This is equivalent to a deceleration of 16%.

# 9 Electrical equipment and accessories

## Starter motors

The starting characteristics of a compression ignition engine are different from those of a spark ignition engine. Although electric starter motors are mainly used for starting compression ignition engines fitted to heavy vehicles, other means are also available. Because of the varied operating conditions of these engines and their size, other power sources are used to turn the engine.

*1 Compressed air* This can be either an air type motor which drives a conventional Bendix pinion or compressed air directed into one or more of the engine cylinders.

*2 Hydraulic motors* Where hydraulic pressure is available, this can be used to actuate a hydraulic motor to drive a conventional Bendix pinion.

*3 Petrol engine* Large CI engines can be started using an auxiliary or 'donkey' engine to rotate the crankshaft.

*4 Cartridge starters* Used to generate gas which acts against an auxiliary piston which in turn is used to engage a starter dog and turn the main engine's crankshaft.

## Electric starter motors

Design considerations require that the starter motor engages, is retained in mesh with the ring gear, and is retracted at the correct time. These problems can be reduced if a separate engaging solenoid is used for advancing the pinion into mesh and an automatic withdrawal device or clutch used to limit the armature speed.

Under cold-start conditions, the starter motor for a CI engine will be required to turn the engine over for a longer period than for a petrol engine. When the engine begins to 'fire' the acceleration of the CI engine flywheel would be sufficient to throw an inertia type of starter pinion prematurely out of mesh. This problem can be overcome if a separate solenoid is used to pre-engage the pinion with the flywheel so that the engine can be turned over until it starts and begins to run. An automatic withdrawal device or overrun clutch should also be incorporated to limit the armature speed which would otherwise be damaged – with a gear reduction of 10:1 between flywheel ring-gear and starter pinion, armature speed could reach 10 000–12 000 rev/min when the engine begins to run regularly. Because of these considerations, the starter motor requires to be more robust and is often a 24-V motor which gives more torque with a comparatively small size of motor.

Two main types of starter motor are used for starting engines fitted to heavy vehicles:

*1 Axial starter* The complete armature assembly moves to engage the pinion with the ring gear.

*2 Co-axial starter* The pinion only moves into mesh axially with the ring gear.

## Principle of operation

A starter motor is a device that converts electrical energy into mechanical energy. The main components are an armature, field coils and brushes. All the wiring is heavy duty to be able to cope with the very high current which passes when the motor is operated under load.

The starter motor is turned by the interaction of two magnetic fields – one produced by the field coils and one produced by the armature windings (Figure 396). When the field coils are energized, a magnetic field exists between the two pole pieces; when the armature windings carry current, a magnetic field surrounds the windings. When these two are placed together, the distortion created by the two magnetic fields produces movement.

In practice four field coils surrounding four pole-shoes are used to produce a concentrated magnetic field. These field coils are wound so as to produce alternate north and south poles. After passing around the field coils the current passes through two brushes to the armature windings and then via two more brushes to earth to complete the circuit.

### Internal connections

Two main circuit layouts are used for starter motors: series wound and series-parallel wound (Figure 397).

The series-wound motor is suitable for use as a starter motor because of its ability to generate a high torque which is necessary to turn the engine from rest and to overcome the first compression stroke. It is then able to continue turning the engine at a speed that is high enough to start the engine. In order to give this initial high torque under starting conditions, using a reasonable size of motor and battery, a small pinion gear engages with the large ring gear mounted on the flywheel. This gives an equivalent gear ratio of approximately 10:1.

### Axial starter motors (Figure 398)

In this sliding armature type of starter motor, the meshing of the pinion and cranking of the engine are actuated by a solenoid switch mounted in the motor itself. This is operated by a push-button on the dash board (Figure 399).

*Operation* Surrounding the armature of this starter motor are three field coils:

1　Main field coil to turn the motor.

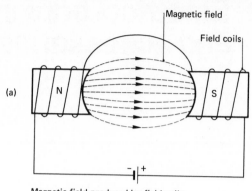

Magnetic field produced by field coils

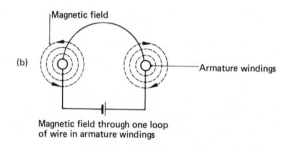

Magnetic field through one loop of wire in armature windings

When current is passed through armature and field windings the armature is moved as shown

Figure 396　*Principle of starter motor*

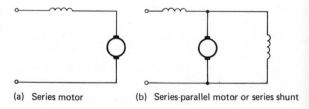

(a) Series motor　　　　(b) Series-parallel motor or series shunt

Figure 397　*Internal circuits*

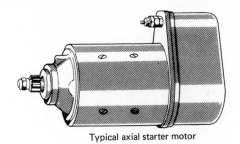

Typical axial starter motor

Figure 398   *Typical axial starter motor*

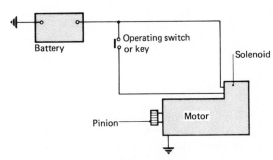

Figure 399   *Layout of starter circuit*

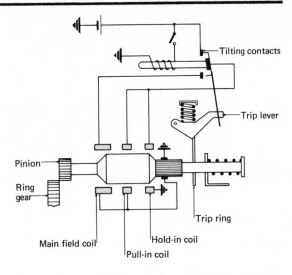

Figure 400   *Stage one: trip lever hold tilting contact, current passes to pull-in coil which draws armature into mesh*

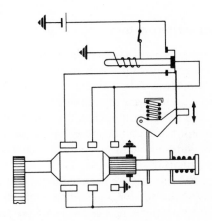

Figure 401   *Stage two: strip releases trip lever to allow full contact of points. Main field coil receives current to turn motor*

2   Auxiliary field coil used to slide the armature and pinion into mesh.

3   Hold-in coil to prevent the pinion from being flung out of mesh.

When at rest the armature is held slightly out of the field coils which therefore holds the pinion out of mesh with the ring gear. When the starter button is operated the solenoid operates the starter motor in two stages.

*Stage 1 (Figure 400)*   When the starter button is depressed, the solenoid attracts the contact bridge but only one half contacts because the trip lever holds the lower half away. This energizes the auxiliary and hold-in coils. The armature is then drawn axially into the main field coil by the auxiliary field coil; for this movement a long commutator is required because the brush gear is common to both operations. At the same time as this axial movement, the armature is rotated slowly; this ensures that the pinion will mesh with the ring gear irrespective of the position of the meshing teeth.

*Stage 2 (Figure 401)*   When the pinion is meshed with the ring gear a trip ring on the armature shaft operates the trip lever which in turn allows the contact bridge to make full contact which energizes the main field coils. As soon as the main field coil is energized, the motor develops its full torque and begins to turn the engine. The hold-in

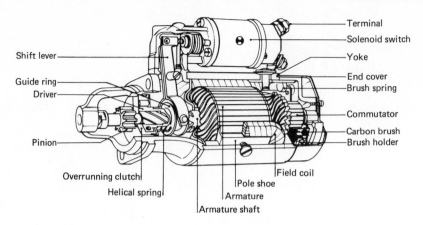

Figure 402   *Coaxial starter motor with external solenoid*

coil keeps the armature in the engaged position until the starter button is released. This prevents early disengagement as the engine begins to 'fire'.

## Co-axial starter motors

This is a pre-engaged type of starter motor, with the pinion only moving axially to engage with the flywheel ring gear. Two main types are used, both having electromagnetic meshing devices: one has the solenoid switch mounted on the outside of the starter motor body, and the other has the solenoid and switching mechanism mounted co-axially with the armature shaft.

Figure 402 shows a pre-engaged motor with an externally mounted solenoid switch. This design gives a short overall length and yet incorporates a roller type of overrun clutch.

*Operation (Figures 403–5)* A push button or ignition-type switch is used by the driver to energize the solenoid. The solenoid has two windings connected in parallel – a pull-in coil and a hold-in coil, both of which are used to attract a plunger into the solenoid. This movement pulls the shift lever which, because of its pivot, pushes the pinion – via guide ring and driver – into mesh with the ring gear. Whilst the pinion is being pushed into mesh, a turning movement is also given to the pinion because of the effect of the

coarse thread. This helps to ensure correct meshing of pinion and ring gear.

When the pinion is in mesh, the plunger in the solenoid closes the main contacts and current is then fed to the armature and it begins to turn. The pull-in coil is short-circuited and the hold-in coil keeps the pinion engaged until the starter button is released.

If the pinion meets tooth-to-tooth with the ring gear, the solenoid switch closes normally. The shift lever, however, only compresses the helical spring between its guide ring and overrun clutch so that when the contacts close, the armature rotates and the pinion engages under the force of the compressed spring.

In order to shorten the overall length of a starter motor even further and to simplify the drive arrangement, a special type of solenoid can be fitted. The special features of this solenoid are:
1   The engagement spring is located inside the plunger.
2   A two-stage switching arrangement is used. The starter motor itself has a four-pole layout and, under normal conditions, the pinion is engaged by the solenoid and shift lever before both pairs of contacts close simultaneously, and current is supplied to all four field coils which provides full cranking power.

If the pinion fails to mesh with the flywheel ring gear when the solenoid is operated, the engage-

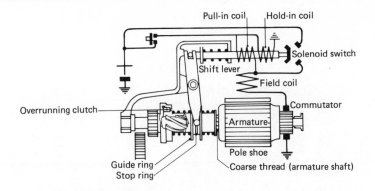

Figure 403   *Coaxial starter circuit*

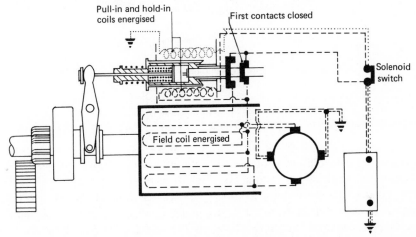

Figure 404   *First contacts closed, one field coil energized. Pinion moves into engaging position*

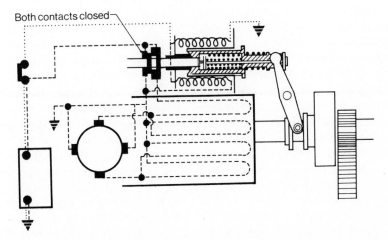

Figure 405   *First and second contacts closed, full power delivered to starter, drive fully engaged*

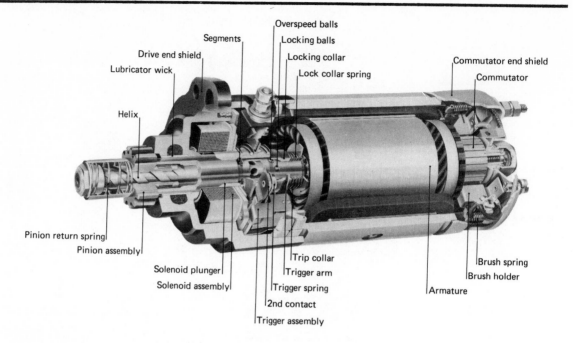

Figure 406    *Coaxial starter with enclosed solenoid*

ment springs inside the solenoid are compressed sufficiently to allow only the first set of contacts to close. This allows current to flow through only one field coil which causes the armature to rotate very slowly, so that the pinion is rotated until the teeth mesh together.

When the pinion is in the fully engaged position the second set of contacts in the solenoid close and current flows to the other three field coils which then provide full cranking power.

Figure 406 shows a co-axial starter motor with the solenoid and switching mechanism mounted co-axially with the armature shaft. Engagement of the pinion is carried out in two stages. The first ensures engagement at low power and the second allows full power when the pinion is fully meshed.

A special locking device is provided to hold the pinion in mesh when the engine is firing. This consists of a set of steel balls which are located in holes in the pinion sleeve.

*Operation (Figure 407)*    When the starter switch is operated, the solenoid is energized. This draws the

plunger forward and the pinion teeth begin to mesh with the flywheel teeth. At the same time a first set of contacts which are mounted on the plunger, close and current passes via a resistance to the field coils. Because the resistance limits the flow of current the armature begins to turn only slowly. The pinion is prevented from rotating because of flywheel teeth and is therefore drawn into full engagement by the screw action of the helix and the slowly rotating armature. Towards the end of this movement the collar on the pinion sleeve trips the trigger to close the second set of contacts. When this contact is made, the resistance is short circuited and full current passes through the field coils and armature windings to give full starting torque.

At the same time as the pinion sleeve moves forward to the fully engaged position, the locking balls in the sleeve drop into the dimpled recesses of the armature shaft. The spring-loaded lock collar then moves over the top of the balls to lock them in position. This means that the pinion cannot move out of mesh with the ring gear until the

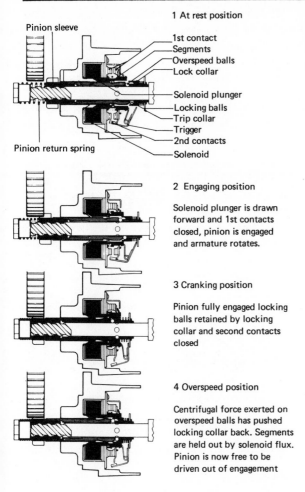

Pinion sleeve

**1 At rest position**
- 1st contact
- Segments
- Overspeed balls
- Lock collar
- Solenoid plunger
- Locking balls
- Trip collar
- Trigger
- 2nd contacts
- Solenoid

Pinion return spring

**2 Engaging position**

Solenoid plunger is drawn forward and 1st contacts closed, pinion is engaged and armature rotates.

**3 Cranking position**

Pinion fully engaged locking balls retained by locking collar and second contacts closed

**4 Overspeed position**

Centrifugal force exerted on overspeed balls has pushed locking collar back. Segments are held out by solenoid flux. Pinion is now free to be driven out of engagement

Figure 407 *Stages of operation of enclosed solenoid starter with hold-in and overspeed device*

solenoid is de-energized. The plunger then returns to its normal position and takes with it the lock collar which releases the balls to allow the pinion sleeve to disengage the pinion.

A mechanical overspeed protection device is fitted which consists of four steel balls and segments. Beyond a pre-determined armature speed, i.e. when the engine is driving the starter motor, centrifugal force acting on these balls pushes the locking collar back and allows the pinion to be driven down the helix out of engagement with the ring gear.

## Clutches

Two types of clutch arrangement are used on heavy-duty starter motors:

1 A multi-plate clutch which has several functions:

   *a* It provides a cushion device which ensures a smooth pinion engagement.

   *b* It incorporates an overload protection which limits the torque transmitted to a pre-set maximum valve.

   *c* It includes an overrunning device which prevents the engine from driving the armature.

2 A roller clutch which prevents the armature from being rotated at high speed when the engine starts.

*Multi-plate clutch (Figure 408)*

This consists of several steel discs – one set keyed to a driving flange which in turn is keyed to the armature shaft – alternate discs are keyed to a pressure sleeve which can slide along the coarse thread of the pinion spindle.

*Operation* When the pinion is engaged, the rotation of the armature forces the pressure sleeve to slide along the coarse thread which compresses the clutch discs until there is sufficient pressure between the discs to give sufficient friction to transmit starting torque.

Unless some initial pressure exists between the discs, the pressure sleeve would not be rotated and forced along its thread to give the positive clutch action. This initial pressure is caused by the helical springs which push the sliding disc against the stop disc and against a stop ring which is formed in the starter bearing casing.

Torque from the starter motor is normally transmitted from the armature shaft via driving flange, outer discs, inner discs and pressure sleeve to the pinion.

*Overload protection* Normal transmission of torque depends upon the resistance felt between pinion and starter ring gear which in turn forces the pressure sleeve along the coarse thread to compress the clutch plates against the pressure

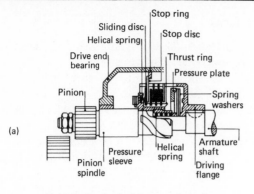

(a)

Multiple-disc clutch with torque limitation —
initial stage (rest position)

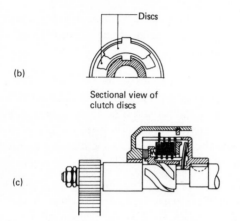

(b)

Sectional view of
clutch discs

(c)

Torque limitation in the multiple disc clutch

Figure 408   *Starter motors clutches*

plate. This pressure plate normally acts against the spring washers as shown in Figure 408. If the effort acting against the clutch plates – the ring gear becoming too hard to turn – reaches a point which causes the thrust ring to bend the spring washers away from the pressure plate, the clutch will momentarily slip. If this condition continues the clutch will overheat and the starter must be switched off immediately.

*Speed protection* As previously stated the pressure acting between the clutch plates depends upon the resistance offered by the flywheel ring gear – the more resistance the greater the pressure exerted by the pressure sleeve via the helical drive threads. If however the pinion is driven by the flywheel ring gear the tendency is for the helical drive gear to move the pressure sleeve in the

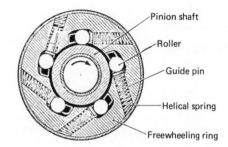

Figure 409   *Outer-wedge type overrunning clutch*

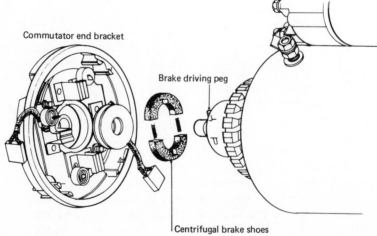

Figure 410   *Armature brake*

opposite direction which relieves the pressure against the clutch discs. This means that the inner plates can rotate free from the outer plates and therefore no damage is done to the armature and starter motor by the engine turning the motor.

### *Overrunning clutch (Figure 409)*

This is usually a rotor type of clutch which consists of a driving and a driven member with a number of spring-loaded cylindrical rollers running in a wedge-shaped track.

When the motor is at rest, the springs push against the guide pins which push the rollers into the narrow portion of the wedge between the driver or free wheeling ring and the cylindrically shaped part of the pinion. This ensures a positive connection between the pinion and driver when the starter motor begins to rotate.

When the engine starts, the pinion, which is still held in mesh, begins to rotate faster than the driver. This moves the rollers, against spring pressure, into the larger part of the wedge, the drive is disconnected and the pinion runs free.

### *Armature brake (Figure 410)*

This can be either a radially acting shoe brake mounted in the commutator-end bearing or an axially acting disc type of brake mounted at the drive end of the armature.

The main purpose of this is to stop the starter motor as quickly as possible after it has been cut off to allow immediate restarting if required.

## The alternator

The electrical loading in heavy vehicles has generally increased beyond the normal and economic conditions suitable for a d.c. generator. In order to supply these load demands and to keep the battery fully charged an alternator system is used. Alternating current systems have two main advantages: they provide higher maximum output than equivalent d.c. systems and an increased output when the engine is idling. Modern advances in semiconductor devices mean that an alternator and its control equipment are very

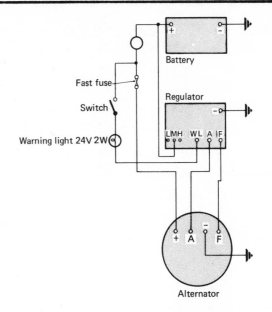

Figure 411  *Alternator circuit diagram*

reliable and provide a very efficient and compact unit.

The alternator circuit (Figure 411) consists essentially of an alternator, warning light, voltage regulator and battery. Other items which can also be fitted to this circuit are an ammeter, field isolating switch or relay, heater load relay and a fast fuse.

An alternator has two main parts (see Figure 412): a stator and an electromagnetic rotor. The rotor is usually turned by a crankshaft driven pulley, and revolves inside the stator windings where an alternating current is produced. This alternating current is unsuitable for charging the battery and has therefore to be changed to d.c. This process is called rectification and involves the use of a device which will pass current in one direction only. In modern semiconductor rectifiers, six silicon diodes are used to convert a.c. to d.c.

A cut-out is not required because these same diodes prevent the battery from discharging through the stator windings when the alternator is at rest or when generating less than battery voltage. A further important feature of an

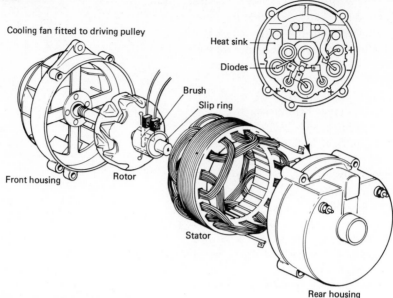

Figure 412   *Construction of typical alternator*

alternator is its inherent self-regulation as regards current output – as speed increases current output is limited. This means that the regulator has to control only voltage which is achieved by regulating the alternator field current and therefore output voltage.

### Principle of operation

The basic principles of operation of any means of producing an electric current apply. Simply this begins from the fact that if a conductor is moved through a magnetic field, an electric current is induced into that conductor. The amount of current induced into the conductor depends on:

1   Number of turns of wire on the conductor.
2   Strength of magnetic field.
3   Number of magnetic poles.
4   Speed at which the magnet rotates.

In practice, it is normal to use three separate coils of wire called phase windings (Figure 414) to form the conductor, which simply means that when the magnet is rotated, it produces a higher output. These three phases can be connected in two ways, but whichever system is used, the resultant three-phase output is the same.

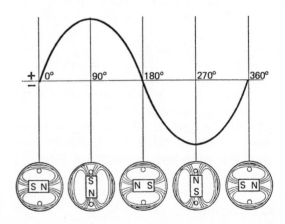

Figure 413   *Magnetic field moving across a conductor to produce a.c. current*

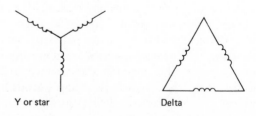

Figure 414   *Phase windings*

## Principle of rectification

The simplest form of rectified circuit is the 'half-wave' connection as shown in Figure 415.

In an alternator this rectification is carried out by a diode which is a semiconductor or solid-state device which has the capacity of passing current in one direction only and will 'shut down' if the current tries to pass in the opposite direction. It thus acts as a one-way valve and is represented by the symbol ➤┤ .

Half-wave rectification is very inefficient because only one half of the cycle is providing useful power. It is therefore usual to use 'full-wave' rectification by means of a bridge system (Figure 416).

In a star connected stator, one end of each coil is connected to a bridge between a pair of diodes as shown in Figure 417. The other ends are all connected together and held inside the body of the alternator.

When all the windings are connected together in this bridge system, the diodes are connected in pairs in parallel with the battery as shown in Figure 418.

The rotor consists of a coil which is wound on an iron core. The ends of this coil are connected to two slip rings which collect a 'current' from the regulator. When this current flows through the windings an electromagnet is formed on the iron core but each end of this core is formed in segments as shown in Figure 419.

Because of the shape of the rotor, the segments are alternate north and south poles. The greater the current flowing through the winding, the stronger is the magnetism experienced in the rotor poles. When these magnetic poles pass a conductor – stator windings – a current is induced into these windings. These magnetic poles

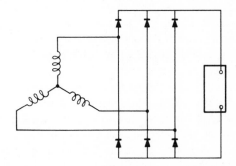

Figure 418    *Full bridge system*

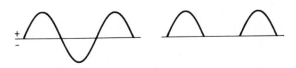

Figure 415    *Alternating current and half-wave rectification – direct current*

Figure 416    *Alternating current and full-wave rectification – direct current*

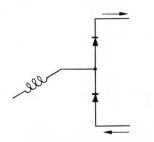

Figure 417    *Bridge with two diodes*

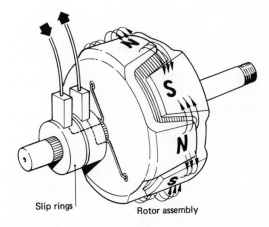

Slip rings            Rotor assembly

Figure 419    *Rotor assembly*

alternate between north and south and therefore the current induced into the stator windings will flow in alternate directions as these poles pass the windings and produce alternating current. But because the ends of these windings are connected to the bridge between two diodes, current can pass only one way, as shown in Figures 420 and 421.

Figure 420 shows a circuit with a north pole passing one of the stator windings. Magnetic lines of force are being cut by the stator and therefore current induced in the winding is flowing as shown. This cannot pass through the lower diode therefore it passes through the upper diode to the battery. To complete the circuit, current passes through the lower diodes and stator windings as shown.

When the following south pole on the rotor passes this same winding, a current is again induced into the winding but in the opposite direction. Because the other end of the stator winding is connected to the other two stator windings, current flows through these, but again can only pass through the upper diodes and pass to the battery as shown in Figure 421.

The same rules apply to the other two windings, and therefore all current reaching the battery is travelling in the same direction. This means that the current induced into each winding by alternate north and south poles and flowing in both directions has been *rectified*.

## The regulator

Because an alternator is generally self-limiting in current output, a regulator has to control only the voltage produced by the alternator. This is done by controlling the strength of the magnetic field in the rotor which is achieved by controlling the current passing to the field windings.

The regulator itself is usually fully transistorized and therefore has no moving parts which will wear out or require adjustment. The transistors and diodes are mounted on a printed circuit base in an aluminium body which conducts away the heat generated when the regulator is operating. Operation of the regulator is such that a flat battery will be charged in a minimum of time and a

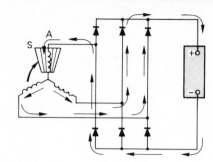

Figure 420

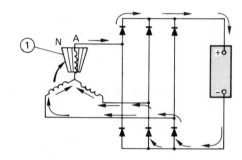

Figure 421

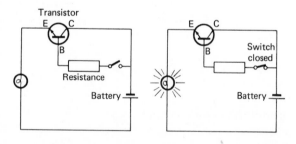

Figure 422   (a)   *When base current is switched off, bulb does not light;* (b)   *Even when base current is very small, controlled by resistor, the transistor is switched on to light the bulb*

battery in good condition would be maintained in a charged condition by a trickle charge.

*Principle of operation (Figure 422)*
Two other kinds of semiconductor device are used in a transistor regulator: transistors represented

by their electrical symbol  and avalanche

diodes represented by the symbol ⇥.

*Transistors* A transistor is an electrical device that is used in a circuit to control current flow and is capable of switching on and off up to 7000 times per second. The main current flow through a transistor is between the collector and emitter in the direction shown by the arrow in the symbol. This current will not flow however until the transistor is switched *on*, and this condition exists only when a current flows between base and emitter. This base/emitter current need only be very small in order to switch on a much higher current flow between collector and emitter. As soon as the base/emitter current is stopped the transistor 'switches off', the current between collector and emitter is automatically switched off.

*Avalanche or Zener diode* This is a specially designed type of diode that, under certain conditions, *will* conduct a current in the reverse direction.

The internal connections of a simple transistor regulator will be dealt with. As illustrated in Figures 423 and 424, other components – resistors, diodes, transistors and capacitors – are used in practice to deal with various induced voltages, voltage variations and changes in temperature, and the result is an efficient and long-lasting component.

The object of the regulator is to control the field current to the alternator. Maximum current will provide maximum voltage and no current will produce no voltage. Consequently, taking time as a controlling factor, the longer the time for which the field current is switched on compared to the time for which it is switched off, the higher will be the output voltage of the alternator.

## Operation

*Stage 1: Current flowing through field windings*
When the switch is switched on, current will flow through resistor R1, through base/emitter of T1, through resistor R2 to earth. This switches

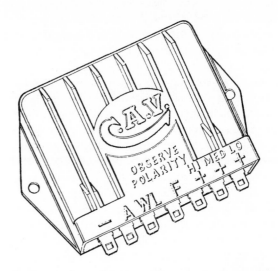

Figure 423 *External view of transistorized regulator*

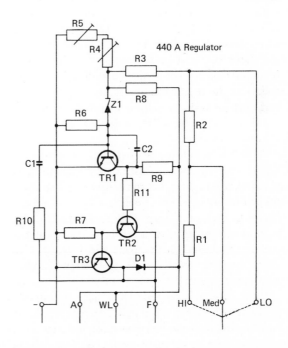

Figure 424 *Theoretic circuit of transistorized regulator*

on T1 which will now allow current to flow from A, through the field windings of the alternator to F through the transistor to earth and give maximum voltage output of the alternator.

*Stage 2: Current through field windings switched off*
By including a second transistor, an avalanche diode and further resistances, transistor T1 can be made to switch off and therefore stop current flowing through the alternator field windings.

As the battery terminal voltage rises, the voltage at resistors R3 and R4 will also rise. When this voltage rises sufficiently to allow the avalanche diode to conduct – current passes in reverse direction to normal – current will then flow in base/emitter of T2. This switches on T2 and current from R1 will now pass through collector/emitter of T2 and straight to earth instead of through base/emitter of T1 through R2 to earth. This switches off T1 which stops the current flowing through the field windings and the alternator voltage immediately drops. This reduces the voltage at the battery which in turn reduces the voltage at R1 and R2, and this voltage is not sufficient to overcome D1. Current then stops flowing through base of T2, switches the transistor off, and current begins to flow again through base of T1 which switches it on and energizes the field windings again.

The steps in the switching operation proceed in rapid succession to maintain the battery in a fully charged condition.

In order to allow the battery to provide the initial field current and ensure a consistent build-up of alternator output, an ignition type or some other form of isolator switch is used in conjunction with a warning lamp. This usually uses a low-voltage bulb which gives a very low flow of current to the regulator which opens the transistor to allow a similar current to flow through the field windings to earth.

As the engine/rotor speed increases, the current generated from this initial field current is rectified by three auxiliary diodes (nine-diode alternator) in conjunction with the main diodes (see Figure 427) to supplement the field current through the warning lamp. This rapidly builds up alternator

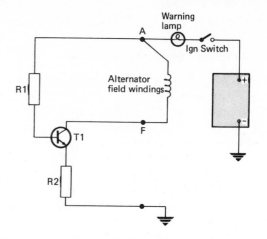

Figure 425   *Principle of operation: stage 1*

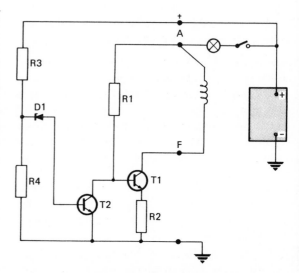

Figure 426   *Principle of operation: stage 2*

voltage to equal battery voltage at which point the warning light is extinguished. All current now fed to the field coil is supplied from the alternator terminal A and normal voltage regulation takes place.

*Precautions to be observed on vehicles fitted with alternators*
Transistors and diodes are sensitive to voltage changes and high temperatures so that safety

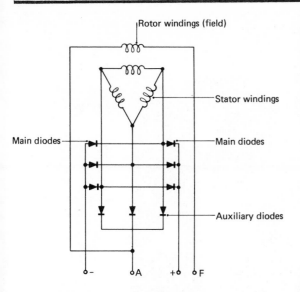

Figure 427  *Nine-diode rectification*

precautions should be taken to prevent damage when carrying out maintenance.
1  Make sure the engine is stopped before disconnecting the leads.
2  Make sure that the leads are correctly refitted – short-circuit and reverse polarity, no matter how brief, will cause damage.
3  Never disconnect the battery with the alternator running.

## Battery

The battery is an essential part of a heavy vehicle. More and more electrical energy is required for the starting, lighting and accessories which are fitted to a modern vehicle. A battery provides the means of storing electrical energy in chemical form whilst being charged, and releases this energy back into electrical energy whilst being discharged. A battery is discharged when it is no longer capable of releasing or changing chemical energy into electrical energy at a satisfactory voltage.

The size of a battery is directly related to the amount of work expected from it. Because the starter motor is the greatest user of electrical energy it follows that the size of battery is mainly decided by the size of the starter motor. In view of the higher pressure (voltage), a 24-V electrical system is often used in heavy vehicles. This means that more and therefore heavier batteries are needed but this is countered by the better efficiency given by a 24-V system.

Two types of battery are available for use in heavy vehicles – lead–acid and alkaline – but the lead–acid type is most common.

### Lead–acid battery (Figure 428)

A working cell consists of several positive and negative lead plates which are separated from each other with the whole unit submerged in dilute sulphuric acid. A chemical reaction between the lead plates and the sulphuric acid during the charge and discharge process converts the electrical energy to chemical energy and *vice versa*.

The battery case is made from a hard moulded rubber or a mixture of pitch and asbestos fibres. A 12-V battery is divided into six separate cells with interconnecting lead links. Each cell contains at least seven lead plates with PVC or glass fibre separators. When fully 'charged' each cell has a voltage of approximately 2.2 V and even when fully discharged its value falls to only approximately 1.8 V. The capacity or rate of discharge of a battery depends upon the surface area of its plates. This means that the larger the plates or the greater their number per cell, the greater the capacity of the battery. A heavy vehicle may have batteries with a capacity of 130 Ah, the ampere hour (Ah) being the unit used to measure battery capacity. This is established by discharging a fully charged battery until it is fully discharged, usually over a period of 10 or 20 hours. For example a 130 Ah capacity battery will be capable of discharging at the rate of 13 A for 10 hours. This may not be the reason for choosing a battery for a heavy vehicle but it has a direct relationship with its ability to discharge over a very short time period, e.g. when operating the starter motor. It follows then that because of the large engine and starter motor required to turn this, a high-capacity battery is required.

A lead–acid battery must be kept in a reasonable state of charge otherwise it will deteriorate

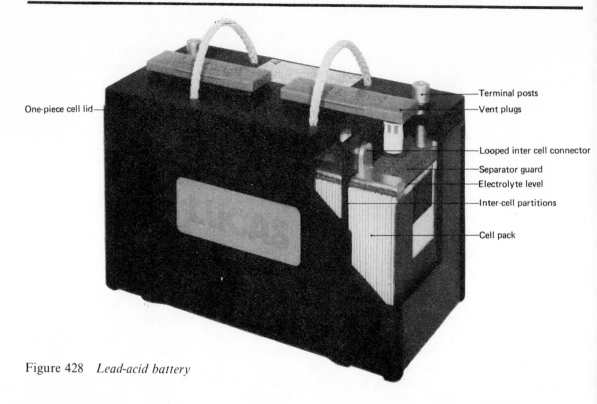

One-piece cell lid

Terminal posts
Vent plugs
Looped inter cell connector
Separator guard
Electrolyte level
Inter-cell partitions
Cell pack

Figure 428   *Lead-acid battery*

and loose its efficiency. It must not, however, be overcharged or the plates may be damaged. The only maintenance required is to keep each cell topped up with distilled water and to keep the terminals clean.

### Alkaline battery

The working cell consists of nickel–cadmium plates separated by plastics rods submerged in a solution of potassium hydroxide. A chemical reaction between the plates and electrolyte takes place whilst charging and discharging. Each cell is formed in its own steel case and is usually carried in a hardwood or plastics case. This gives this type of battery very great strength and resistance to vibration and shocks. Unlike the lead-acid battery, each cell has a voltage of approximately 1.4 V, therefore nine cells are required to make up a 12-V battery.

This type of battery has a very long life – up to 10 years – and needs very little maintenance, normal topping up uses conventional distilled water. Also unlike the lead–acid battery, an alkaline battery is not affected by under or over charging and the electrolyte does not promote corrosion of the case or terminals. The advantages of this type of cell are offset however by the weight and the very high initial cost.

## Battery condition indicator (Figure 429)

This is a very sensitive voltmeter which indicates the condition of the battery and often is fitted in place of an ammeter. The scale on the dial is split up into two main sections – *off charge* and *on charge*.

When no electrical equipment is being used, the pointer – in the *off charge* area of the scale – shows the state of charge of the battery. When the engine is running, the pointer would normally be in the *on charge* area of the scale which indicates that any electrical energy which is taken from the battery is being replaced by the alternator or generator to keep the battery fully charged.

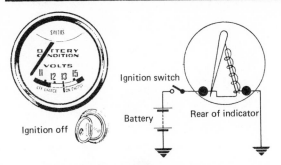

Figure 429   *Battery condition indicator*

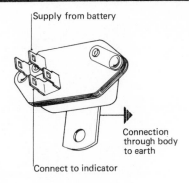

Figure 430   *Voltage stabilizer*

## Voltage stabilizer unit (Figures 430 and 431)

Used in conjunction with temperature-sensitive instruments, this unit is designed to give a constant output to the instruments irrespective of fluctuation in battery voltage.

This is a bimetallic type stabilizer which depends upon the heating effect of an electric current to heat a bimetallic strip. When heated, this bends and separates the contacts. When the contacts are separated, current supply ceases to flow and the strip cools down to close the contacts. This causes current to flow and the strip heats up again. The operation is repeated so that in effect a pulsating voltage is provided to give an average voltage to the instrument panel. As supply voltage falls the rate of oscillation of the contacts falls to increase the period of contact closure thus maintaining the voltage to the instruments.

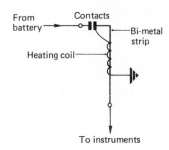

Figure 431   *Internal wiring of voltage stabilizer*

and is visible from outside to give a direct reading of contents.

2   *Electrical*, consisting of a transmitter unit mounted in the tank and an indicator mounted on the dashboard.

### Moving-iron type fuel gauge (Figure 432)

A transmitter unit mounted in the tank consists of a float arm which rises and falls according to fuel level. This movement slides a contact over a resistance in a flame-proof chamber, as the float

## Fuel gauges

Two main types of fuel gauge are used:
1   *Mechanical*, which is mounted in the fuel tank

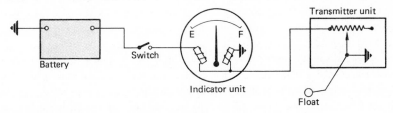

Figure 432   *Moving-iron type fuel gauge circuit*

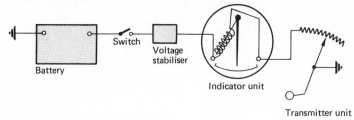

Figure 433   *Bimetal resistance fuel gauge circuit*

rises with fuel level, more resistance is brought into the circuit.

The transmitter unit is connected to an indicator unit which contains two coils, one acting as a control coil and the other as a deflector coil. Current passing through these coils produces a magnetic field which attracts a soft iron armature connected to the pointer.

In the empty position the tank unit resistance is at a minimum, and the easiest electrical path is through the control coil, through the transmitter to earth. As the float rises, the transmitter resistance is increased and more current will pass through the deflecting coil which attracts the armature towards F on the indicator scale.

*Bimetal resistance fuel gauge (Figure 433)*
Because a moving-iron type of meter is sensitive to movement of fuel in the tank, the indicator tends to swing and give inaccurate readings. A bimetal indicator is less sensitive to this type of movement as it relies upon the heating effect of a current to deflect the needle.

Current passing through the heater winding is controlled by the amount of resistance in the transmitter unit. This in turn is controlled, as before, by the position of the float and slider to increase or decrease the resistance in the circuit. Any quick variation of current flow due to surging of fuel in the tank is not sufficient to produce enough heat to alter the position of the bimetal strip and therefore register on the instruments.

A disadvantage of this system however is its sensitivity to voltage. Lowering of voltage means less current flowing and therefore less heating of the bimetal strip and inaccurate readings. To over-

come this, a voltage stabilizer unit is fitted to the circuit. This supplies a constant voltage to the instrument irrespective of battery voltage.

## Flashing indicators (Figure 434)

The law requires that flashing indicators be fitted to all new vehicles, with the rate of flash of the lamps between 60 and 120 flashes per minute. The rate of flash of the lamps can be controlled by an electric motor driving a rotor similar to a distributor or a transistorized unit but a simple and less expensive system uses a flasher unit.

This unit houses contacts which are operated magnetically by a heat-sensitive wire. When the indicators are switched on, a circuit is completed through the flasher unit to the indicator bulbs. An initial current passes through the thermal wire, resistor, 'L' terminal to indicator switch, through the bulbs – not enough current to light because of resistor – to earth. This initial current is sufficient to heat the thermal wire which expands and allows the main contacts to close. Sufficient current can now pass through the coil to light up the bulbs and the magnetism attracts the second contact to illuminate the warning light.

When current is passing through main contacts, no current passes through the thermal wire circuit because of the resistor. This means that the wire cools down, contracts and opens the main contacts and therefore puts out the lights. The thermal wire is again in circuit which heats up, expands and closes the main contacts once again. The whole process is repeated at a rate determined by the wattage of the bulbs in the circuit whose current consumption determines the time required to heat up the thermal wire sufficiently and close the contacts.

## Hazard warning system (Figure 435)

This is a device which allows all four indicator lamps to flash simultaneously in cases where the vehicle is a hazard to other road users, e.g. in case of breakdown or accidents.

Because it will be used in unusual circumstances, the system is fed directly from the battery without passing through a separate switch. It incorporates its own flasher unit and warning light and bypasses the normal indicator switch. Because all indicator lamps will operate at the same time – or all those which are working – a special non-load-sensitive flasher unit is used which will effectively operate any number of bulbs in use.

By operating the switch, the normal flasher unit is isolated from the circuit and at the same time the flasher lamps are connected to the hazard system and flashing commences.

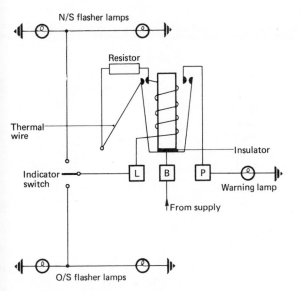

Figure 434 *Wiring diagram for a flashing indicator circuit*

## Horn

A horn produces its note by vibrating a metal diaphragm to produce a low frequency note, which is increased in frequency by a tone or oscillating disc mounted in front of the diaphragm. The diaphragm is connected to an armature which is attracted by an electromagnet when the circuit is earthed by the horn button (see Figure 436). When the armature is attracted a set of contacts are opened which break the circuit, the armature is released and the contacts close again to attract the armature. This is repeated very quickly to produce

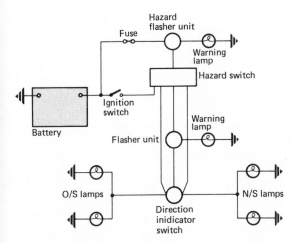

Figure 435 *Layout of hazard warning system*

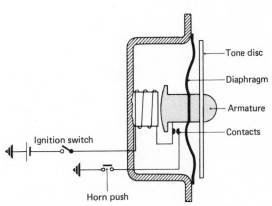

Figure 436 *Principle operation of horn*

a high rate of vibration. A condenser can be fitted to reduce 'arcing' at the points.

When two horns are connected together – one high frequency and one low frequency – the current consumption can be greater than 10 A. In order to overcome the effect of excessive voltage drop in the horn circuit and to give the push button contacts a longer life, a relay is usually fitted (Figure 437). The relay carries the heavy current directly to the horns, like a solenoid in a starter circuit. When the horn button is pressed, a circuit to earth is completed which operates a solenoid in the relay and connects the battery directly to the horns.

### Electrically operated windscreen wiper motor (Figures 438–41)

A two-pole or permanent magnet motor is usually used with conventional brush gear, commutator and armature. The end of the armature is formed into a worm gear which drives a nylon wheel and operating crank. Most modern wiper motors are self-parking and may operate at two speeds. The rotary movement of the crank is converted to a to and fro movement of the wiper blades, by using a suitable linkage.

A two-speed motor has a three-position switch. When switched on to the first or normal position, current can pass directly to earth. When switched to the fast position, a resistor is switched into the circuit which has the effect of increasing the motor speed.

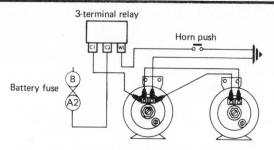

Figure 437    *Windtone horn circuit with relay*

When a wiper motor is switched *on*, the circuit is earthed by the switch circuit. If this earth circuit is broken only when the wiper blades are in a parking position – irrespective of manual switch – then a self-switching or automatic parking feature is obtained. When the switch is moved to the *off* position, the circuit is still completed until the contact acting against the wheel housing contact is insulated from earth.

### Windscreen washer

Legislation makes it compulsory to have some form of windscreen washing equipment fitted and in working order. The simplest form is a pump that is manually operated by the driver. An easier and more efficient system is to use an electrically driven pump which operates for several seconds from a single press on the switch.

A permanent magnet motor is used which is mounted on the cover of the water reservoir. A

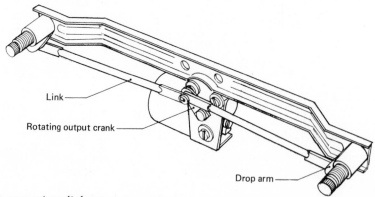

Figure 438    *Link-type wiper linkage*

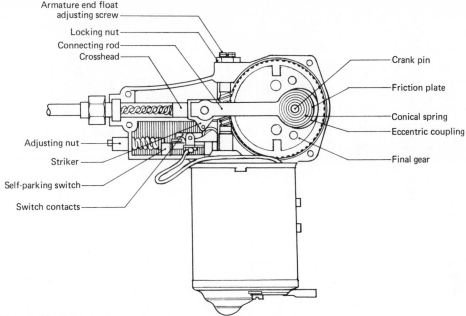

Figure 439   *Cable-linked wiper motor*

spindle from this motor drives the impeller which is located in an auxiliary reservoir inside the main container. When the switch is operated the motor drives the impeller and the contents of the auxiliary reservoir are discharged through nozzles on to the windscreen.

The motor is designed so that when it is rotated the spindle is lifted. This closes the inlet to the auxiliary reservoir, and electrical contacts are closed which allow the motor to rotate until the water in the auxiliary reservoir is exhausted even when the manual switch is released. When the reservoir is empty, the spindle falls to stop the motor and open the inlet valve which allows water to refill the reservoir ready for the next operation.

## Insulated return

Many modern heavy vehicles are using a double pole or insulated return system of wiring. This means that the chassis frame is not used as a return path to complete an electrical circuit, a return wire being used instead. This system of wiring is compulsory on tankers that carry inflammable liquids

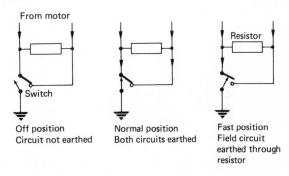

Figure 440   *Three-position switch for two-speed motors*

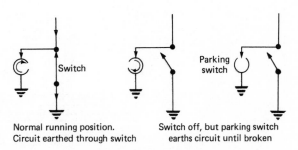

Figure 441   *Principle of self-parking wiper motor*

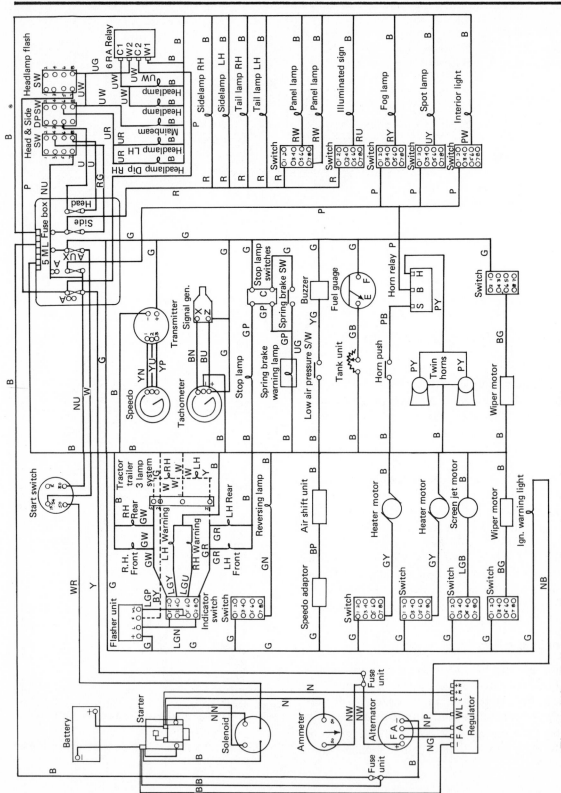

Figure 442   *Full wiring diagram for an insulated return system*

and on public service vehicles. Although the system is more expensive it is much safer, as the possibility of a short-circuit or a spark from a loose wire is virtually eliminated.

## Brief summary of lighting regulations

All vehicles must be fitted with:
1  Two side lamps showing a diffused white light to the front. Each lamp must be within 305 mm (1 ft) of the extreme edge of the vehicle (except tower wagons) and not higher than 1.52 metres (5 ft). Maximum wattage is 7 W.
2  Two matched headlamps capable of adjustment and able to show either a dipped or main beam. The lamps should be no higher than 1.07 m (3 ft 6 in) or lower than 610 mm (2 ft) and not more than 400 mm (15 in) from the outer edge of the vehicle. Minimum wattage of bulb 30 W.
3  Two rear lamps showing a red light to the rear. Minimum wattage of bulb 5 W.
4  Number plate illumination lamp which illuminates the plate to make it easily visible from a distance of 60 ft.
5  Flashing direction indicator lamps with amber lenses flashing at the rate of 60–120 flashes per minute. Bulb wattage between 15 and 36 W.
6  Two stop lamps with red lens showing a diffused light. Bulb wattage between 15 and 36 W.
7  Two red reflectors with the reflecting area vertical and facing squarely to the rear. They must be at least 38.1 mm ($1\frac{1}{2}$ in) diameter. Two amber reflectors facing sideways must be fitted if the vehicle exceeds 8 m (26 ft).

Many of the above regulations can vary with special applications.

# Index